W9-DCG-105

WHAT PEOPLE ARE SAYING ABOUT BRIG. GEN. (RET.) JULIA JETER CLECKLEY AND HER STORY...

"General Cleckley is without a doubt a woman of God and a woman of great faith. I have witnessed what one might consider the most challenging time in her life; however, she was able to overcome that challenge and many more she faced in life; she forged ahead with faithful service to God and God's people. God is her strength and refuge in the present time of trouble. She keeps a smile on her face; a prayer on her lips and the joy of the Lord in her heart. This is a great woman of God to emulate and my sister friend."

—REV. DR. FAYE S. GUNN

"General Cleckley epitomizes resilience dealing with life challenges with grace, dignity and humility all while maintaining her personal commitment to help others. She has instilled a sense of selfish service and obligation to open doors for those who have the desire to work and contribute."

—LT. COL. (RET.) ALFRANDA DURR

"Julia's concern for people covers varied cultural and social-economical levels. She shows patience and caring behavior while working with all individuals whether supervisors, subordinates, or peers. Her personality allows her to set all individuals at ease... Julia Cleckley, has always been an initiator, goal setter, planner, and a pace setter."

—MARY L WILLIAMS, PH.D.

"General Cleckley always made time to teach, coach, and mentor soldiers. While working with her, lived by the values she taught; that my success and happiness will always be determined by me;

that my faith, family and friends are what really matter, to never miss an opportunity to help someone else; that it is so important to build people up and never put them down, but that it is even more important to have achieved success the right way.

—COL. (RET.) ROGER ETZEL

"Julia was faced with challenges in her personnel life as well as while in the military. She always had a can do attitude and faced her challenges head on. Who would have imagined a young lady from our small steel mill town—a single parent challenged on every hand—would make it to the rank of General."

—BLANCHE BYRD ROBERTS

A PROMISE FULFILLED

A Promise Fulfilled: My life as Wife and Mother, Soldier and General Officer

First Edition

Copyright ©2013 Julia Cleckley

ISBN: 978-1-4947-6375-6

www.cleckleyenterprises.com

Book design: Brion Sausser of Book Creatives

A PROMISE FULFILLED

MY LIFE AS A WIFE AND MOTHER, SOLDIER AND GENERAL OFFICER

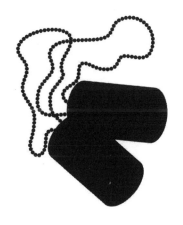

Julia Cleckley
Brigadier General (Ret.)

with M.L. Doyle

INTRODUCTION

By Lieutenant General (Ret.) Roger Schultz,

former Director of the Army National Guard

You are about to embark on a journey of discovery, one that charts the growth of a very special individual, a "one of a kind" human being. Julia Cleckley embodies the best qualities of a devoted wife and mother as well as a superb soldier and admired general. From her early days as a shy recruit in the Women's Army Corps during Vietnam to a leadership position as a Brigadier General in the Army National Guard, Julia led others by her example. Her approach to serving was actually quite straightforward: standards apply to everyone and should be universally applied to everyone; doing what is right and for the right reasons is always the place to start. This framework is the foundation of her strength. She willingly accepted every tough job that was given to her. Even when she was a bit uncertain about the future and her fit with the task, she never wavered, thanks to her strong belief in equal opportunity for everyone. As an African-American woman, Brigadier General Julia J. Cleckley is a living example of the diversity our armed forces have sought to achieve. But you will see that her story goes well beyond any questions of "glass ceilings"; Julia's performance of duty as a soldier and her devotion to her faith and her family are what this amazing memoir is all about.

During the forty-two years and nine months of my own active duty, I was proud to have worked by General Cleckley's side. I closely observed her as we worked through any number of complex issues. She always had a unique ability to focus on the priorities and the intent of the leadership team. At the same time, she demonstrated an ability to appreciate individual soldier issues and dealt with them objectively, seeking the fair-minded solution to every problem by applying the appropriate rules and regulations or developing new rules and regulations if that was needed to reach the fair-minded solution. She was first and foremost dedicated to helping others. And I can honestly say, in our years together there was not a single occasion when I questioned her judgment. She was that good.

Even as General Cleckley was dealing with difficult issues professionally, she was confronting staggering losses and grief personally. The triumph of Julia's story is that she not only survived the loss of the people closest to her, she did it while achieving things no other African-American female officer had ever accomplished in the Army National Guard. Her tenacity in the face of such great loss distinguishes her as among the best. Her resilience serves as a model for all of us.

General Cleckley's storied career is chronicled in these pages. You will come to understand how she inspired other soldiers to follow her and I can tell you this: the impact she had on the Army National Guard is a lasting legacy. Brigadier General Julia J. Cleckley ranks in a class all her own. But Julia's personal story will surely also have an impact, inspiring all of us to find the strength that abides within so that we may face obstacles in a straight-forward but compassionate way.

Well done, my Friend.

CONTENTS

My promise 1

Part one: Life-changing decisions

The first 7
Growing up timid 11
My greatest sin 21
I went up the stairs 35
My own bed 47
My name is Julia 53
The new me 61
The Presidio 69
After the Army 81
New opportunities 93
Back in uniform 103
An Officer and a Lady 111
Teaching and training others 119
Gustavus 131
A Widow 141
Helene 151

Part two: Military life

Changes 161
A School of Higher Learning 165
A call from Bobbie 175
Making the choice permanent 179
A new signature block 185

Career moves and success 197

Qualified but unwanted 211

My friend Ellen 223

Not the black messiah 229

My biggest regret 235

Earning the Star 239

Retirement 247

Hospitals and doctors 257

Ellen 263

Saying goodbye 277

What does a General look like? 283

Life now 285

Acknowledgments 291

About the Authors 293

Photo Album 295

MY PROMISE

At first, hope felt tangible. Like a solid presence I could wrap my arms around and embrace when I needed it. After several treatments, CAT scans and surgeries, hope became more elusive. It slowly condensed to smaller than the thinnest thread, a tiny filament that cut into my fingers when I tugged on it, and I felt reluctant to pull. I constantly feared that hope would snap at any second.

Now hope became a mist, and trying to grab it was like reaching for a cloud. I could see it and want it, but there was no way to gain real purchase.

I hadn't relied totally on hope. Prayer was my other anchor. I had clasped my hands together and squeezed until my knuckles were white, mumbling promises, trying to make deals, my eyes squeezed shut.

Please, God. Please, God. Please, God, if you would only do this one thing for me, I will never swear again, never lose my temper, never sin, never do anything bad. Please, God...

Hope and prayer. Prayer and hope.

There had been other times in my life when I had searched for hope. Other times when I had been on my knees making promises to God.

At nineteen, I had a feeling there was something terribly wrong with my first baby, Helene. I prayed then, too. *Please let me be wrong. Please let her be okay, please Lord, please Lord.*

And another time, when my husband, Gus, fell ill, I had prayed until

I was hoarse, my fear for the worst almost paralyzing me. I wore a brave face for him and kept my prayers to myself, but my begging never ended. I was willing to make any deal to keep him safe and with me. *Please don't let him die. Don't leave me alone. Don't take him away from me. Please, Lord, please, Lord, please!* Oh, how I had prayed.

Maybe the deals I offered weren't sweet enough, or maybe I hadn't prayed hard enough or God simply had some other plan I couldn't hope to understand. Those battles were lost to me, but I was a fighter and I was determined to keep my hold on hope this time, no matter how thin or how misty it might become.

Fighting for what I want is in my nature. I expect a struggle and had faced many throughout my life and military career, first as an enlisted soldier, then as an officer. I earned promotions quickly and passed many qualified men as I made my way up the rank structure, until, finally, I wore a general's stars on my shoulders. The rank brought with it much responsibility and a few privileges, but now, sitting in the hospital again, there were no orders I could issue to correct this nightmare, no policy I could change, no waiver I could file to make this right. Despite my rank, I was powerless to help my second daughter, Ellen-Lizette.

Her hand felt warm in mine as we sat in the hospital while she went through another chemotherapy treatment. Her beautiful hair was mostly gone now, her skin grey, all cheek bones and deep eye sockets. She turned her bright gaze to me.

"You okay, Momma?"

"Of course, baby. I'm alright."

The oncologist, standing in the doorway in her white coat, asked to speak to me and I knew that wasn't a good sign. I let go of my daughter's hand and stepped into the hallway, ignoring the hustle bustle of the hospital around us.

She gave me facts about the surgery my daughter had just been through. Medical terms, procedural information—none of it was good.

A neurologist had taken a laser knife to my daughter's brain. The surgery, while non-invasive, was still petrifying, but not going through with it offered a far worse nightmare.

"You should take her out. Have some fun. Do things she loves to do," the doctor said.

She was telling me that the surgery hadn't worked and my beautiful, 31-year-old daughter was going to die, far too young and with far too much life unlived. In my mind, my hands grabbed at the cloud of hope and came up empty.

"I understand," I managed to say. "But we're not ready to give up. Please, continue to do everything you can. And thank you. Thank you, for everything you've done."

I squared my shoulders, put a calm look on my face, and went back into the room, taking hold of my daughter's hand again.

"What did she have to say, Momma?" Ellen had participated in every aspect of her medical decisions, knew clearly what the chances and risks were, and was well aware of her prognosis.

"She said they think they got most of it, but it's hard to tell. We're not giving up." I squeezed her hand. "We're not giving up on this fight."

We sat together quietly, my younger daughter and I, like we had for most of her life. She was my best friend. My confidant. My rock. I was losing her, and I wondered how I could go on living without her.

After a few minutes, Ellen turned her gaze to me. "You have to write the book, Momma." Ellen, the avid reader, a graduate of Cornell University, had always wanted to write my story. She knew, with the labor of her breathing and the effort it took to simply hold my hand, it wouldn't be possible now.

"People will want to read it," she said.

"I will, honey," I said.

"Really, Momma. You have to promise me you'll write it. *Promise* me."

"Okay, baby. I'll write the book."

It took me several years to come to terms with Ellen's passing, several years to understand all that I had lost and to struggle with the reasons she was taken so early from me. Now, I grab at that misty hope again. Clench my hands in prayer again. It's time to fulfill my promise to my daughter and my hopes and prayers are that I can tell it the way she would want it told.

For my Ellen, this is my story.

PART ONE

LIFE-CHANGING DECISIONS

THE FIRST

"Being the first in anything is not worthwhile if you don't open doors for the others who come after you."

That's what I said during the ceremony on September 3, 2002, when more than four hundred people crowded into a room at the National Guard Bureau in Washington, DC to see my promotion. I wore a silver star on the epaulets of my uniform as I became the first African-American female General Officer of the Line at the National Guard Bureau on that day. My promotion was a bit unusual in that I was selected to serve at the federal level at the National Guard Bureau, rather than for my state leadership, as was the case for most National Guard general officer promotions. The crowd was unusually large, even for a general officer's promotion ceremony, but it was an historic event and lots of folks wanted to be part of it.

"Being first is not so important unless there is a second and a fourth and a tenth," I said.

I had marked many firsts during my twenty-eight years in uniform, but the promotion to general had been long in coming and every bit as sweet as I expected. Someone was shooting video so that my mother, who couldn't attend, would be able to watch the ceremony later. My daughters, Helene and Ellen, sat beaming in the VIP section. I knew they were proud of me, but I was even more proud of them. I made sure they were both part of the ceremony. Ellen, along with my boss, Lieutenant

General Roger Schultz, pinned the silver stars on my epaulets while Helene, with the help of my niece, Lisa, pinned the star on my beret.

The promotion ceremony was one of the biggest events of my life. If you had asked me years before, when I first raised my right hand and swore to protect and defend the United States of America against all enemies, foreign and domestic, how far I would go in my military career, the answer would have been simple. I would have said the plan was to serve my three-year obligation, take my discharge papers and start the rest of my life with the experience and education the military helped me gain. But life often throws us curve balls we don't expect.

I looked about the crowd and saw many familiar faces, men and women I had led, men and women with whom I had served. There were men who had mentored me, now standing amongst other men who had tried and failed to get in my way.

Much of my career had been filled with hours and hours in briefing rooms, armories, in the field and operation centers at the Pentagon surrounded by men and women, mostly white. It wasn't something I took much note of anymore, but it was interesting to think that even on the date of such a milestone, my race was still significant in the Army. Some of the people assembled that day were instrumental in my success; others had been obstacles. Many of them, I'm sure, were a bit surprised.

After all, I had enlisted seemingly on a whim. The option presented itself and I took it. I knew nothing about service in uniform. Had no idea what to expect of the life, of the training, of the obligation. What I did know was that I could get an education and do something other than what a lot of the other girls at the time were doing: getting married, raising children, living predictable lives with few choices and sometimes no excitement. When I signed my enlistment contract, I was attracted to the notion of travel and the lure of an adventure, the opportunity to do something different.

But the most important reason for joining was one I hadn't discussed with anyone, not even my mother, who was the closet person to me in the world. I was desperate. Desperate to change my life. Desperate to get an education. Desperate to get out of the small Pennsylvania town I called home. At the time, of course, I had no idea where my desperate decision would lead.

GROWING UP TIMID

To say that I was timid would make me sound more brave then I felt. The unknown frightened me, but it was the dark that held the most mystery and I wanted no part of it. As a small girl, I slept with a light on. Still do. Flick all the lights off in the middle of the night and I will pop up from a deep sleep because of some instinctual warning. I hate the dark.

So many things intimidated me while I was growing up that I relied on my mother for support and remained glued to her side as much as possible. We talked all the time, laughed with each other and went to church together every Sunday. I refused to be separated from my mother and, when I was frightened, which was often, it was to her side that I ran. My timid nature had been a bone of contention between my mother and father for as long as he was around. My parents, Robert and Lizzie Mae Jeter, would argue about my need to cling to her and during my father's frequent drinking binges, he turned violent.

My father was a wandering soul. He couldn't stay in one place for long and would pack us up and move us around according to whatever whim directed such things. I was born in Carlisle, South Carolina on September 30, 1944, but we lived in Carlisle for only a year before we moved to Knoxville, Tennessee. A few years after that, we moved to Washington, D.C. to live near my great-aunt Sister. Since I was so young, I don't remember Carlisle or Knoxville. Living in D.C. is where my childhood memories start.

I was too young to know it, but a lot was happening at that time. It was 1949 and the Marshall Plan was in full swing, Harry Truman was President of the United States, and the North Atlantic Treaty Organization was established. There were rumblings of war on the Korean Peninsula, and that year the Yankees won the World Series.

Those were the news headlines when my father moved our family to the nation's capital where we ended up staying for several years. At five years old, I was only beginning to understand how hard my mother worked to keep us clean and fed. What I did know was that our mother was in a constant struggle to take care of us. My father was rarely around, so Momma supported me and my two brothers and two sisters on the income she earned as a nanny and general domestic worker.

In the summertime, we would take the train from D.C. to South Carolina to visit my parents' families, spending time surrounded by aunts, uncles and cousins. Like most kids, I wasn't always clear about who was related to whom and how. I never became schooled on the deep family history, where we came from or how our family came to be the way we were. Up until my early teenage years, learning about my roots wasn't at the top of my priorities.

One of the few things I do remember is that my father's father was of mixed race. Our summer get-togethers with family often included a lot of white people, many of them related to me in some distant way. When my grandfather died, the church during his funeral service was filled with white people.

I didn't have to know a bunch of family history to know where my height came from. I'd always been far taller than most of the young girls I knew. Lizzie Mae Jeter was tall and lean, stylish in her pageboy hairdo that curled slightly at her jaw line. She was frugal in her shopping but managed, on our weekly visits to church, to wear the latest styles, cute little dresses with matching hats, shoes and gloves. I wanted so much to be like her but didn't think I would ever have her poise and grace.

Instead, I was an awkward bean pole, skittish at my own shadow.

At home, my mother stayed in constant motion, always wiping counters, sweeping floors, cleaning every nook and cranny. Momma believed in keeping a spotless home which meant she rarely sat still. And when she wasn't cleaning our house, she was out earning a living, working one job or another.

Along with her height, I inherited her need to be busy all the time. And from the time I was a child, I wanted to help ease some of her burden, so I sought out ways to earn money by finding little jobs to do around the neighborhood. It wasn't long before I found my first steady job. At age eight, I began to run errands for a white lady in the neighborhood, Mrs. Greenwood, who was confined to a wheelchair. I would visit Mrs. Greenwood after school, run to the store for her and do her shopping, and sometimes wash her feet for her when she needed me to. That kind old woman paid me ten dollars a week, which I immediately handed over to my mother to help with the bills. Momma let me buy myself a hot dog with my weekly earnings, but the rest went to contribute to the upkeep of the household.

I never minded the work. It seemed natural for me to head to Mrs. Greenwood's directly after school, to run her errands and to sit with her for a few minutes. We would sit at her kitchen table, dunking wheat bread in milk, a snack I quickly learned to love. While the money wasn't much, it was enough to teach me to appreciate earning a wage, to be proud of a job well done and to be dependable and reliable. Throughout the rest of my life, I never went long without some kind of employment.

My little weekly pay helped my mother as she struggled to support us and pay rent on the two bedrooms and tiny living room our entire family lived in on the second floor of a small home. We shared our kitchen with the homeowners, a family living on the main floor.

At the time, I didn't realize how poor we were, how much my mother's small paycheck had to stretch or how devastating it was when my father, someone who was already unreliable, disappeared for good. All I knew at the time was that our home looked spotless, we were never hungry, and we were always clean and well cared for.

I shared a bedroom with all of my siblings. My sisters Barbara and Robbie, who we called Cat, shared a bed on one side of the room. My brother Robert, who we called Mickey, had a bed on the other side of the room. My youngest brother, Larry, was just an infant at the time and slept in a crib. The other bedroom belonged to my parents, but since my father was gone most of the time, only my mother stayed there. She was rarely in the room since she was constantly busy, sometimes taking in laundry and caring for other people's children in our small home.

I don't remember a lot about those early years in Washington, but the few memories that stick were not altogether happy. Maybe that's why they come to mind when I think of the city, because of the fear and uneasiness that accompany them. Like my first frightening day at kindergarten. My mother put ribbons in my hair and held my hand as she took me to Sumner Magruder Elementary school. She took me to the little girls' room when I needed to go out of nervous energy. She waited for me outside as I went into the restroom. When the toilet flushed by itself, an automatic trigger sending the water rushing away, I became so frightened, I ran out of the room crying and continued running straight past my mother. She chased me down the hall, finally catching me.

Automatic flushing toilets weren't the only things that frightened me. The dark, strangers, things I didn't understand, and just about anything that happened when my mother wasn't around could reduce me to tears. One day, my mother dressed all us girls in our Sunday best to attend a birthday party. Momma walked Barbara, Cat and me a few blocks away to the home of a family who attended our church. This family was much better off than we were and their home was large, with all the modern conveniences of the time, including a black-and-white television. My sisters and I had never seen a television before and we weren't alone in our ignorance. After arriving, the kids all wanted to see the magical box and gathered in front of the grainy image that danced across the console set, watching *The Lone Ranger.*

Not only was I seeing television for the first time, I'd never seen men on horses before, let alone riding them in a full-out gallop. One of these men was wearing a mask and his Indian friend had a painted face. They were speeding away from a mob of Indians right on their tails. During the pursuit, the Indians fired arrows and rifles at the men, and the men spun in their saddles to fire back.

As crazy as it sounds now, at the time I was convinced those Indians, with their scary painted faces and their blood-thirsty yells, and the loud bangs from all the guns going off, were going to come crashing out of that television and get me. I screamed and cried and begged for my mother. I was about nine years old at the time, and, looking back on it now, I am deeply embarrassed by the way I ruined that birthday party, by the fact that one of the adults at the party had to walk me home (Bobbie and Cat stayed to enjoy themselves) and, despite everyone's kind attempts to help, my inability to stop crying until I was in my mother's arms.

As easily frightened as I was then, I do remember that I enjoyed school and looked forward to learning new things, hearing about the world outside my tiny sphere of experience. But my sister Barbara had other ideas.

My oldest sister, whose given name was Bertha Mae after our paternal grandmother, was an aggressive sort, to put it mildly, and tended to get her way by force if threats didn't work. She was the oldest, the biggest and unafraid of using her fists if necessary. Bertha May hated her name, and if any of us called her by the name she was christened with, she would beat us up. A violent punch to the shoulder, a smack across the face, a sharp pull of a handful of hair—she would dole out the punishment without guilt or self-recrimination. When my sister began to call herself Barbara, we all complied with her wishes under threat of bodily harm. It was Barbara or Bobbie or else.

Barbara hated school; hated it so much she skipped often and sometimes forced me through intimidation and sheer menace to join her in her truancy. Momma would dress us for school and send us out the door to walk the three blocks to Sumner Magruder. If Bobbie decided she didn't want to go to school that day, she didn't. I remember several times when she'd grab me and force me to hide with her under the house.

"Be quiet," she'd warn with a fist in front of my face, "and don't you say nothin'." She would shove me under the porch and into a little crawl space there. "And you better not tell."

I never did tell and felt I had little choice but to comply with Barbara's demands. Given the choice between feeling the wrath of Bobbie's anger in harsh slaps or worrying about being caught, I chose to worry about being caught. Kowtowing to Barbara under the porch, my silent little prayers were answered. We were never caught.

Despite the occasional skipped day of school, I always brought home report cards I could be proud of. But just when I began to get really comfortable in school, my father made another appearance.

Robert Jeter would disappear for days and months at a time, and when he did return, he'd be stumbling drunk and ready to fight. I don't remember what most of the fights were about, but he usually managed to turn my gentle mother into someone ready to go to combat to protect her children. Blows were thrown on both sides. It would get ugly. Very ugly.

The worst fight I can remember was when my youngest brother Larry was still a baby. My father came home after being away for several weeks. He was drunk. So drunk he stumbled around the apartment, cursing loudly and slurring his words with no regard for waking up his children. When my father was in such a state, the slightest provocation, and sometimes no provocation at all, made him angry and combative. This instance wasn't any different.

He came in the apartment and went straight to find Larry, who was sleeping peacefully in his crib. Perhaps he just wanted to see his son after being absent for so long. But no matter how good his intentions may have been, my mother naturally jumped to her child's defense, knowing her husband was too drunk to be near the baby.

"Leave me alone, woman!" he shouted, pushing my mother violently against the wall. He could barely stand without swaying or speak a coherent sentence. Worse, he was too drunk to see reason.

"Stay away from my baby," my mother shouted.

They pushed and shoved each other, screaming and crying while my father threw wild swings at our mother. I was shocked when Barbara jumped onto my father's back, trying to stop him—one of the few times I was grateful for my sister's violent tendencies. Then Cat joined in, hitting, screaming and desperate to protect our mother. I stood against the wall, my hands covering my face, crying, frightened and too petrified to move. I could only imagine how the entire sordid ruckus sounded to the neighbors downstairs.

Things escalated before they calmed down. With Bobby on his back, Cat hitting him, my mother pulling on him, and as drunk as he was, he eventually wore himself out. They forced him to back away from the crib where he stumbled to the floor, cursing them with every four-letter word imaginable. Momma grabbed Larry from his crib and clutched him to her chest as she warned our father to stay away. He sputtered and yelled for her to come back, but she ignored him.

We all piled into our mother's room and crowded onto her bed for a restless, uncomfortable night. I can only assume that with us out of the room, our father quickly passed out. The next morning, we wandered out of our mother's room wondering if our father was still in the house. We found him curled up and sleeping in Larry's crib.

Robert Jeter disappeared for the longest time after that. He simply left and didn't come back for several months. And while his disappearance brought far more peace to our home, the absence of what little money he contributed to the household budget caused us to lose our apartment. Momma couldn't afford it any longer. To avoid eviction, we moved into the basement of a friend of my great-aunt's. Aunt Sister was the sister of my paternal grandmother. She helped arrange it so that we could live in the crowded, unfinished, dark basement of her friend's home for several months, existing on the charity of a stranger. Our mother was able to get welfare assistance and scrimped and saved while she searched for a decent place to live. After a lot of searching, she finally found a place for us.

When I saw the apartment for the first time, I could barely contain my excitement. To my young mind it was the most beautiful apartment I'd ever seen, with a porch, two bedrooms so the boys and girls would have their own rooms for the first time, a full kitchen we didn't have to share, and a living room. The prospect of living there thrilled me. I smiled from ear to ear, so eager to live in such a place.

Then, just before we were to move into the apartment of my dreams, my father came back.

"I've changed," he said. "I'm not drinking anymore."

He begged for forgiveness and claimed that everything would be better and that he wanted to be part of our family. He had found work hours away in another state, in a town where his brother lived, and he wanted us all to move there. The plan was for us to live with my uncle and his family for a time, until we could find a place of our own.

My father spent several days trying to convince my mother to go with him and move to that other state. He begged Aunt Sister, begged our mother, worked his charm, made promise after promise. I had my heart set on the new apartment and, while I didn't know what the move to another state would mean, I knew that at the very least, we would be giving up the home I'd wished for so hard.

When my mother finally gave in to his wishes, I was disappointed, but I didn't have a say in the matter. I said goodbye to Mrs. Greenwood and my little job with her. I withdrew from Sumner Magruder elementary school with its automatically flushing toilets and we packed up what few belongings we had and moved out of the basement. I was eleven years old when we moved to Aliquippa, Pennsylvania—the place I would always call home.

MY GREATEST SIN

Tall and lanky. I'm sure when people saw my skinny body, all knobby angles and loose clothing, they wondered if we had enough food to eat at home. I loved food but couldn't ever seem to eat enough to make it stick. By the time I turned seventeen, I was six feet tall. Awkward was too kind a word for how I felt. My height attracted attention and that was the last thing I wanted, so I hunched my shoulders, tried to slink around unnoticed, keeping my eyes to the ground. I rarely spoke unless I had a good reason.

In our small neighborhood in the suburban town of Aliquippa, Pennsylvania, no matter how much I slumped and tried to be invisible, people still knew everything about me and my family, as neighbors do in small towns everywhere. Aliquippa was a town run by steel. The steel mill jobs were steady and well paying. My father took us there because of the work he knew he would find at the mill and the extended family he had in the town. There were several Jeter families in Aliquippa, not all of them related to us. Those that were, like my father, didn't play much of a role in my life.

In those days, when a man found a job at the steel mill, he and his family were set for life. Steady income meant the ability to own a car and a home, raise children and, after a few decades of dedicated labor, look forward to a sound retirement. Those were the days when the American landscape was filled with factories and foundries, places where people who wanted to work could find it, and with that work, build families and secure lives. In Aliquippa, generations of families had built their lives around the steel mill.

Most everyone worked for the Jones and Laughlin Steel Company, one of the largest steel mills in America. The entire town seemed connected to the powerful enterprise. Aliquippa drew its life blood from the corporation that employed the men, fed the children and kept the town alive. The huge factory complex, surrounded by rail lines and heaps of raw materials, incessantly belched smoke and noise every hour of the day. Late at night, the lights from the factory stayed on, steam billowed from the stacks and train cars delivered parts and supplies then took away finished product in a constant, never-ending stream of factory life.

The pulse of the entire town flowed through and around that factory. There was even a J and L Store, where employees could make purchases and have the charges deducted directly from their pay.

Despite his well-paying job and the security it meant to his family, not long after we arrived my father again found comfort in a bottle of alcohol. Once he started drinking, work was less important and, eventually, his wanderlust took hold again. And in an unexpected way, the very company that provided the essentials to life for most everyone in town also helped to keep our father supplied with drink. Anywhere else, once he ran out of money, he wouldn't have been able to buy alcohol. Because of the company store, when his pockets emptied, he literally began to take food out of his children's mouths to feed his addiction. Along with his pay, came credits that could be used in the J and L store to buy food and other necessities. Our mother took charge of the food credits to keep good meals on the table. Sometimes, she would be surprised to find that Robert Jeter had already used all of those credits without bringing any food home to his family, and she would have to stretch what we had to keep us fed.

One day, Bobbie and I were in the store and we saw him buying a large ham, a steak and other high-priced items. He paid for the food using credits then turned and saw his daughters watching him. He bent down and put his index finger up to his lips. "Shhhhhh," he said, telling us to keep his secret. He picked up his purchases and left the store.

"Don't you say nothin'," Bobbie said, squeezing my arm until it hurt.

"Okay, okay! I won't say anything," I promised.

Later, after selling the ham and the steak and the other food his children could have eaten, he came home drunk, belligerent and stinking of liquor.

Robert Jeter left his wife and five children for the last time when I was twelve years old. I wouldn't see him again until I was twenty-eight and a mother myself. At the time, he had suffered a stroke and I was asked to visit him in the hospital. I had so few memories of his role in my life, most of them negative, that I felt little when I looked at him, sick and helpless in his hospital bed. The next time I saw him, several years after that hospital visit, I was staring down at him tucked neatly in his coffin. To this day, I don't think of Robert Jeter as my father for the simple reason he was never a father to me. He was my mother's wayward husband. I regret that I didn't have a father, but I'm not angry about it. Robert Jeter was simply not up to the task.

Even after he left, our schools, our church, our work remained in Aliquippa. So my mother, sisters and brothers and I stayed in the small town and made it our home. It was so different from the city life we were used to in D.C. that Momma never hesitated to send us all outside to play with our friends. She would stay inside, cleaning, tidying, dusting, wiping down counters, and probably enjoying it more without us underfoot.

Once a week, on Sundays, we would have a huge family meal together. On most of those Sundays, I was the only child who wanted to go to church, so I would go with Momma and after, she would cook a special meal. Whether they went to church or not, my brothers and sisters were required to appear for dinner. As we grew older, as other interests began to drag our attention away from family conversation, sitting down to the Sunday meal wasn't always voluntary, but it was the only regular time we were together as a family.

As children, our neighborhood was our playground and in those days, no one hesitated to let kids play on their own outside, as long as they were in the house by dark. We took advantage of every minute of sunlight. Our neighborhood games of hide and seek, marbles, jump rope, hopscotch and tag involved every kid on the block and sometimes neighboring blocks. After school most afternoons you'd find kids racing through backyards, challenging each other to one competition or another in games that would go on for hours.

My siblings and I all had our little groups of friends we played with, both black and white. The three girls I spent most of my time with, Rena Mae, Helen and Annie, felt the same way I did. Our schools were integrated and we didn't really care about color. We had friends of both races. So by the time I was in high school and we began to see the newsreel footage of the troubles in the South—the water cannons and people attacked by dogs—we were surprised and horrified. That sort of racism wasn't part of my life in Pennsylvania and we didn't understand how it could go on.

While our teachers were all white, I never felt any discrimination from them or from the white students. We played together during recess, met each other outside of school and generally got along. My closest friends were black, but I never felt any hatred leveled against me simply because of my color. Not in Aliquippa.

I was unaware of it at the time, but Robert Jeter's influence continued to affect my life after he left. All through high school I avoided dating, never trusting the boys I grew to know. The only example of a man I had known had turned out to be untrustworthy, violent and more trouble than he was worth. I had watched the bitter fights between my parents and didn't want any part of a tumultuous relationship like theirs. I went to dances now and then, let a couple of boys walk me home, but my fear of the consequences of allowing a boy to get too close never wavered.

Besides, my two sisters Barbara and Cat made up for any disregard I had for men. They were both vivacious and outgoing, surrounded by friends and looking for fun. Bobbie dated a lot and was always out, spending time with friends and socializing. I always thought she was beautiful, much better looking than I was. She was average height, shapely and confident, and could pretty much have any boy she wanted. She and Cat both had warm brown skin, long, thick hair and always took time to look their best. They would come home late after dates, often missing their curfew. My mother became stressed over the antics of her beautiful girls. The first signs of future problems came when Cat would occasionally come home intoxicated after a late night.

While Barbara and Cat were out, I preferred to spend my time with my mother and sometimes with a couple of girl friends. I just never felt that I was attractive like my sisters. One day, I overheard a neighbor lady say something that I could never shake: "It's a good thing that girl has a cute face and that long pretty hair, because she's almost too dark."

Those words affected my self-image, but it wasn't just my color that made me feel unattractive. I was too tall, too skinny, and felt too awkward to converse with anyone other than a small group of school friends and my mother. When I wasn't with my mother, I would be in the library reading books about places and things I could never imagine on my own. I became kind of a dreamer, thinking about other possibilities, other places, something different. I wanted to *be* something. I didn't have any idea what that something was, but books made other worlds seem more possible.

And then it was 1962 and John F. Kennedy was President. He launched the Bay of Pigs and the world held its breath during the Cuban Missile Crisis. The Berlin Wall had been built the year before and we were learning to live with the idea of a Cold War. Each night on our small, black-and-white TVs, we watched the grainy footage of Freedom Riders in the South, heard the stories of murdered civil rights workers and the violent riots that stemmed from the attempts to desegregate of the University of Mississippi. I graduated from high school that year at seventeen and spent my summer listening to the Supremes, Smokey Robinson and the Miracles, Aretha Franklin and Curtis Mayfield. But Aliquippa offered little in the way of diversion. Once I graduated, I kept working and tried to figure out what to do with the rest of my life. There weren't too many options.

My love of books was so great that I thought myself lucky to find work that allowed me to keep my nose buried between pages while earning money. My job at Prather's Pool Hall and Barbershop gave me plenty of opportunity to read, while waiting for opportunities to rack balls for the start of new games. I could hide behind my counter, where I sold gum and snacks to the pool players, quietly observing what was going on around me while keeping my nose buried in a book. I would listen to the constant banter of the people who hung out at Prather's, until someone yelled for me to get to work.

"Slim! Rack 'em, table four," the customers would yell. I'd go over and rack the balls in the wooden triangle, making things ready for another game.

"Rack 'em tight, Slim," they would instruct and tip me when I finished.

Mr. Prather, the barber who owned the pool hall/barbershop, kept close watch over me. He always had one eye on the heads he was styling and one eye on me, making sure the customers treated me like a lady. I liked the pool hall job—I could read while I worked and I could watch the goings-on while sitting anonymously behind the counter. The extra tips helped, too. It was far better than my previous job as a short-order cook, flipping hamburgers from ten at night until four in the morning.

Prather's Pool Hall was a pretty good gig.

I'd sit on a high stool against the wall, my attention bouncing between the books and magazines I was reading to the friendly banter and boastful talk of the men and young boys who hung around the place. If they weren't sitting in Prather's chair draped in a barber's cape, they were hanging around the billiard tables, squinting through cigarette smoke to aim their pool cues at an impossible shot. They popped their fingers to the music, joked and teased each other and generally spent a lot of time doing very little but hanging out. I was the observer in the corner, sitting quietly, watching and listening to the activities around me. Invisible.

Invisible until Walter Ingram took notice of me. His skin was milk-chocolate brown and he was taller than me, which was unusual for a six-foot teenage girl. His height was a definite plus. When he turned his bright smile and smoky eyes my way, I would blush and look away. He always caught me looking though and would saunter over, share a few kind words with me, ask what I was reading and offer to walk me home at the end of my shift. I had recently turned eighteen and Walter made me feel like a woman, a pretty and desirable woman. He made me feel things I hadn't felt before and I liked it. The problem was, Walter was seven years my senior. My mother had no idea a twenty-five-year-old man had taken an interest in me, and I never told her, preferring to hold my secret to myself.

Walter was persistent and spent months working his charm. He talked to me, seemed to confide in me and, on the rare occasion when I did have something to say, he listened as if my ideas were important. Most nights, he would wait for me to finish my shift and walk me home, playing the gentleman, making me feel special. Eventually, I invited him inside.

In addition to the occasional domestic work she was doing, my mother had been working as a waitress at the local Elks Club in the evenings. Walter and his buddies often hung out at the club, drinking, dancing and flirting with women. My mom had already heard that an older man had been walking her daughter home from Prather's. So when Walter showed up at her door in his fancy clothes, she wasn't impressed.

Still, when I brought Walter to the house, Momma didn't send him away. Maybe she knew he was my first real romantic interest. Maybe she figured if she said no, I'd only want him more. Whatever her reason, she gave me a stern warning but allowed him to come into the house. She pulled me into the kitchen to provide her cautionary words: "He can visit for a little while, but he better not put his processed head down on that sofa. Do you understand?"

"Yes, Momma." I had every intention of following her instructions.

Momma went upstairs and left us alone in the living room. It was late, but we sat on the sofa, watching television, talking, holding hands and feeling the closeness that had been building between us. Eventually, he kissed me. I had never been kissed like that before. My heart fluttered in my chest, and I felt so beautiful, so special, that this handsome, older man would take such an interest in me. It was magical.

And then it all turned ugly.

I don't know how it happened. My mother was right upstairs and I could have cried out to her, but I was so ashamed, so frightened that I had allowed the situation to get completely out of my control. One minute we were kissing and I liked it. The next minute he had pushed my skirt up and I felt helpless to stop him. The details are fuzzy, but I remember the piercing pain and then shame, total and complete shame.

There was no such thing as date rape in 1962. No one to explain to me what was happening, no language I could use to express how power-less I felt. I wasn't drunk or drugged. I wasn't beaten or restrained, but fighting him off didn't seem possible. I couldn't even bring myself to say no to him. I think he would have ignored me if I had.

When it was over, Walter acted as if everything was normal, like there was nothing wrong with a twenty-five-year-old man having his way with an eighteen-year-old girl on her mother's sofa. I rushed him out of the house, wanting to get rid of him. At the time, I was certain of two things. That I had sinned, had committed the greatest sin of my life, and that I was pregnant.

The next day, I went to the only black doctor in town, bringing my underwear with me. I'm not sure what I thought he could do with the panties, but they had blood on them. After Walter left, I had hidden them under the porch, afraid my mother would see the evidence of what had happened. I brought them to the doctor as proof that the sin had been committed.

"I'm pregnant," I told the doctor. "I just know it."

"You said this was the first time you've had intercourse," he said.

"Yes," I managed to say. "And I shouldn't have done it."

"Well, don't be ridiculous," he said. "You don't automatically get pregnant your first time. Just be sure to take precautions next time."

Later, when my initial fears came true and I was weeks late, my sin was confirmed and I knew God was punishing me for it.

Of course, I was petrified to tell my mother. As frightened as I was, I knew I needed to tell her before she discovered my predicament herself. I figured she would question me soon because I usually suffered severe cramps. I wanted to tell her before she noticed the time passing and came to her own conclusions. Finding the courage to tell her was one of the hardest things I'd ever done. She wasn't just my mother; she was my best friend. There was no one else I could confide in.

When I finally told her, she appeared just as shocked as I feared she would be. She shouted "No," then ran from the room crying. After spending sometime on her own to think things over and to calm down, she had lots of questions. She wanted to know how I knew.

"I'm over three weeks late," I told her.

She called me stupid, and I felt stupid. Stupid for falling for Walter's smooth talk. Stupid for the predicament I was in. I told her the specifics of that awful night with Walter and it made the sordid details all the more real. Eventually she insisted that we go to the doctor as soon as possible.

Momma had always trusted that I would do the right thing. I was the good girl. I was the one who accompanied her to church, the one who came home after work and the one who shared all of my secrets with her. Now, I felt I was her greatest disappointment.

As I walked out the door that day to go to Prather's for work, she told me to stay away from Walter and I did, until several days later when I finally had to tell him. He had a quick solution to the problem: "I'll do anything you want. Let me pay for the abortion. Everything will be okay."

Abortion was never an option for me. Yes, I had sinned, but I felt abortion would be an even greater sin. I never considered giving the child up, either. Once I gave birth, the baby would be *my* baby. I knew it would be hard, but I felt determined to figure out a way to keep the child and raise it. I had made the mistake, but I wasn't going to make my child suffer because of what I had done.

I continued to work at Prather's and each day my mom had my brother Mickey walk me home to ensure I made it there safely. I went from work to home, home to work, up to the seventh month of my pregnancy.

Walter still spoke to me at the pool hall, still came by the house now and then. He would give me money to help pay doctor's bills and wasn't ashamed to tell his friends that he was going to be a father. He acted as if fatherhood was something he was proud of, but he never mentioned marriage. I wouldn't have accepted him if he had. The more I got to know Walter, the more I saw him for who he truly was, a fast-talking dandy who took advantage of a young girl. Far from feeling ashamed, he was proud of his conquest. It became clear that Walter wasn't a nice man.

By the seventh month, there was no question how pregnant I was and I could no longer walk around town with my head up. Everyone knew everyone else's business in Aliquippa. Everyone knew who I was and everyone knew what Walter had done, but I always felt that I was the one who carried the sin. I wasn't a fast and loose girl, but that didn't matter. I had committed the sin and it was mine to bear.

I quit the job at Prather's and stayed home Monday through Saturday. On Sundays I went to church with my mother and prayed for forgiveness and tried to come to terms with the coming of my child. There was nothing joyful about my pregnancy. I was so racked with guilt, so filled with shame, that I was sad and fearful much of the time. I never actually prepared for delivery, never learned anything about what to expect, how to breathe, how to ease the pain of labor. When I finally delivered my daughter on September 25, 1963, it was after hours of fear and pain, hours of screaming. I cried and prayed that the punishment of the delivery would finally cleanse me of my transgression, that somehow the pain of labor would absolve me.

Walter came to the hospital, smiling proudly at his little girl. I called her Helene, and looking at her brought such a complicated jumble of feelings. Guilt. Responsibility. Fear. She was a beautiful baby, with bright eyes and a head of curly red hair. I expected to experience a welling of maternal love, but that didn't come until later. My overall feeling was that Helene was my responsibility and that I would care for her to the very best of my ability and be as good a mother as I could. My mother had set the example for me, providing a constant, kind, caring and supportive home for me and my siblings. I intended to provide the same for my own daughter, no matter how sinful I still felt.

Walter would come to the house to visit, bringing money for Helene's care. I didn't want any part of his money. I made him give it to my mother, who had started to warm to his charm. "He's not so bad," she said. "Look, he's contributing. He's trying to do the right thing."

But I knew it was all for show. Walter was seeing lots of women in town, bragging about his daughter. It wasn't long before I realized two things: that Walter would never leave me alone, now that I had his daughter; and if I was ever going to get away from him and his influence, I had to get the hell out of Aliquippa.

I was on the bus, coming home from my six-week check-up, when I heard the news that President Kennedy had been shot. The world suddenly seemed more unstable, more vulnerable to the unthinkable. We had advisors in Vietnam and there was constant talk of war. The civil rights movement was stirring up violent reactions in other parts of the country. None of that touched Aliquippa, but uncertainty was multiplied many fold when the President was assassinated. None of us knew what would happen next.

After Helene's birth, my mother remained the main breadwinner in the home. I couldn't return to work and didn't have any idea where I would find work that would support me and my child. I spent my days caring for Helene and wondering what I would do with my life.

One evening, Walter came by to visit. Helene was three months old at the time, and as usual hadn't fussed when I put her down for the night. When I joined Walter downstairs, he was his usual, charming self, talking, laughing, not giving up on the fact that we would never have a physical relationship again, let alone one in which I could ever trust him. As we sat there talking, something told me to check on Helene. She had only been in bed an hour or so, but by some instinct I knew I needed to check on her.

I went upstairs and could tell immediately that something was horribly wrong. Helene lay in her bassinette, a beautiful white-laced cradle with pillows all around. She lay on her stomach, her face turned to the side, buried into the pillow padding of the bassinette. When I rolled her over, her face was blue and her eyes were rolled back. She had stopped breathing.

I screamed so loud the entire neighborhood must have heard me. "Oh, my God! She's not breathing. My baby's not breathing."

I snatched her up, trying to bring some life back into her, but she seemed completely lifeless.

We didn't know anything about Sudden Infant Death Syndrome (SIDS) at the time and certainly nothing about administering CPR to an infant. All I knew was that my baby was either dead or near it. I was as close to panic as I'd ever felt.

A neighbor heard the ruckus and came to help. He drove all of us, Walter, my mother, Helene and me to the hospital. I had wrapped Helene in a blanket and we all piled into the car. As we raced down the street, jostling against each other in the back seat, I finally felt Helene take a deep shuddering breath. By the time we got to the emergency room, her color had begun to return to normal and she seemed to be breathing normally. The doctor made a cursory examination but didn't find any reason to worry.

"She's fine," he said. "Her color is back and she looks perfectly normal. You can take her home. There's nothing we can do for her here."

Mother and Walter looked relieved, but I knew better. I looked into my baby's eyes and knew something was missing. Her eyes were open, but she didn't seem to be seeing me.

"Are you sure, doctor?" I asked. "Shouldn't you do some tests or something?"

My worries were dismissed and we all went home, relieved that Helene was still with us. But I knew better. As the days wore on, I sensed the change in my daughter. Even at three months old, Helene had been a bright, smiling child who followed me with her eyes, grabbed at things the way curious children do. Now, when I held bright shiny things in front of her, she had no reaction. Once I touched her hand with the object, she might grab at it, but she didn't react as before, didn't seem as curious. A mother knows when things aren't right and I knew Helene had suffered some damage as a result of the lack of oxygen.

I made frequent visits to the doctor, trying to convince him that things weren't right.

"You're working yourself up over nothing," he said. "She's an infant. They develop differently sometimes. Give her time to grow. Everything will be fine. You'll see."

But everything wasn't fine. She was such a beautiful baby that no one wanted to see past her cuteness to that lack of reaction she displayed. Soon, Walter, my mother, and all of my siblings were telling me it was just my imagination.

"What is wrong with you?" my mother asked me. "There's nothing wrong with that baby. Why do you keep taking her to the doctor?"

I would attempt to demonstrate for them what I had observed. I would light a match and slowly move the match closer and closer to Helene's face, just to the brink of burning her. She never flinched, never showed any reaction of any kind.

"Just stop it," my mother yelled. "You're being ridiculous and looking for trouble. You have to stop this nonsense."

As the months went by and Helene didn't begin to crawl as soon as other babies, when she didn't walk as expected, when she never learned to form words, my fears were proven true. I still couldn't get anyone to speak about it, but it was abundantly clear that Helene wasn't going to be like other children. She attempted to communicate with sounds and gestures. Her vocabulary was restricted to monosyllabic words that came out more like grunts than speech. Her inability to properly communicate her needs eventually led to some mild behavioral problems as her frustrations mounted.

In those early days, my concern for my daughter and what her future might hold was constant. I was completely alone in the realization that Helene would need special care and that I didn't have the means to provide it for her. I felt alone with my worry.

They say desperate times call for desperate measures and I was feeling desperate.

I WENT UP THE STAIRS

One thing I knew for sure, I was never going to be able to provide for my daughter if I didn't get an education. Bobbie hadn't graduated from high school—she simply lost interest and quit. Quitting wasn't an option for me. When I graduated, in 1962, I was the first member of my family to get a high school diploma. Being the first person in the family to finish high school turned out to be the first of many firsts I would achieve in my life.

I knew a high school diploma wasn't enough. Helene was going to need more than normal childcare. I didn't know the extent of her condition, but her development wasn't progressing the way it should and I knew, even if no one else would admit it, that we were going to need professional help.

I tried to get a job as an airline stewardess – that's what we called them back then. I went to Pittsburgh to apply and interviewed with several airlines. They all told me I was too tall—once they put the pointy-toed high-heeled shoes on me along with a hat, my six-foot frame wouldn't fit in the plane! I suspected the real reason for the rejection might have been more about my color than my height. Stewardesses were thin, pretty and white in those days. There wasn't much I could do about that so I quickly set my sights on something else.

Thinking I could use my height to my advantage, I decided to try modeling. The modeling agents said that while I'd work well on a runway, the gap in my teeth would prevent me from getting any catalogue work. There were very few African-American models around at that time, and I wouldn't be surprised to learn that race had played a role in that rejection, too.

Still, I wasn't ready to give up. I had a baby to think of, and Walter was coming around the house, visiting whenever he wished. He had changed his tune and was now trying to convince me to marry him. I was nineteen and I didn't want my life to turn out like other young girls I knew—married and raising babies in that steel mill town. The last thing in the world I wanted was to be tied forever to Walter. Almost every week he came by, handing out money and trying to convince me to include him in my life. I didn't trust him and I knew he was selling me the same line he was hawking to other girls in town. I would never be happy as Mrs. Walter Ingram.

Staying in Aliquippa would lead to a totally predictable future. First one baby, then another baby, until before I knew it, I'd be stuck in a place I didn't want to be, looking like a train wreck, with no future, no past and no hope. I never wanted to end up on that treadmill of predictability. It wasn't long before I was desperate to get out. I was still reading, still dreaming, still imagining myself with something greater to look forward to. My twenties were approaching, and if I didn't do something quick, I knew my hopes could quickly dim to nothing.

So I racked my brain, trying to come up with a solution to my problem. How would I earn a living, get an education and get my child the help she needed to thrive?

I finally decided that I would apply to the police force. They had just started hiring women, even minority women. My mother wouldn't have approved had I talked it over with her, but at that point I was too desperate to worry about her approval. So I went downtown, heading for the police station to ask some questions to see what it would take to get into the police academy. It was midday and few people were out and about.

I was almost to police headquarters when I looked across the street and saw a life-sized cutout of Uncle Sam. He was dressed in his red, white and blue tuxedo and tails, wearing the striped top hat and a serious look on his face. The cardboard cutout said, "Uncle Sam wants YOU!"

That 'YOU' written in capital letters felt like Uncle Sam was speaking to me. He stood out on the sidewalk and his cardboard arm was pointing up the stairs to a second-floor recruiting office. I'm not sure how long I stared at that sign. It had stopped me in my tracks and I remember standing there, contemplating it. I had walked the streets of downtown Aliquippa countless times, but I didn't remember ever seeing that sign before.

I crossed the street and went up the stairs.

I walked into the recruiting office where a white man in a military uniform sat behind a desk. He wore his hair in a precise crew cut. A name tag and a rack of colorful ribbons were pinned on his chest. I didn't waste any time. "I want to join the Army."

His eyebrows shot up in surprise and I'm not sure, but I think he restrained himself from laughing. "You do, huh?"

"Yes." Now that I had climbed the stairs, I was completely sure about the decision.

"How old are you?" he asked, that laugh almost escaping him.

"I'm nineteen."

"Well, why don't you come and sit down and we'll talk about your options."

So I sat down and we talked. He told me about different career choices I could make, about basic training and about the pay, free room and board, medical care and promotion potential. When he talked about the GI Bill and the education benefits, saying I could even take college classes part-time while I served, he didn't need to go any further. I had made my decision. Still, he wanted to know why I wanted to join the Army.

"I have a daughter," I said. "And I want to give her a good future. I won't be able to do that without an education. I think this is the perfect solution."

"I think this is a good fit for you, but there are a couple of problems," he said.

My heart sank. It had taken me only minutes to be convinced that the Women's Army Corps was the answer to all of my prayers. I braced myself to hear about the obstacles. Whatever they were, I couldn't allow them to prevent me from reaching my goal.

"To join the Women's Army Corps, you have to be twenty years old. Since you're only nineteen, you have to have your parents' permission."

That, I thought, was a deal breaker. I could imagine my mother's reaction and it wasn't pretty. Momma was a kind and gentle person, but she didn't suffer any nonsense. I knew the idea of her daughter in an Army uniform would seem totally unseemly to her sensibilities.

"I'm not sure my mother will ever agree."

"Well, you'll have to discuss it with her. If you can't convince her, let me know. I'd be willing to come and talk to her myself if you want me to."

My eyes got big at that suggestion. I wasn't sure what worried me more, the thought of telling my mother what I intended to do, or the thought of this man coming to our house.

"But there's a bigger problem," he continued. "Women with children under fourteen years old are prohibited from joining the Army. Who would take care of your daughter while you are away?"

"My mother would, of course." My mother and Helene were very close. If I could convince her to let me join, the matter of Helene's care wouldn't be an issue. It would be hard to be away from Helene so long, but I would come home as often as I could and in only three years, our futures would be secure. It would be a small sacrifice compared to the opportunity the separation would bring.

"If you can convince your mother to allow you to join, and if she agrees to be the guardian of your daughter while you're away, I think we can make this work," the recruiter said.

Those 'ifs' seemed almost insurmountable to me. What words could I possibly say that would persuade my mother that this was the right thing to do? I didn't know, but I knew I needed to try.

That night, I found the courage to tell my mother my intentions.

"WHAT? You are not joining the military. No."

When my mother said no in that definitive way, then added the shake of her head with the crazy look in her eye, I knew it would take a great deal of convincing to get my way.

"Don't say no right away, Mom. The pay is great and, with the GI bill, I can get an education. How else could I ever pay for college?"

But she wasn't listening to me. I counted on the fact that she would care for Helene while I was away. My plan was to send most of my pay home, knowing it would be more money than I could ever hope to earn in Aliquippa. And it would be for only three years. Three years of service, three years of sacrifice and I'd have the ability to get the education that would lead to a much better life for all of us. My daughter and I would have a good start at something better. My hopes and dreams were tied up in convincing my mother of the rationality of my decision, but I knew I had my work cut out for me.

"The Army is no place for a girl like you. You'll end up a bull dagger," my mother said.

I had no idea what a bull dagger was but it didn't sound good, and I knew nothing I said after that was going to sway my mother's opinion.

The next day, I went back to the recruiter and told him about the conversation.

"She says I'll turn into a bull dagger," I told him.

This time he did laugh, covering his face with his hands as he tried to swallow the laughter, but it was a losing battle.

"I don't understand, sir. What's a bull dagger?"

He finally gained control of his laughter and answered me. In a very dignified way, he said, "I'm afraid your mother thinks you might become a lesbian. You know, a woman who wants to be with other women."

"Well, that's ridiculous! I would NEVER…" At that point in my life, I wasn't that crazy about men, but I knew I wouldn't ever change so much that I would want to be with women.

"I want to join the Army," I told the recruiter. "I know this is the right decision for me."

I wish I could remember his name now, the white man who recruited me into the Women's Army Corps, since he helped me make the most important decision of my life. He looked to be in his thirties with a ruddy complexion and blond hair. His uniform was immaculate and he carried himself very upright, as if he were constantly at attention. He could easily have decided that I was more trouble than I was worth, but he volunteered to do something that I thought at the time was very brave: "I'll talk to her."

"You will?"

"Don't worry about a thing. You just make us some tea and leave us alone, and I'll see if I can convince her to agree with this decision you've made."

We agreed on a time and date for him to come by the house when I knew my mother would be home. We never served tea in our house, but I was determined to do everything as he instructed, so I went out and purchased what I would need to make some instant iced tea, even hiding the stuff from my mother, thinking it would somehow clue her in that something was up. I never told her he was coming. I had been trying to gain the courage to warn her, but I never did. Finally, on the day of the appointment, he came walking up the sidewalk in his dress uniform. I almost panicked since I still hadn't told her that he was coming. I finally spit out the words as fast as I could say them. "Momma, the recruiter is coming over to talk to you about my joining the Army."

"He's WHAT?" Momma said. "I don't want to talk to him. You're not going to join the military. There's no reason to talk to him."

"But Momma, he's coming up the sidewalk right now!"

At that moment he knocked on the door and it was too late to back out. Momma, obviously exasperated with me, threw open the door.

"Hello, Mrs. Jeter." He removed his hat and tucked it under his arm. "May I speak to you for a few minutes?"

He stood there in his green jacket, his shiny brass buttons, gold stripes on his sleeves and ribbons on his chest. He was very erect and formidable. My mother could be intimidating, but the recruiter wasn't deterred. He just stuck out his hand and introduced himself very politely.

"Ma'am, I'd like to speak to you about your daughter. She would like to join the Army."

"My daughter is not joining the military." Momma sounded adamant.

But the recruiter was not going to be turned away so easily.

"Please, Mrs. Jeter, I'll only take a few minutes of your time. This is very important to your daughter and I think you should hear me out."

She looked him up and down for a minute, but she was too polite to bar him from entering. "You can come in if you want to," she said.

They went into the living room together, and I dashed into the kitchen. I made up a batch of the iced tea, following the instructions on the package and putting glasses and a pitcher on a tray. I carried the lot into the living room.

"Tea?" I asked.

"Tea?" My mother looked at me like I was from another planet. She watched me put the tray down with lips pressed together and her arms crossed. I laid out the tea things and poured with shaking hands. My mother and the recruiter were quiet as I went through the motions.

When that task was done, I left the room as fast as I could and returned to the kitchen, where I paced and bit my nails and wondered what the heck he was saying to her. There weren't any raised voices, which I took to be a good sign. I couldn't hear a thing he said, and as the minutes ticked by, I grew more and more nervous. Finally, after about an hour, my mother called my name.

When I entered the living room, Momma was leaning over the coffee table, signing the papers. The recruiter stood and turned to me, a smile lighting up his face.

"Looks like you'll be coming to Pittsburgh for your physical," he said.

I looked at my mother, who avoided my eyes. I could hardly believe what he had just said.

"I am?" I restrained myself from jumping up and down and clapping my hands in joy. Momma had signed the papers, but she could change her mind if I made too big a deal of the concession. So I just smiled.

"Yes, you are." There was the tiniest bit of triumph in his voice, but I couldn't blame him. He had done what I thought was the impossible—convinced my mother what I knew in my heart to be true, that the Army was the answer to my prayers.

He had already completed the contract and went over it with me page by page. My mother sat with me as he explained all the details, but one detail in the contract had to be explained further. The yes or no question asked if I had any children. The box next to 'no' had a large X on it. I questioned him about it.

"Remember, I told you that you can't join the Army if you have a child under fourteen."

"Yes, but I do have a daughter."

He turned to me, a very serious expression on his face. "This document assigns guardianship of your daughter to your mother. Are you both willing to sign this?"

My mother and I exchanged glances, Momma nodding her head. "Of course, I'll be guardian to my granddaughter. You don't have to worry about that."

"Then once we have this letter, technically, at least for the three years you are away, you won't have a child. Your mother is legally responsible, so you can answer no to this question."

Looking back on this moment, it's clear that my recruiter was helping me. From its inception in the 1940s, the Women's Army Corps discriminated against women with children. By the 1960s, they were still discriminating. Male military members received benefits for their dependants, both their wives and their children. Female military members didn't receive any benefits for dependants because the assumption was that a man in the house would be the primary breadwinner of the family. If a woman became pregnant while a WAC, she was immediately given a general discharge, and if she was married, she had to have her husband's permission to join. Even if her husband agreed to allow her to join, if there were children in the household who were under fourteen, regulations prohibited her from joining.

The rules were that I couldn't join the Army because the norms demanded I stay home to care for my child, but I felt I couldn't care for my child if I didn't join the Army. I relied on my recruiter's guidance and chose to do what was required to provide the best future for my daughter. My mother and I signed a guardianship letter and I signed the contract.

He gave me more details about shipping off to basic training at Fort McClellan, Alabama, about attending the Advanced Individual Training school there to learn to be an administrative clerk, and about opportunities to come home and visit my family in between. But I barely heard anything he said. My life was about to change in ways I could never have predicted.

I sometimes wonder now what the daughters of today say to their mothers when they've made the decision to join the military. I like to think mothers have fewer objections. Friends of mine have often said it would be easier for them to approve their daughters joining the Navy or the Air Force, making the assumption that those services would be easier on their girls than service in the Army or Marine Corps. Yet, plenty of women are joining the Army and serving with distinction and valor.

Serving in uniform still offers great benefits, like healthcare, education and the possibility for advancement, that make it an attractive place to start a career, especially for someone who may have trouble paying for a college education. While many parents may not consider it a first choice, the military is still a place where they see a second chance for the child who may have dropped out of college for one reason or another, for the child who can't get a scholarship and will have trouble paying for college, or for the son or daughter who may not be ready to go to college right out of high school.

It's been my experience that minority parents are usually more supportive of the idea, understanding the military as a place where equality is well established with mechanisms in place to ensure individuals are recognized for their abilities. The recent elimination of Don't Ask Don't Tell policies and the changes which allow same-sex couples to receive family and dependant benefits are examples of just how far the Department of Defense is willing to go in terms of equality. The DoD has always been a trail-blazer in terms of equality and it continues to be so.

At the writing of this book, we've been at war for more than ten years, a great portion of that time at war on two different fronts. In light of these wars, I'm sure there may be fewer parents who would be supportive of their children joining, but unlike the mood of the country in 1964 when I joined, there seems to be overwhelming support of people in uniform. The country loves our men and women in uniform and recognizes them for their noble sacrifice. How many parents could object to their children choosing to be a part of that?

That said, it's clear that modern warfare doesn't have a front line. There is no rear echelon, no "safe" military jobs. A woman in any military role can be in danger when the bullets start flying. In addition to the growing murky nature of the front line, women will soon have greater choice in the types of roles they will play and could volunteer for the kinds of combat roles previously excluded from them.

There is no doubt a woman's role in the military is far different today than it was when I joined and those changes mean that the potential leadership roles women could play will be much higher in the future. At one point in my career, it became clear to me that the lack of a combat patch would essentially stop my career progression. And while combat may not be for every woman, I know that at some point, like all glass ceilings, the one preventing women from attaining four-star status will shatter along with so many others.

MY OWN BED

I ran into a small complication when I gave my recruiter a copy of my birth certificate, part of the mountain of paperwork needed to complete my enlistment contract.

"This says your name is Julia, not Judith," he said.

"No, my name is Judith. Everyone calls me Judy."

"If this is your real birth certificate, then everyone is wrong." He handed the document to me.

I stared at the name *Julia* silently and, not knowing what to say, returned the certificate to him. The name spelled out plainly in black and white was indeed Julia. Why hadn't I ever known that before? Why hadn't my mother ever called me Julia? The document left me filled with questions, but it didn't seem to faze my seasoned recruiter. "We'll make it work," is all he said.

He typed the remainder of my paperwork using the name on my birth certificate and I signed it with the name I grew up with, Judith Jeter. I figured everything would sort itself out.

Of course, I went directly home and asked my mother about it. She said her intention had been to call me Judith, but the mid-wives who helped her when she gave birth to me at home assumed she meant to say Julia, since that was my grandmother's name. Evidently it had been a long and difficult labor. The mid-wives figured Lizzie Mae wasn't in her right mind, must have made a mistake, must have meant to say something else, so they took it upon themselves to put Julia on the birth certificate. My mother had simply ignored the legal document and used the name she wanted me to have. When anyone in my family wanted me, they hollered Judy. That's what Momma called me. That's what my sisters and brothers called me. Even my high school yearbook has the name Judith Jeter in the caption of my graduation photo. Right there, under my picture it says Judith Jeter, followed by what I had chosen as my highest aspiration, which was to be a secretary.

Despite the paperwork problems, less than a month after my mother gave her permission, I looked forward to traveling, and for the first time, traveling by plane. Unfortunately, I slept the entire flight. I was hung over.

The night before I shipped out, my brother wanted us to celebrate by giving me a good send off. Mickey came home with a six pack of Colt 45 Malt Liquor. He convinced me to drink one can. I felt like someone had injected the alcohol straight into my head. I became so drunk I could hardly read the writing on the can. I wondered if God sought to punish me. I was frightened and out of control and I didn't enjoy the feeling one bit. To this day, just hearing about malt liquor or beer makes me nauseous.

The next morning I woke up on the biggest day of my life with a head full of cotton, a mouth dry as ash and an unsettled stomach. I felt like crap. I was angry with myself and ashamed. I had grown up with an alcoholic in the house—I never wanted my life to be affected by alcohol the way Robert Jeter's had been. My sisters and brothers all drank, but I simply wasn't comfortable with how it made me feel. I swore to never get that drunk again.

I boarded the plane, happy but still feeling hung-over. As soon as my head hit the back of the airplane seat, I went to sleep and didn't wake up until we landed in Alabama. In the end, it was a good thing that I had caught several hours of sleep. I had a big day ahead of me.

I will never forget the first time I saw a woman in uniform. She wore a narrow hat that sloped down to a point on her forehead. Her light green shirt with its sharp darts, rounded collar and sculpted sides, fit snuggly. Her perfectly pressed, slim-cut skirt reached just above her knees. She wore flesh-colored pantyhose and her feet were in smart-looking low-quarter shoes. She appeared to be a hard, serious-looking thing and I wondered if this was what my mother feared would happen to me. There wasn't a hint of a smile on her face. I should have been afraid of her, but I was just so happy to see her. I felt so excited to be starting this adventure that I smiled at her.

"What's your name, recruit?" she asked me.

"Judy Jeter."

"Wipe that smile off your face, Jeter, and stand right here."

I stood where she directed but getting rid of the smile was harder. My journey was beginning and Aliquippa was behind me. I couldn't help but smile.

The drill sergeant tipped her head back to look up at me, but she wasn't the least bit intimidated by my height. Instead, she used it to her advantage.

"Okay, Jeter, you're now a squad leader," she said. "All of you recruits assemble on Jeter here. Do it now."

Most of the other women were white, although I spotted a few brown faces in the crowd. They all looked nervous. Some were crying. It puzzled me that everyone wasn't as excited and happy as I was. The women lined up in rows, whispering words of encouragement to each other. Once we were all lined up, the drill sergeants began to call out our names, expecting us to respond with, "Here, Sergeant." When they got to my name, the unfamiliar name was used.

"Jeter, Julia," the sergeant said.

I immediately decided that if the hard woman in the uniform wanted to call me Julia, I wasn't going to correct her. I called out loudly,

"Here, Sergeant."

The next few hours went by in a blur. We were hustled onto a bus under a flurry of orders and instructions. The drill sergeants talked fast and robotically, wasting no time as they recited a litany of what we could and could not do—one list much longer than the other. Eventually, we were seated in a classroom to fill out paperwork. Life insurance, naming beneficiaries, financial paperwork, medical and dental files—we had to fill out and sign page after page of documents. Of course, I used the name I had been raised with and signed in my usual way, not thinking it would matter.

Everywhere we went, we were lined up and marched from place to place, and every time we lined up, I was first. I learned quickly that being singled out as a squad leader meant when other women had questions, they turned to me for the answers. Through most of that first day, I was just as full of questions as everyone else, but everyone still expected me to know the answers. It was unusual for me to be the focus of so much attention, for people to look to me for information. I had spent most of my life trying to be invisible. The moment I stepped off the plane, I couldn't hide anymore. Jeter was the tall, black squad leader. Everyone learned my name, everyone knew who I was. It was a strange feeling. I grew to like it.

We were issued uniforms—hats, skirts, blouses, and a set of fatigues for field training —all of it shoved at us in an assembly line of efficiency. The people working in supply ran into all kinds of problems as they tried to fit my six-foot, one-hundred-and-ten-pound frame. Pants and sleeves were too short, shoes and boots didn't fit, waistlines were too large and shoulder seams hung down like weeping willow branches. Eventually, I left with an approximation of a uniform and promises that other parts would have to be specially ordered.

At the end of the day, we were all dressed like WACs and standing in our barracks building in an open bay surrounded by narrow metal beds with thin mattresses and footlockers. The final instruction our drill sergeants gave was to find a bed and get a good night's sleep because the next day was going to start long before the sun was up.

Their words were lost on me. At that point, my attention was focused elsewhere. It wouldn't be long before someone would turn out the lights and, squad leader or not, I was still afraid of the dark. I was about to spend my first night in a bed without my sister Cat next to me. The thought of being in such a large, unfamiliar room, alone in bed, surrounded by darkness was too much. If I didn't find a bed near some kind of light, things could get ugly.

The large red exit signs at opposite ends of the room were the only lights I was sure would stay on all night. My goal was to take a bed directly under one of those. When we were finally dismissed, I ran for one of the beds and claimed it, but I needn't have panicked. No one else seemed to be quite as desperate for a nightlight as I was. I sat on the bed I would use over the next few weeks, giving it a bounce, checking out the footlocker, feeling relieved.

And as I sat there it all really began to sink in. I had made it out of Aliquippa. I was a squad leader. I was a WAC. I was about to sleep alone in my own bed. I could have been worried about what the next few weeks would bring, and what kinds of challenges I would face, but none of that mattered. My new life had begun. I was happy.

MY NAME IS JULIA

The next morning, the drill sergeants decided that if the uniforms didn't fit me, they were going to change me to fit the uniforms. As I moved down the tray line in the mess hall, the breakfast servers were instructed to pile on the food.

"Give her more bacon," they said. And the strips were piled on my plate until there was a pound of crispy bacon stacked there.

As soon as I finished one glass of milk, someone placed another large glass in front of me. It was unbelievable to me that I could have as much milk and bacon as I wanted.

"Eat, Jeter, eat," they shouted at me. "We gotta put some meat on those bones."

We were allowed only minutes to eat, so we shoveled the food in our mouths, barely stopping to taste or chew with drill sergeants constantly berating us to eat faster, stop talking, eat, eat, eat! For me, the instructions were to eat more bacon, drink more milk. I was too skinny and was in danger of not meeting the weight requirements. Every week I had to step on the scale and show progress toward reaching the minimum weight standards for a woman in uniform. If I didn't put on some weight, there was a good chance that I would be booted out of the service.

So I complied with their demands. It was easy to do. I've always loved bacon, and milk was always my favorite drink, so it wasn't a problem to eat or drink as much of both as I could.

With the drill sergeants hovering around the tables, it became clear that as long as I was here in the Army, fading into the background, as was my custom, was not an option. The drill sergeants, the other recruits, even the people who served the food in the mess hall, all knew my name and they used it. "Jeter, Jeter, Jeter." I heard it over and over again. I wasn't accustomed to so much attention, but instead of cringing from it, I greeted it all with a smile.

This is what I wanted, wasn't it? A new start. A new life. A new chance to be the person I knew I could be. When I was instructed to stand at attention, my head went up, shoulders went back, chest out. The new, upright posture forced me to lose my customary hunch. It wasn't long before the hunch disappeared forever.

"Jeter, get in here," the drill sergeant snarled.

I stepped into the office, saluted and wondered what the drama was about. I had been pulled away from training and the other women had stared at me, wondering what was up. I wondered about it, too.

One drill sergeant sat behind a large, green metal desk. Another stood in the corner, her arms folded across her chest. Neither of them smiled, and the one in the corner gave me the command I had quickly grown accustomed to hearing: "Wipe that smile off your face, Jeter."

"Yes, Sergeant." Getting rid of my constant grin wasn't easy.

"What does this say, Jeter?" The one seated behind the desk pointed to my name on a document, her eyebrows raised in a quizzical accusation.

I leaned over the document and read the name typed at the top. Suddenly I understood what was going on. "It says Julia Jeter, Sergeant."

"Okay, and what does this say?" She pointed to my signature block.

"It says Judith Jeter, Sergeant."

"Is that your name, Judith Jeter?"

"Yes, Sergeant."

"No, it isn't. Not according to your birth certificate." She pulled a copy of the document from my file. "Your birth certificate says your name is Julia Jeter. Isn't that what it says right here?"

"Yes, Sergeant, but my mother always called my Judy. Everyone calls me Judy."

"That may be true, but we can't argue with a legal document. Now, I'm going to ask you again. What is your name, Jeter?"

"Judith... I mean, Julia Jeter, Sergeant."

"That's right. Your name is Julia Jeter. Now practice it. What is your name?"

"Julia Jeter."

"Again!"

"Julia Jeter," I shouted.

She nodded, glad the lesson had finally sunk in. "Now, I want you to practice it until it is part of you." She pushed a blank sheet of paper toward me with a pen. "Sit here. Print it and write it out, like you're signing a legal document, one hundred times."

A hundred times? I thought it was a silly exercise, but I didn't have much choice. I sat there and wrote my name, one hundred times. Julia Jeter, Julia Jeter. No matter how many times I wrote it, the exercise wasn't going to change the fact that the other women in my platoon had already grown accustomed to calling me Judy. They weren't going to start calling me Julia just because the drill sergeants were demanding it. I also knew my mother, siblings and hometown friends would continue to call me Judy. How was I going to write the name out of their minds?

But the sergeants were determined. From that day on, I was constantly tested.

"Jeter, what's your name?"

"Judy, I mean, Julia Jeter," I would stumble.

"You obviously need more practice writing your name!" they would say, shaking their heads at me, and I knew I was in for more punishment. Late at night, while everyone else was asleep, they'd call me into the office so I could write my name a hundred times. You'd think after writing it so many times, I'd finally get it, but they would leap at me at the most unexpected times, making it a game as well as a test. At first, I often failed.

My name wasn't the only thing I was learning. First aid, drill and ceremony, rank structure and military hierarchy were only a few of the items on the long list of things we had to learn on our road to becoming WACs. We spent hours a day in classrooms. A few times I was roused long before everyone else for kitchen patrol, KP it was called, where I peeled potatoes and wore a hair net.

We were issued gas masks and taught the proper way to wear them. They assembled us in a darkened chamber where a tear gas canister was released. The smoke hissed loudly and quickly filled the room. The drill instructors spoke to us through the thick fog, their voices eerily mechanical and muffled behind the cumbersome gas masks. We stood in the darkness of the chamber for several minutes to become accustomed to the mask's function, and then were forced to remove the mask and recite our name, rank and serial number before we could leave. One by one, we went through the routine and came stumbling out of the chamber, our eyes on fire, coughing and choking on the horrible gas. Some of us puked. All of us cried and choked.

We marched for miles in formation out to the field training area and spent nights in the woods, learning to set up a camp and to survive in the outdoors. I combined my canvas shelter half, tent pegs and rope with the gear another woman had to create our two-person pup tent. I had never spent the night in the woods before, but I was comfortable, tucked snugly in my sleeping bag, surrounded by insect and animal night noises.

We were taken to a land navigation course to be tested on our ability to use a map and compass to get from point A to point B. They split us into teams. For some reason, the women in my group decided I should hold the compass and be in charge. I honestly had no idea what I was doing, but as the designated leader, I had no choice, so I bluffed my way through the exercise. We stomped through the brush, slogged through mud, counted paces and followed the direction of the quivering arrow on the compass and successfully arrived at our destination point. I was a bit surprised but also proud that we had made it through the course.

Every day, no matter whether I was muddy or tired, or covered in potato peels, a drill instructor was shouting at me. "What are you smiling about, Jeter?"

"I'm just happy, Sergeant."

"Wipe that smile off you face or I'll have you peeling potatoes until your fingers bleed."

I would do the pushups and keep on smiling. The whole experience was an adventure and I was determined to succeed, but there was one challenge I couldn't conquer—swimming.

I had always been afraid of the water. I couldn't dog paddle, couldn't float, and absolutely couldn't dunk my head without sputtering and flailing in panic. Our schedule required several days of training in the swimming pool. It didn't take long for the instructors to recognize my fear. Most of the women dove in and glided smoothly from one end of the pool to the other. I stood in the shallow end, fearing for my life.

After the first day in the pool, while everyone else was turning in for the night, one of the drill sergeants told me to put on my swim suit and meet her in the showers.

"Hold your nose and stick your head under the water," she said.

Unlike taking a shower, she wanted me to stand directly under the flow, to try to mimic what it would be like to dunk my head in the pool. It didn't work. I continued to sputter and cough but she didn't give up, determined that I keep trying. Eventually, even she realized it was hopeless. I was never going to get over my fear of water.

The next day, when everyone else was swimming, I was ordered to pick up rocks. I walked around the pool area, picking up tiny rocks and moving them from one place to the next for no apparent reason.

The senseless task was meant as punishment for my failure, but when the drill sergeants saw me hard at work, they were still giving me the familiar order. "Wipe that smile off your face, Jeter!"

On two occasions during our training, we were issued our monthly pay and given a day pass to go into town. While the pay was meager, it was more money than I had ever earned in thirty days. I sent most of it home and still had enough left to go into town, do some shopping, have a meal and some fun. But before we were allowed to leave, the drill sergeants put us in formation to receive our safety briefing. The senior drill sergeant paced back and forth in front of us, issuing her instructions in her thick southern drawl.

"Some of you ladies are from the North, and you may not understand how things are done around here, so I'm going to explain it to you. On this base, you live together, you work together, you eat and you sleep together. But when you leave this base and go into town, all of that will change. In this town, white and colored do not mix. You colored ladies will stick together. You white ladies will stick together. Do not look at each other. Do not talk to each other. You may not like it. You may not agree with it. But this is the way things are done down here in Alabama. Am I understood?"

"Yes, Sergeant!" We responded in unison.

"I do not want to get a call from some sheriff in town that there is inappropriate color mixing going on. Am I understood?"

"Yes, Sergeant!"

I said yes with everyone else, but the news shocked me. This was 1964 and the civil rights movement was always in the news. The year before, Dr. Martin Luther King, Jr. had written his "Letter from a Birmingham Jail" in which he advocated breaking laws if they were morally unjust. Later that year, he led the march on Washington, D.C. Despite the marches, the protests and the prominence of the issue in the news, I was relatively ignorant of it all. I had never felt or been exposed to blatant racism. Sure, I knew there were times when I might have been treated differently because of my color. Looking for a job, shopping in fancy stores, even in school, there were occasional instances when I could tell someone didn't like me or didn't trust me because I was black. The idea that we were going into a town where I would be defined first by my color made me a bit nervous.

Properly cautioned, we boarded buses and headed to town. It was an uneventful excursion. The town was very small and there wasn't much to see or do. Still, I wondered what would happen and how I would react if I were confronted with some kind of racism. We saw the signs we had heard about—Whites Only. We elbowed each other and skirted those establishments like they were road kill, something you didn't want to look at too long. And it felt strange to see the white women in the company walk by us like we didn't know each other. One thing was clear, I was glad I hadn't been raised in a town like that; glad I could leave it behind at the first opportunity. Little did I know, if some people had their way, I would be staying in Alabama a lot longer than I had planned. But at the time, I knew I would be going home on leave very soon and was looking forward to the more accepting color blindness of Aliquippa.

After eight weeks of training, we finally graduated. We dressed in skirts and blouses, polished our shoes, put on our hats and formed up in rows to accept our certificates of completion. I was proud of my accomplishment and excited to have a future ahead of me, with my small town now behind me.

We were given thirty days of leave after basic, before our individualized specialty training would begin. I looked forward to going home— couldn't wait to see Helene and my siblings, and to show my mother I hadn't turned into a bull dagger. The training had been challenging and, while I always knew becoming a WAC would have a lasting effect on my future prospects, I wasn't aware of how much it would change me as a person. Even as we marched off the parade field following the graduation ceremony, I didn't realize how much I had changed. My head up, my shoulders back and leading my squad, you would think I had made the connection that Julia Jeter was a different person.

I found out pretty quickly that my changes were obvious to everyone else.

THE NEW ME

The pride in my mother's eyes when she first saw me in uniform made every punishment, every potato I peeled and every rock I picked up worth it. I had missed her so much. The hardest part about being away from home, aside from missing my daughter, was not having my mother around to talk things over with, to confide in. I was accustomed to sharing everything with her and basic training had given me a lot to talk about.

I wore the Army green service uniform—a hat, shaped just like the men's overseas cap, fitting snuggly on my head and dipping down my forehead, an A-line skirt hemmed just above the knee, a short-sleeved and cuffed blouse with a rounded collar and rounded bottom in light green cotton. A dark green jacket fit snugly, like a well-tailored little suit. My highly-polished black lace-up shoes finished the uniform. I had been promoted during the graduation ceremony and the rank of Private E2 was pinned to my collar. Two medals were pinned to my chest—a rainbow-colored medal they awarded me for graduating from basic and another for good conduct. Maybe my constant smile had something to do with that.

In addition to my uniform and shiny shoes, I wore a little makeup—foundation, powder, eyebrow pencil and red lipstick. I wore my hair in a perfectly coifed bun at the back of my head, slicked back, neat and according to regulation. If the uniform and medals weren't intimidating enough, the makeup and perfect hair made me look much more sophisticated than the scrawny, awkward kid who had left home only months before.

My mother's eyes were huge and her smile beaming as she threw her arms wide for me. Mickey, Larry and Cat all teased me about my uniform, but it was obvious they were proud of me. I'm not sure I can describe Bobbie's reaction. She was married by this time and lived in Midland, Pennsylvania. She seemed distant, unsure, as if she didn't recognize the woman standing before her. Perhaps she recognized my new confidence.

I barely recognized myself. I had filled out a bit, gaining the weight my drill instructors insisted upon with the piles of bacon and glasses of milk that had been forced upon me, but the changes went far deeper than that. I found myself looking people in the eye, responding to their questions in full sentences, answering them in a tone well above a whisper. After weeks of standing at attention with my head up and chest out, after shouting out responses to commands issued by my drill instructors, and after helping so many of the women in my platoon who were even more frightened than I was, nothing anyone back home could say to me ruffled my feathers.

Judy, the unsure and frightened girl, had left Aliquippa. Julia, the soldier and woman, had returned.

Everything seemed different when I got home. Our house, the room I had shared with my sisters, the whole town seemed to have changed somehow to something vaguely unfamiliar. Reflecting on it now, I was probably seeing my world more clearly because I was looking at it straight on instead of glancing quickly and then hiding my eyes.

Graduating from basic training was one huge step on my road to securing the kind of future I dreamed about for myself and my daughter. The two paychecks I had already received were more money than I could ever have hoped to earn at the little jobs I was able to scrounge around

Aliquippa. Most of the money I had sent home to my mother and I knew it was only the beginning.

The most exciting thing about being home was seeing Helene for the first time. Two months is a long time in an infant's growth. Helene's changes were amazing. What hadn't changed was my awareness that she wasn't developing the way a child her age should be. Everyone still insisted there was nothing to be concerned about, which worried me all the more. If they didn't acknowledge the problem, they wouldn't provide the special care and attention my little girl needed to fully develop. Part of the problem was that she was so darn cute and she charmed everyone. They enjoyed holding her and accepted what she could do, but they didn't encourage her to do more than what she was willing to do herself.

"She'll walk when she's ready," my mother said.

"No, Momma," I insisted. "She's twelve months old now. We have to help her to walk. She can't get there on her own."

We never argued about Helene, but while my mother wanted to allow her to progress on her own, I was determined to insist on her development. The few improvements we made during my visit were minor, but they demonstrated to my mother that Helene would make more progress with a little more encouragement.

"Mom, she needs to ask for things, not just grab for them," I would say.

I spent every minute I could with Helene and my mother because I knew it would be months before I would be able to see them again.

The local paper ran a story about me. A woman going off to the Army in my town was a big deal. No one had heard of such a thing before so the newspaper article was a big deal and included the official photograph I had taken with the American flag behind me and my uniform looking perfectly starched and put together.

Lots of people stopped by the house, curious to see what changes my time away had made. They all ooh-ed and ahh-ed over my uniform. Their reactions were interesting. Most of them seemed to know that something about me was different, but they couldn't quite figure out what it was. I still didn't like being the center of attention, but I wasn't afraid to speak up anymore. I looked people in the eye, answered them without looking away and towered over them without rounding my shoulders.

Of course, Walter had to come by the house to see me. I had gone to say hello to Mr. Prather and let him get a look at me in my uniform. The guys in the barber shop and the pool hall made a big deal over how I had changed, how different I looked.

"Look at Slim," they said. "Girl, you're looking good in that uniform."

Some of them were veterans themselves and wanted to share their war stories with me. Now that I had been through the training, had marched in formation and wore a uniform, I had earned their respect. They went on and on about the way I had changed. I heard later that they had given Walter a hard time about my leaving.

"She don't care about you no more, Walter," the guys said. "Slim's off seeing the world. Left you behind. She don't need you no more."

They were right, but Walter wasn't listening. He was angry that I had ventured out on my own and he wanted the quiet, shy and timid Judy back. That Judy was gone for good. His offers of money to assist in taking care of Helene weren't necessary anymore and his marriage proposals fell on deaf ears.

I was moving on.

Boot camp was only the beginning of my training. After my thirty days of leave, I said goodbye to my family again and returned directly to Fort McClellen to complete my training as an administrative clerk. My military occupational specialty or MOS was 71L. Using military-speak, they called it seventy-one lima, administrative clerk. By this time, I was familiar with McClellen, but the school house where my training took place was on a different part of the military post. We weren't new recruits anymore. We had more privileges, more freedom, but the training was serious and presented daily challenges. There were several tests along the way and if you didn't pass, you would be removed from the course and possibly sent home. That was not going to happen to me.

I had an advantage over some of the women in the training since I already had taken four years of typing classes in high school. Typing in those days was not for the weak. The manual typewriters were heavy, unwieldy things and you had to give each key a good punch to make it click. I was already fast and accurate, but a military clerk had to be able to handle countless forms, not to mention multiple carbon copies. Our days ended with blue ink coating our fingers from the carbons.

We spent day after day learning which forms were necessary for which actions. Learning how to process pay, insurance, transfers, orders, the bureaucracy seemed endless, but I caught on quickly. After several weeks of training, when graduation was just around the corner, it was time for us to begin to wonder what would happen next. Where would our next duty station be?

For days, it was the main topic of conversation. We constantly discussed the possibilities of where we wanted to go, where we could possibly go, what it might be like, on and on. Since almost every company in the Army needed clerks, the possibilities were endless.

Finally, the day came when we were assembled and the instructors started calling out names and duty stations.

"Jones."

"Here, Sergeant."

"Fort Bragg, North Carolina."

"Bradley."

"Here, Sergeant."

"Fort Bliss, Texas."

After each one was read, I kept thinking—Texas, I've never been to Texas; or North Carolina, I've never been to North Carolina. Of course, I'd never been anywhere, so thinking about going to any of those places was exciting.

After several people learned where they were going, the announcements were called to a halt. "That's all we have for today. We'll have more to announce tomorrow," the sergeant said.

Everyone buzzed about what they would find out the next day, what they had already learned. I tried to imagine what life would be like if I had orders to a place like Fort Bragg or Fort Bliss—until one of the instructors interrupted my thoughts.

"The commandant would like to see you in her office, Jeter."

The commandant! The officer in charge of the school wanted to speak to *me*? A million possibilities ran through my head. I was in trouble. I had done something wrong. I didn't know what she wanted to speak to me about, but I was nervous as I made my way to her office.

After knocking, I stepped into her office, stood at attention in front of her desk and saluted. "Private Jeter reporting, ma'am."

"At ease, Jeter." She shuffled papers around on her desk, looking everywhere but at me. "Congratulations, Jeter. You are going to be graduating at the top of your class. You're the best typist we've seen for a while. I have an offer for you."

I stood stone still, but my heart raced. Sure, I was proud to be considered the best in the class, but I was nervous, too. I didn't know why I had been ordered there.

"We'd like you to stay on here as a typing instructor."

I was speechless. One of the reasons why I joined the WACs was to travel, to see new places. I had already spent ten weeks at Fort McClellen, Alabama. She was asking me to spend the next three years of my life there. I wanted to say *No, ma'am, I don't want to stay here*, but I didn't know if I could. I didn't want her to be mad at me. I didn't know what to do.

"I can see you are indecisive about this," she said. "You don't have to answer now. Think about it overnight and let me know tomorrow. Dismissed."

I saluted, did an about-face and left her office, exhaling deeply as I stepped into the hallway. I was relieved I would have some time to think about it. There was no way I could make this decision without talking it over with my best friend. As soon as I had the chance, I telephoned my mother.

"Mom, I don't want to stay here! I want to go someplace different."

"Well, tell her that," she said.

"But she's the commandant. The officer in charge. How can I say no to her?"

"Just be honest with her. Tell her you want to travel and see the world."

Hanging up the phone, I was determined to take my mother's advice. Over and over, I rehearsed in my head what I would say the next day. When they called me back to the commandant's office, everything I had practiced disappeared. I could barely speak, my nerves getting the best of me.

Again, she didn't seem to want to look at me, just kept messing around with stuff on her desk. "Well, Jeter, have you made a decision?"

"Well, ma'am," I began, "I really appreciate the offer, but I..."

"That's okay, Jeter. I understand. Dismissed." With a flip of her hand she dismissed me.

"Ah, yes, ma'am," I stuttered. "Thank you, ma'am." I left her office as quickly as I could.

Later that day, we were assembled again and the sergeants began calling out names and assignments.

"Hughes."

"Here, Sergeant."

"Fort Dix, New Jersey. Jeter."

I jumped when I heard my name, but managed to respond, "Here, sergeant."

"Presidio of San Francisco, California."

Goose bumps ran up my arms and my mouth hung open in shock. California? California! I had never in a million years imagined myself in such a place. What would California be like? Everything about the name and the place seemed magical, as if some miraculous thing had been bestowed upon me. I was going to California.

The news put a permanent smile on my face, and no orders to wipe it off would change a thing. The other girls were equally in awe. Most of the assignments were to places like Fort Bragg, Fort Campbell, Fort Benning. I was the only one on my way to California.

"Jeet, you're going to California," the girls said as if I had won the lottery.

And it felt like I had. The more they said it—*California*—the more unreal it seemed. I would spend the next three years of my life in that magical place, looking at San Francisco Bay, under the Golden Gate Bridge. Those three years would lead to the happiest days of my life.

THE PRESIDIO

And then, there I was at The Presidio. Stately brick officers' quarters march up tree-lined, winding roads. Thick morning mist rolls in from the bay to the rhythm of bleating fog horns. Orange and purple sunsets ripple across steel-grey water. The continuous call of sea gulls, the views of Alcatraz, the parade of ships and sailboats gliding across the bay, all of it watched over by the majestic Golden Gate Bridge. The Presidio, my new home, was the most beautiful place I had ever seen.

My assignment was company clerk to the captain who commanded the medical headquarters company. I did all the administrative work for the commander, as well as processing paperwork for the WACs who worked at Letterman Army Hospital. They were nurses' aides, laboratory and pharmacy clerks and supply personnel. It didn't take me long to adapt to my new job, to fall in love with the place, to love my little corner of the barracks where I lived, and to look forward to seeing the views of the bay every morning.

I made friends with several girls. Felicia, Sonja and Delores all worked at Letterman and we shared the same barracks building. We spent much of our free time together, forming friendships that have endured the decades. Sonja, my best friend, still lives in San Francisco and to this day, whenever I visit the city by the bay, I usually stay with her.

Even in this new place, the girls looked to me when they needed help or advice, when they had questions or worries. Basic training had taught me that people tended to expect me to lead and I wasn't about to back away from the responsibility. I found myself passing on wisdom I had learned from my mother. I reminded them to keep their rooms clean, to pay attention to their personal hygiene, to go to church and to work hard no matter the challenge. Back home, I had been the quiet one, too timid to speak up and too frightened to call attention to myself. My role as a leader was new to me, but it didn't take much effort to continue to play that role.

The women were my friends and confidants, but this was the '60s. Being an unwed mother was uncommon and unaccepted. At first, I couldn't tell them that the beautiful little girl in the pictures I had all around my room wasn't my niece, but my own little girl. I thought about Helene every day. Shopping for her was one way I could feel closer to her, although my new friends were surprised at how many clothes and toys I sent to my niece. I wish I could have been truthful with them, but I had to think of my three years away from my little girl as a sacrifice I was willing to make for our future. And that in the end—it would all be worth it.

For the next three years, the duration of my military contract, I fully enjoyed my life in San Francisco. I not only had my own bed, I had my own little room. The walls were thin and the "door" was only a curtain, but it was my own space. I kept it neat and tidy, and a few personal touches and pictures of my family and my daughter made it feel homey. The barracks inspectors even recognized my room as being the best in the barracks. They announced it with a picture in *The Fog Horn*, the newspaper published by the hospital. Maybe it was because it was my first room of my own, or because my mother's constant cleaning habits rubbed off on me, but I took pride in my cozy little space.

The Presidio and Letterman General Hospital were busy places. While it wasn't the biggest news story yet, our conflict with a little country called Vietnam was already producing casualties. Wounded were transported to Travis Air Force Base, then brought into Letterman for treatment or shipped to other hospitals around the states. The longer I worked there, the busier the place became as the war effort steadily escalated.

In those early days, though, I served as the company clerk and had regular office hours. My duties included typing forms and memorandums, processing paperwork, and compiling reports. The first sergeant was my direct supervisor and while I can't remember her name, I do remember that she expected perfection and showed little patience for anything less. She never hesitated to let me know exactly where I screwed up. If something failed to meet her standards, I would hear about it. And in those days, typing forms on manual typewriters with three carbon copies, perfection was a challenge. Now and then there would be some emergency, and the first sergeant would send someone to get me out of bed.

"Jeter, the commander needs you now," the runner would say. "You need to come to the orderly room."

I'd drag myself out of bed and go save the day, put out whatever clerical fire that had sparked. I worked hard at my job and never resented the high demands. My life had changed for the better and a little criticism, especially if it made me better at my job, seemed a small price to pay.

While I did work hard, my off time was fun time. All the girls, Sonja, Felecia, Delores, and I as well, were into the mod clothing popular at the time. Some nights we would get dressed up in matching outfits, deciding it was black-and-white-polka-dot night for instance, and we'd wear some variation of the pattern in miniskirts, blouses, bellbottom pants. We would meet up with other friends and go shopping, go someplace nice for dinner, then hit the clubs and dance until we couldn't dance anymore.

San Francisco was an exciting place in the '60s. There were rumblings from the Black Power groups on one side and Flower Power on the other. Angela Davis sported her afro in Oakland and men wore waist-length hair at hippie love fests in Haight-Ashbury with the likes of Jack Kerouac. And there was Bob Dylan, Beatnik jazz and the Beach Boys, too. The city was the epicenter of all the movements and musical changes.

I admit to not paying much attention to the radicalism of the time. I was too busy enjoying California and growing accustomed to my new life to get mired in any of the counterculture movements. I was a long-distance mom, a woman on her own for the first time, and a soldier. There was plenty to keep me busy.

The pay didn't make me rich, but since room, board and medical coverage were all part of the compensation, I had plenty of money to send home and still have enough leftover to afford fun on the town. Soon, I was able to buy my mother a new refrigerator, a stove and a washer and dryer. Each time I went home, I arrived with gifts for Helene. One time I even brought my mother a coat with a real fur collar.

I wanted to do more for my family, though, so I started taking on babysitting jobs to earn extra money. Before long, word spread that Jeter was willing to babysit, and soon I spent some evenings of my off-time watching the children of captains and majors, doctors and other officers around the Presidio. They would stop by the office, peeking around the corner at me.

"Ah, Private Jeter, I understand you do some babysitting on the side?"

"Oh, yes, sir. I can babysit for you."

I would be asked to go to their homes, places I thought of as mansions, to babysit. The stately, historic buildings with large white columns and brick exteriors impressed me. I had never seen any place so beautiful. One night, when the kids were in bed and it would still be hours before their parents came home, I walked around the beautiful home, admiring the furnishings, the wide staircase, and the drapes. The next day, I told Sonja about the mansion, and added, "Someday, I'm going to have a big house like that."

"Girl, you're dreaming!" She laughed at me through the thin walls of my little cubical, as the curtain I had for a door fluttered in the breeze.

I lay on my little single bed in the barracks, thinking about living in a large beautiful home. It seemed like a distant dream at the time, but still not impossible. In fact, to me, everything seemed possible.

With dreams of doing more for my family, the babysitting wasn't enough, so I decided to take a part-time job at the non-commissioned officers' club on post. My experience working at the diner in Aliquippa came in handy as I waited tables and eventually became a lead waitress.

People commented on my constant need to be working. It was the only way I knew how to be. I hated being idle and the busier I was, the better I felt about things. Between the Army, the NCO club, babysitting and fun with my friends, I was constantly in motion and I liked it that way.

After less than a year at the Presidio, I was called into the commander's office. The captain sat behind her desk, a serious frown on her face.

"Jeter, I have orders for you from Washington. You're doing a great job for me and I need you here. Are you happy here?"

"Yes, ma'am, I like it here."

"Well, I have to tell you that we've received orders that would send you to Vietnam. But if you want to stay, I can make this go away."

Vietnam? Every chance I had, I went back to Pennsylvania to see my daughter. There would be no way to do that from the war zone. I didn't know the details of the orders, like where I would go or how long I would be required to stay. I knew only that it might be a very long time before I saw my daughter again.

"Yes, ma'am, I want to stay here."

So I stayed on as company clerk until the commander left for her next assignment. When she left, I was transferred to Letterman Army Hospital to be an admissions clerk where a different set of demands awaited me, some more challenging than others.

At the time, I was excited about the job change. It would mean I could stay in San Francisco, be near the friends I had made and keep my job at the NCO club. I had no idea the new job would lead to meeting someone who would become the center of my life.

I ducked and ran toward the Chinook helicopter, holding my skirt down in the wash of the still-rotating blades. Another load of wounded had arrived. We met them as soon as they landed on the airfield to begin the process of admitting them to the hospital. Some of the men were so badly injured they couldn't talk, so we had to take their information from the medical records hanging on their litters. Others were able to answer our questions and it was typical for these soldiers to flirt. We were among the first women they had seen for months, perhaps. They joked and flirted and were usually very happy to be back in the USA.

As determined as some of them were to take us out, the unwritten rule was pretty clear: dating patients was frowned upon. That didn't bother me. I wasn't interested in dating anyone anyway.

But, eventually, one man did catch my eye.

I was walking through the admissions office of the hospital, checking a long list of names on the clipboard I held, when I glanced down to see him laying on a stretcher. He immediately snagged my attention because he smiled directly at me. His smile was so charming, his open admiration so apparent, I couldn't help myself. I had to smile back. His infectious grin lit up his large, brown eyes, which were partially hidden behind thick black glasses. He was a big, burly man, with smooth, caramel skin, one arm draped over his forehead, displaying large hands and a muscular physique. His head was shaved in a tight military cut. His shoulders were far wider than the stretcher and when I turned back to my clipboard, I remember smiling to myself, thinking that he was very handsome. I went about my business, but from that moment on, I watched out for the big guy as I walked through the hallways of the hospital.

And I kept my ears and eyes open, finding out his name, checking out his files to see the nature of his injuries. I learned his name was Gustavus W. Cleckley. He was a combat medic and was in our hospital because he had stepped on a landmine and lost most of the calf on one of his legs. Over the next several months, I watched as he progressed from being confined to a wheelchair, to using crutches, then to walking with a pronounced limp. His recovery required a year of treatments, surgeries and physical therapy. That's a long time to be in a hospital, to prowl the halls and go from one appointment to another. Through most of that time, we smiled at each other and spoke politely, conscious of the attraction to each other and aware of the unwritten rule against dating.

"Why are you looking at that man?" one of my friends said one day. "He's a patient."

"He's very nice. I'm just being nice back."

"Yes, but he's a patient!"

I couldn't argue with her. She was right and I knew he should be off limits, but that didn't stop me from continuing to look, to smile, to appreciate the attention from him. Eventually, after several months, he didn't need crutches anymore and I was surprised when one night, he came into the NCO club where I worked. Still, we didn't speak to each other. He came into the club several times after that. We still didn't speak. Eventually, he got a job at the club as a waiter, and when he finally did speak to me, it was to give me instruction.

"You just wrap them in foil like that?" he asked.

I was in the kitchen with my friend Sonja, who was also a waitress at the club, preparing potatoes for the dinner rush. We were laughing and joking while we completed the task, working our way methodically through the pile of potatoes that would be served baked alongside the steak that was on special that night. Gus came in, looking over our shoulders.

"Yes," I said, wondering what the issue was.

"Oh no," he said. "You need to scrub them first before wrapping them in foil. A lot of people like to eat the peel."

I rolled my eyes at my girlfriend, wondering who the heck this guy thought he was, giving us instructions like that on his first day. But we dutifully scrubbed those potatoes and, from then on, we always scrubbed potatoes before wrapping them in foil.

Not long after that, he started walking us back to the barracks after the club closed. The NCO club sat right on the water of the Presidio, with a beautiful view of the bay. In the wee hours of the morning, a group of us would stroll along the water, several women and Gus, escorting us home, laughing and joking and enjoying each other's company. Eventually, one of the girls commented that Gus liked me.

"You think so?" I said.

"He's obviously into you," she said. "But he is a patient."

He would always be a patient and, as such, would always be off-limits to me, but that didn't stop me from looking at him and from thinking about him. He was an intelligent, kind man. I liked being around him.

Eventually, he asked me out.

"I'm sorry, but I can't go out with you," I said. "You're a patient."

"I'm not staying in the hospital anymore. I'm almost fully recovered."

"That doesn't matter. You're still a patient and that means you're off-limits."

When he hosted a party at his sister's apartment, he asked me to attend as his date. I wanted very much to say yes. His sister, a social worker who lived in the city, had a great apartment and everyone we knew planned to go. It was one of those events you couldn't miss, so I definitely planned to go—but not as his date.

My rejection of his invitation didn't slow Gus down. He asked another girl to come as his date, someone who lived in my barracks. I'll never forget her. Her name was Cherry and I hate to admit it, but I was jealous and disappointed that he had simply asked someone else when I turned him down. I also wondered why she didn't feel the same compulsion I felt to comply with the unwritten rules about dating patients.

In any case, I went to the party along with a bunch of friends. It was a big, noisy gathering with music blaring and everyone dressed up, dancing to the latest Motown music, everyone jiving and partying and generally having a good time. Cherry, probably knowing that I had feelings for Gus, smiled from ear to ear whenever she saw me.

"He is such a nice man," she told me. "He even cooked dinner for me tonight."

"Oh, how nice." I tried not to show the intense jealousy I felt.

I started thinking more about the whole no-dating-patients thing and wondered if I was making too big a deal out of the unwritten regulation. Maybe, since he wasn't an in-patient anymore, it would be okay. But I knew I was only second-guessing myself and I couldn't change the decision I'd already made. Since I'd rejected him once, I figured he probably wouldn't ask me out again. I was disappointed, but I tried not to let it ruin my fun.

That night I tried very hard not to watch everything Gus and Cherry did, but I could barely keep my eyes from them as they danced, and I stared at Gus as he mingled with the people at the party while playing host. At one point, I went to the kitchen, only to find Gus there. Alone. It was awkward for a moment.

"I heard you cooked a nice dinner for Cherry," I said, the heat rushing to my face.

"It was nice," he said, smiling. As tall as I am, there are few men who could make me feel small, but Gus did. He stepped closer to me. I was conscious that we were very much alone. My heart raced. I knew I should get out of there, fast. But I didn't.

"That's wonderful." I was desperately looking for something to say that would help me with my exit. Finding nothing, I forced a smile and turned to leave.

Those big hands of his were suddenly on my shoulders. He spun me around, pulled me into an embrace, and kissed me.

I was lost for a moment, but I managed to push him away. "Don't do that. You're with Cherry."

He smiled at me anyway as I left, feeling flustered. I made my way out of the kitchen, still feeling his arms around me, still feeling the effects of that kiss. I couldn't deny that Gustavus Cleckley had become a distraction, one I wanted to know more about.

I stayed at the party for a few more hours, pretending the kiss hadn't happened, pretending that I wasn't completely preoccupied with the big man. It wasn't easy.

The next morning, I got a call at the barracks.

"Jeter, there's a call for you!" one of the women yelled.

I had a brief flutter of hope that it would be Gus, but quickly convinced myself that on a Sunday morning, it was probably my mother, calling to give me the latest update on Helene. But it wasn't my mother.

"Julia, this is Gus. How are you this morning?"

I was speechless for a moment, my heart doing little flips as I found myself smiling.

"I'm great. How are you?"

"I was wondering if you would like to go to church with me."

"You go to church?"

He chuckled, one of those deep, chest-rumbling chuckles.

"Yes, every Sunday. Will you go with me?"

Of course I agreed to go. And that was the first time we went out alone together. We took a cab to a Baptist church in the Filmore district with a large, multi-ethnic congregation. After the service, we strolled through the neighborhood looking at shops, people-watching and talking. That day we talked a lot and I learned so much more about the man who had captured my attention.

Gus told me that his mother was a Pentecostal minister. When I thought of Pentecostal, I immediately pictured a holy-roller church with lots of music and shouting by people feeling the spirit. It was a completely different image from the one I had of Gus, who was usually very even-tempered, patient and calm. With a minister for a mother, Gus had been raised with the bible in his hands and knew the book from cover to cover, quoting scripture from memory. While he'd spent a great deal of time in church, as an adult, Gus had become more spiritual than religious, although he did attend church regularly.

We talked about all of this as we strolled the streets that day, getting to know one another. There was no awkwardness between us. I felt comfortable with him, trusting and safe.

Our relationship changed that day. We didn't need to discuss it or talk about it—from that moment on, we were a couple. We did everything together after that and either saw or spoke to each other on the phone every day.

On our first evening date, Gus took me to dinner at a rather formal restaurant in downtown San Francisco. I'd never been to a place quite so fancy—linen tablecloths, more silverware than I knew what to do with, fancy waiters, and a menu full of things I had never heard of. Although I was intimidated by the place, Gus seemed perfectly comfortable, the consummate gentleman. He took a quick glance at the menu and ordered wine and frog legs as an appetizer.

I thought, "Oh Lord! What have I gotten myself into?"

I ordered chicken, because it was the only thing I recognized. Gus knew, of course, how nervous I was and he led me through the meal. I watched him pick up the salad fork, watched what knife he used and which glass he drank from and which plate he used for his bread. I copied him and learned.

Gus came from a family that was solidly middle-class, where education was valued and the finer points of social particulars were observed. His older sister, who I learned didn't approve of her brother dating a Specialist in the Army with no education and a questionable family background, had a graduate degree in Social Work. His brother was a lawyer serving in the Navy at the time. His father had passed away long before I met Gus, but his mother's strict standards and high expectations guided her children as she guided the congregation of her own church in West Virginia.

Although Gus had begun his studies at Marshall University in West Virginia, he'd quit school to volunteer for the Army. He was a medic in uniform, but his interests were varied and he read extensively. He never earned a formal degree, but he was frequently absorbed in a book, or engaged in deep discussion about a concept or controversy he had read about. Knowledge wasn't a means to achieving success for him, he was simply incessantly curious. He learned from reading, observing, asking questions and listening. Gus had worked at a country club while in high school and he had observed how the rich lived. He mimicked their manners and absorbed their sensibilities.

He was a rare, lovely, kind, gentle person. Most of all, he was a very patient man. I needed that. Trust was hard for me. Eventually his tender ministrations drew me in. I fell totally and completely in love. I had found my soul mate.

AFTER THE ARMY

Gus received his honorable discharge from the Army almost a year before my enlistment contract was up. He took an apartment in San Francisco and found work writing grant proposals for nonprofit organizations and charity groups. We saw each other whenever we could and grew closer as a couple. I told him about my daughter, how Helene was conceived, how she had almost died, and about her as-yet-unconfirmed disabilities. He listened, understood and never passed judgment. After I told him about her, he often expressed his desire to meet her. Before long, he did.

By the time Gus was beginning his civilian career I had been promoted to Specialist E-5 and was the lead admissions clerk at Letterman Hospital. My decision to become a WAC had been based on a need to get educated, to care for my daughter, and to start somewhere fresh—away from people like Walter who wanted to hold me back. I had made the decision to join the Army quickly, but I was fairly certain at the time that it was a good choice because, in addition to my desire for higher education, it would provide me with the means to deal with the problems I faced with Helene. I had no idea that so many other positive things would happen as a result of making that one simple choice to sign on the dotted line.

My rise through the ranks had been rapid and unusual. From the minute I stepped off the plane for basic training in Alabama, women had turned to me when they had questions. Just like that, I became a leader. I quickly learned that leadership felt perfectly natural. The role was unexpected but welcomed. There were times when supervising, leading, directing and even disciplining, were difficult and lonely roles to fill, but I learned that I could do it and do it well. My final year as a WAC in uniform, I was supervising several admitting clerks and I enjoyed my job.

But there was never any doubt in my mind that as soon as my enlistment was up, I would go back to civilian life. The regulations hadn't changed. I couldn't be in uniform and be the mother of a child younger than fourteen. Parenthood was an automatic discharge and three years without my daughter was long enough. But the NCO I worked for wasn't going to give up so easily.

"Specialist Jeter, you realize you could have a very good career in the military," my first sergeant said. "You will qualify soon to be promoted to staff sergeant. After that, your career potential is limitless."

She was right, and with each promotion, the pay and privileges got better, but I couldn't stay in the military. Each time I visited home, it was harder for me to leave Helene behind. I didn't need a doctor to confirm my diagnosis anymore. Helene needed special care and attention and I was in a better position to provide it for her now. Thanks to the G. I. Bill I had money to go to school and the skills and experience that I had acquired would help me start a new career when my military obligation was over. Perhaps the most significant thing that had changed was that I now had the confidence to know that I could do it, that I could provide for Helene and improve our lives, make good decisions and navigate my way in the world. I'd shed the shackles of doubt and fear and was ready to face the world and bring my daughter with me.

In 1967, after three years in uniform, I felt the time was right. I took my discharge papers, changed into civilian clothes and started the rest of my life. After we moved out of the barracks, my best friend, Sonja and

I shared a two-bedroom apartment in San Francisco for just over a year. As soon as I was solidly on my feet and able to afford my own place, I went to Aliquippa to visit my family and to make plans for my mother to bring Helene to San Francisco. By this time, Aliquippa barely felt like home anymore. I had fallen completely in love with San Francisco and couldn't imagine living anywhere else. My mother brought Helene to our new home and stayed with us for two weeks while Helene got settled. My daughter was four-and-a-half-years-old when we were finally able to start our life together.

My apartment on California Street was about three blocks from where Gus lived in a studio apartment near Presidio Heights. Each morning I awoke to the sounds of San Francisco. The neighborhood was vibrant and convenient. I rode the cable cars and buses, easily getting anywhere I needed to go. I didn't drive, so the inexpensive public transportation was important. I quickly learned my way around and grew accustomed to city life.

I soon found a civilian job at Kaiser Permanente Hospital as an admissions clerk, basically doing the same work I had done in uniform only now as a civilian employee, the patients no longer wounded soldiers with injuries and illness associated with war, but civilians with the sicknesses associated with everyday life. The hospitals were very different, but my dedication to the job was very much the same.

Gus and Helene bonded almost immediately. He loved my little girl as if she were his own. I chose to work an overnight shift at the hospital so that Gus and I could share childcare duties for Helene. I would be with her during the day and then while I worked the evening shift, Gus took care of her, spending the night at my apartment until I returned in the morning.

As hectic as most people's lives are today, at least we now have the benefit of easy communication at our fingertips. In those days, long before cell phones and email, coordinating daily and hourly changes to schedules was more difficult. We usually discussed the next day's events over dinner, sharing our schedules and coordinating our plans. To make it work, we both had to pay attention to time, divvy up the errands and chores, and communicate what we had going on. Sometimes I think our experience in the military helped us both stay focused on the mission. We approached our daily lives with the discipline to get the necessary tasks done each day, including keeping Helene happy and well cared for.

With Gus living only a few blocks away and with his constant involvement in our lives, Helene, Gus and I quickly grew to know, trust and love each other. We didn't live together but our separate lives were bonded together, the tentacles of family growing deeper and tighter as the days went on and as we surmounted challenges, worked through problems and got on with the business of life.

The hustle and bustle of the week, however, was left behind on Saturdays, our special time together. We would go to the parks, eat seafood on Fisherman's Wharf, watch the kite flyers in the Marina area or stroll along the water. Those were pleasant, relaxing days and Gus knew how to eke out the most joy in an afternoon by sharing with us the things he liked doing, taking charge and making my daughter and me feel safe and loved. And I know it was that safety and love that helped bring about changes in Helene. Now that I had her with me, I could spend more time working with her, learning more about her. My mother had provided Helene with a loving home, but she had had low expectations of what Helene was capable of. While I knew she could never be like other kids, I was sure she was more capable than we gave her credit for.

She would soon be turning five years old, but she still didn't talk. Her only word, when she moved to San Francisco, was Momma. At first I liked that her only word was Momma, until I realized she only learned it because she heard me and my siblings talking to my mother. When Helene said Momma, she meant my mother, the woman she had, at that point in her young life, spent the most time with. Eventually, Gus taught Helene to call me Mother and she still refers to her grandmother as Momma.

Gus seemed intuitive about Helene's needs and desires. He understood rather quickly that she grew frustrated with her inability to communicate what she wanted, often demonstrating her frustration in crying, screaming and acting out. Still, he remained patient with her and worked with her, even surprising me with the progress they made together.

"Your daughter has a surprise for you," Gus said when I came home from working the overnight shift one day. "Go ahead, honey, show your mother what you learned last night."

Helene knelt at the side of her bed, clasped her hands together and began. "Our Father, who art in heaven, hallowed be thy name." She managed to recite the entire Lord's Prayer that morning, something I would have thought impossible only a few short months before. She paused in places, stumbled a bit, but Gus was there to help her over the difficult parts. I stood watching her, amazed at what Helene was able to do, and I smiled at her and fought back tears, clasping my hands together along with her as she said the prayer. When she finished, she simply stood and went into the kitchen, ready for her breakfast, as if she hadn't completely shocked me.

Even though Helene still didn't speak, didn't express herself in words, she and Gus had worked together over several nights, Helene repeating the words Gus told her until she was able to memorize and recite the prayer from start to finish. While they weren't her words, she proved she was indeed capable of speaking. We only had to figure out how to get her there.

"That's wonderful, Helene," I said to her, hiding just how impressed and excited I was by her demonstration. My daughter wasn't crazy about hugs, but I gave her one anyway. "I love you baby," I said to her and let her eat her breakfast while I showered more hugs on Gus.

In his patient and caring way, he continued to ask more of her—to talk using words instead of sounds and gestures, to ask for the things she wanted instead of just pointing at them, to express what she felt instead of just acting out or crying. As we both worked with her, her socialization skills, her ability to communicate and her temperament progressed.

Despite Helene's steady improvement, Gus made an appointment for her to see a specialist at Children's Hospital in San Francisco at the earliest opportunity. We both realized she needed care and training we were unable to give. We sought guidance to find out what the extent of her disability might be. For several days she was put through a battery of tests and then we sat down with the doctor.

"You are right," he told us, "Helene did suffer some brain damage as a result of lack of oxygen for an extended period of time."

I wasn't surprised by the diagnosis, but the next thing he said was a shock.

"Helene will never be able to care for herself. My best advice for you is to have her institutionalized someplace where she can have around-the-clock care and the attention of specialists."

"No, that's not going to happen," I said. I knew she had obstacles to overcome, but there was no way I was going to have her committed to an institution.

"It really is for the best," the doctor said.

"That is out of the question." I squeezed Gus's hand. I knew he was on my side in this, particularly since he had worked so well with her and had gained such noticeable improvements. Neither of us was going to give up on Helene.

"Her brain damage will mean a lifetime of difficulty, and since she is legally blind, institutionalizing her would give her the opportunity to be around children who have similar difficulties. You see how that could benefit her, don't you?"

"She's blind?" That bit of news stunned both of us. It was obvious that she didn't react to things held in front of her like other children her age, but I hadn't connected that lack of reaction to blindness. Helene's vision is restricted to that of a tunnel and even that vision is low.

As shocking as the information was, having it made me hopeful. It explained so many things about her mannerisms. There had been times when I would ask her to pick something up or to bring me something. She'd often ignored the requests. I would insist, assuming that her refusal to pick up a toy or to bring me the book I pointed to was a willful refusal to follow directions. Now I understood her lack of response wasn't from an unwillingness to follow directions. She simply couldn't see! With her inability to tell me that she didn't see things, I could now understand why she would grow so frustrated.

After that talk with the specialist, Gus and I both felt guilty for not understanding her struggles, for thinking that she was being willful when she simply couldn't see what we were talking about. The new knowledge gave us new perspective on Helene's behavior. It was as if Gus and I had been given the key to a secret code.

We found a pre-school program named Aide to the Retarded which was uniquely qualified to help Helene with her special challenges. I would come home from working my night shift, freshen up and get her dressed to take her to school every day. I'd grab a couple hours of sleep then return to pick her up in the late afternoon. After dinner, and after putting her to bed, I'd get a few more hours of sleep before Gus arrived to stay with her and I left for my all-night shift.

It was obvious that going to school improved her ability to express herself and to care for herself in little ways. The program, combined with Gus's instinctual ability to coach and train, helped her improve markedly. Our discoveries into the mystery that was Helene's world and our constant companionship only brought Gus and me closer together. This was the late '60s, a time when it was slowly becoming more common for unmarried couples to live together. At first, the idea was against my sensibilities. Gus and I were both God-fearing people. Still, the religious teachings we'd both learned as children and the negative reactions we expected from our mothers weren't enough to dissuade us from our decision. Gus, Helene and I were together so much it simply made sense to move in together. We found a three-bedroom apartment and kept our new living arrangements secret from my mother. Gus never answered the phone for fear that it would be a call from her.

I changed jobs a few times, leaving government employment and Kaiser Hospital for an administrative assistant's job in a corporate office downtown. Each job change came with an increase in pay and responsibilities. A better salary meant we could afford the kind of child care Helene required. She continued to thrive and progress as we adapted to her vision problems—she now wore thick glasses and we were more aware of what she could and couldn't see.

I was able to put my G.I. Bill college money to use by taking classes at the University of San Francisco, working toward a bachelor's degree. And Gus landed a job as a healthcare consultant and proposal writer, which eventually led to a job offer for an even better paying position. That job, however, was in hospital administration in New York City.

"Why don't you come with me?" he said.

We had been a couple for almost four years at this point. The city by the bay was home to me and the thought of moving to the opposite coast wasn't appealing. As disagreeable as moving to New York felt, losing my daily dose of Gus was worse. I didn't know how Helene and I would cope without him—didn't want to know. But I couldn't stand in his way and I couldn't make the decision to uproot Helene to follow him.

The opportunity, the promotion, was too good to pass up. It broke my heart to see him leave but his decision was made. We threw Gus a big going-away party. All of our friends came and wished him luck on his new job and new life. Too soon, he packed up and moved to New York. It was clear from the beginning that while he was excited about the job, he wasn't happy there. "I miss seeing you every day," he said during his daily calls. "Won't you come out and see me?"

Every night, seven days a week, we talked on the phone. I tried to put a brave face on things, but there were no words to describe how much I missed him and his big bear hugs. His departure left a huge gap in our lives. After seven months of separation, he didn't want to live with the absence anymore.

"Will you marry me?" he said.

I hesitated. I could picture him on the other end of the phone, his big hands gripping the receiver and absentmindedly pushing the heavy, black glasses he wore up onto his nose.

"I don't know," I said. "Is this what you really want?"

"Yes! I love you. These months away from you have made it clear that I miss you more than I can say. I don't want us to live apart anymore. We're a family already. I think it's time we made it official."

I don't know why I hesitated in the first place. We had already existed comfortably as a couple, sharing the day-to-day challenges of progressing careers, raising a child with special needs and leading an active social life. I had never questioned whether or not we would marry. I was happy and would never have brought up the subject before he mentioned it that day over the phone. And while I hated the idea of leaving San Francisco, to be near Gus I would have moved across the world.

"Yes," I said. "Of course I'll marry you."

Before our ceremony, Gus and I met in Pennsylvania, where he asked my mother for her permission to marry me. I was so flattered by his gesture. So was she and, of course, she approved.

On July 17, 1971, Gus came back to San Francisco and we were married in front of a roomful of our friends. My husband had big taste and insisted that our wedding be a well-appointed affair. A good friend of ours lived in a nice neighborhood in San Francisco in a beautiful home with a long, staircase. We invited a small group of friends to be part of the ceremony at the house and then held a reception for a larger crowd at the NCO club on the Presidio where we had both worked.

Gus wanted my bridal gown to be something exceptional and I wasn't going to argue with him about that. My only caveat was that the dress had to be off-white. We found an elegant designer original at Saks Fifth Avenue that was chiffon with a fitted bodice and long, transparent sleeves, faint yellow, pink and green swaths of color throughout the fabric. It amuses me now to remember that it was a size eight and still required a great deal of taking in to fit properly.

Sonja, who was pregnant at the time, served as my matron of honor; a high school friend, Helen, flew in from Washington, D.C. to serve as a bridesmaid; and my friend Charlene flew in from Los Angeles to be the hostess at the wedding and reception. Helene, dressed in a beautiful little white and yellow dress, was the flower girl, scattering rose petals down the stairs as she walked in front of the wedding procession.

We descended the stairs to meet Gus and his best men, Sonja's husband Eugene and Ricardo, waiting in front of a large fireplace. Gus wore a beige and white designer suit with a wide tie and a vest. He looked handsome and sophisticated. I felt beautiful and proud of him. We stared at each other as we recited the traditional vows, pledging to love, honor and obey, to stay together in sickness and in health. We exchanged wedding rings, wide bands of gold braided together in a twist that symbolized our inseparability. They were wider bands than normal, ones we had custom made in a small jewelry shop when I visited Gus in New York before the wedding. They were such beautiful rings and we received compliments on them as we wore them throughout the years.

"I now pronounce you husband and wife," the minister said. And before he could give us permission to seal the vows with a kiss, Helene piped in, "And now I can call you, Daddy!"

Everyone laughed. I was surprised by her outburst, but I guess I shouldn't have been. She obviously loved Gus and the strong feelings were mutual between them.

After a champagne toast, rented limousines took us to the NCO club where we danced, drank more champagne and partied with friends on into the night. We had a brief two-day honeymoon in Sausalito, where we spent time lingering over long, romantic meals in fancy restaurants, took strolls along the water holding hands and shopped just for the sake of looking.

Gus gave me a special wedding present. It was an outfit that, if worn today, would reduce a woman's respectability in most people's eyes, but in 1971 it was the height of modern fashion—hot pants and an afro. Everyone was wearing them. My gift was a matching outfit of bright yellow hot pants, a long, lacy crocheted vest that went down to my knees and white, high-heeled, lace-up sandals that snaked up my calves to just below my kneecaps. It was an ensemble typical of what Pam Greer wore in her popular blaxploitation films of the era, and my six-foot frame wore it proudly. My new husband loved the way I looked in that outfit and I was proud to be on his arm.

When our honeymoon was over, we spent a few days finishing our packing and then in short order moved to New York City.

NEW OPPORTUNITIES

Gus's work at Montefiore Hospital kept him busy, but his love of the city rubbed off on me. He had fun showing me the nooks and crannies of the city, helped me master the subway and took me out most weekends to explore some new neighborhood. It took a little while, but I grew to enjoy living in our Manhattan apartment.

His new job meant a promotion and a salary that provided for all of us. For a time, I stayed home and cared for Helene, but it wasn't long before I became restless. I was accustomed to working, not just one job but two, or even three, at a time. Staying home simply wasn't in my blood. I had to get a job to stay sane, and I found one as an executive secretary to the director of the United Service Organization in their New York headquarters, which was just two blocks from Bloomingdales.

The director was a busy woman who traveled extensively, visiting every USO in the world. I rarely saw my boss since she was gone so much of the time on travel that I booked for her. She often sent me tapes of correspondence she wanted me to type, and often dictated letters or memos to me over the phone. Between booking her travel and typing all of her correspondence—I was still a great typist, spending much of my day with my fingers flying over the keys—it was a very busy job and I really enjoyed the work.

My home life was just as enjoyable. A year into our marriage, Gus and I were both happy. My husband liked to write me little letters professing his love. I would often find cards in unexpected places, little reminders that he was thinking of me. He was affectionate, thoughtful and a wonderful father. But one day he took me completely by surprise.

"I'd like to have a baby with you. We should give Helene a brother or sister."

I was shocked. It had been Helene and me for so long, the thought of having another child hadn't crossed my mind. It took me time to grow accustomed to the idea of changing diapers again. Gus really wanted a bigger family. He also wanted a traditional wife, one that would stay home and care for the children. While I wasn't onboard with that idea, I did want to give him the family he wanted. To fulfill his desire, I would be a 28-year-old mother of an infant. I was afraid I might be too old!

The more I thought about it, the more I knew that having a child with Gus was the right thing to do. I decided to stop taking the pill, and only a month later, I was pregnant. When I shared the news with Gus, he was thrilled and wanted to tell the world. From the very beginning it was a happy pregnancy, a very different experience from my first time when shame and fear of the future were the prominent emotions. We even threw a party to celebrate it.

I continued to work for the USO until my seventh month. Just before I left, having resigned my position, my boss and all of my coworkers threw me a surprise baby shower at the office. Since my boss was Jewish, she gave me a huge basket of things like gefilte fish, lox and bagels and all kinds of things she loved to eat. There was coffee and cake at the party and all the ladies showered me with gifts and attention.

Two years after we were married, I gave birth to Ellen-Lizette on November 29, 1973.

Gus and I kept Ellen's crib in our bedroom for a long time—too long, actually. I was so fearful that what had happened to Helene would repeat itself that I checked on her constantly, worried about her all the time. But my worries were, thankfully, unfounded.

Helene, Gus and I were overjoyed to have Ellen join our family. She was a beautiful, bright child with a ready smile and lots of energy. I loved taking care of her, but I simply couldn't stand playing the stay-at-home mom for long. I was too restless, too determined to do something else with myself and, despite Gus's wishes, staying at home just would never work for me.

He wanted me to be like some of the other women in our apartment building. We had several neighbors with small children and I would see them in the elevator with their strollers. New mothers should have a lot in common to talk about, but I found myself unable to relate to any of them. They seemed happy with being wives and mothers, as if that was it. That was what their lives were meant to be. They seemed foreign to me, so different from my small-town background and my working-class family. It wasn't just that most of them were white—only one other family that I knew of in the building was black—it was more that I couldn't relate to their desire to build their entire lives around raising their children. They sat in the playground, knitting, watching their children and discussing day care, their daily soap operas, household chores and the other mundane minutia of daily family life. It drove me crazy with boredom. I wanted to do more. I missed being busy, simply couldn't stay home playing mom anymore. I tried to convince Gus that I needed to go back to work. He had other ideas. Instead of working, he wanted me to go back to school. I transferred my University of San Francisco credits to Hunter College and concentrated on finishing my degree in psychology.

We hired a babysitter to come into our home while I was in class for several hours each day. I went to class in the morning and returned home in the afternoon to do my homework and take care of the girls.

My niece Lisa, the youngest daughter of my sister Bobbie, came to visit us over her summer holiday. The idea was that we would take Lisa off Bobbie's hands for a couple of weeks, while Lisa would help care for

Helene and Ellen in exchange for a fun couple of weeks in New York City. Lisa was thirteen and had never been to the city before, so that first trip was a huge treat for her. She flew in an airplane for the first time, which was also a big deal for her.

Lisa was excited about seeing the city and Gus was ready to show it to her. On weekends, he would lead us all on an exploration of one kind or another—poking around in art galleries, walking through small parks, looking at architecture, unique shops and street festivals. Once she learned her way around, Lisa was ready to navigate our neighborhood on her own and take charge of caring for Helene and Ellen.

Each day, I would leave home for class and Lisa would bundle Ellen into her stroller and off the three girls would go. Gus would give Lisa and Helene a few dollars each to spend on their outings and they would buy Sicilian pizza, Italian ice cream or movie tickets.

"I like coming to visit you, Aunt Judy," she said more than once.

"We like having you, Lisa."

Lisa's summer visits became an annual event. Each time she visited, she grew closer to the girls, becoming a fixture in their lives and part of our family. As the years went by, our relationship with Lisa continued. Unfortunately, the closer I became to my niece, the further estranged I became from my sister Bobbie. The love I shared with her daughter added to the list of things she resented me for.

In April, 1975, the world watched in horror as Saigon fell to the Viet Cong. After the violent anti-war protests on college campuses across the country, and the final defeat in Vietnam, wearing a uniform was unpopular. By the mid-seventies, the draft had ended. The U.S. military was an all-volunteer force and that meant incentives for enlistment generated interest from potential recruits. There was also an increased push to recruit women. The idea was to fill as many non-combat roles as possible with women. The WACs still existed, but women could now choose to join the Army Reserve and National Guard, becoming soldiers and serving alongside men instead of being restricted to serving in the WACs which was for women only. Despite the incentives, National Guard recruiters had a hard time selling the notion to enlist.

Vietnam veterans garnered negative responses from students, but students' attitudes toward National Guard members were even worse. The National Guard had shot at peaceful protesters at Kent State University in Ohio, wounding thirteen and killing four students. The National Guard also responded when riots broke out in places like Chicago and Detroit, where civilians looted and burned neighborhoods.

Despite the negative attitude toward the Guard, recruiters from the National Guard Armory, one block from the Hunter College campus, came on campus several times a month to discuss options. I would see them walking around in their uniforms, passing out flyers and talking to students. I hadn't told many people that I was a veteran. My three years as a WAC seemed a long time in the past, not really connected to the life I had now. Still, the visits from the recruiters were hard to miss and one day, I listened.

"If you have prior service," the recruiter said, "you can join the National Guard at the same rank you held during your prior service. In the National Guard, your obligation is one weekend a month, and two weeks each summer."

I'm not one to mull over a decision for long and, frankly, the sales pitch worked on me. I approached the recruiter to confirm what I had heard.

"Oh yes. We can bring you back in as a Specialist, E5." He told me how much I could expect to make, which wasn't much, but I had grown independent during my years in uniform. I appreciated everything Gus did for me and our girls, but I was becoming disgruntled spending my afternoons in the park with the other mothers and their constant discussion of diapers and childhood coughs and the latest thing their exceptional child could do. School kept my mind occupied, but I really needed a challenge.

Before I was pregnant with Ellen, I'd seen an ad in the paper for a job that had sparked my interest. The job prospect occupied my mind for a long time. Despite my unique qualifications for the work, I knew Gus wouldn't approve. I was convinced, however, that I could make a handsome amount of money, so I called the number and made an appointment to go the next day for an interview. When Gus came home that night, I told him about it.

"Honey, I have an appointment for an interview tomorrow," I said.

"Really? What for?"

"It's for a waitress job at the Playboy club."

Before I could tell him how much money I could make, he was already sputtering, "You can't work there!"

"But, Honey... "

"I am a hospital administrator. You can't work at a place like that. What about my reputation!"

"What does it have to do with you? You know I'm a great waitress."

We went back and forth like that for a while. In the end, of course, I didn't go to the interview. After that objectionable job choice, I hoped he would find the Army National Guard easier to accept, but I knew that it would be a long shot. So far, any discussion of my taking a job hadn't gone well.

"I put in so many hours," he said. "Someone needs to be here for the children."

I agreed, but I didn't want that someone to be me anymore. The women's movement was flourishing in the '70s. More and more women were working, becoming independent and, yes, joining the military. I missed the sense of accomplishment I felt from doing a job well. I liked the idea of having money of my own. And I have to admit, the prospect of having a little time away from mothering appealed to me. I loved my children, there was no doubt about that, but I hungered for an adult challenge, something new and different. I had enjoyed my short time in uniform. If I joined, I would no longer be a member of the Women's Army Corps. I would be a member of the Army National Guard, which, like all the other services, no longer discriminated against women with children. I would have full dependant benefits, bring extra pay into the household budget and have a chance to train and contribute.

The choice seemed easy at the time. I joined.

When Gus came home that evening, I tried to get all the information out before he could object. "Honey, today I joined the Army National Guard. It's only one weekend a month and two weeks each summer and I'll go in as an E5..."

"WHAT! You already joined? How could you do that without talking to me about it first?"

We argued for a long time. He was angry and hurt that I hadn't consulted him, discussed it with him first, and he had a right to be. The National Guard represented a sore spot for him—he had tried to join the Guard during Vietnam but wasn't accepted. At the time, the Guard in West Virginia simply wouldn't allow blacks to join. That was one reason the Guard continued to have the reputation of being a white man's club. It was common knowledge that white men like George W. Bush could join the National Guard in the '60s to defer being drafted to Vietnam.

After being rejected by the Guard, Gus had volunteered for his service in Vietnam so that he could choose to be a medic instead of being forced into some other position through the draft. And then he had been wounded. Bottom line: the National Guard was a sore subject for my husband and I hadn't considered his feelings. Joining the Guard wasn't like joining the WACs of my day. I hadn't needed his permission to join and I hadn't asked for it. Fortunately, despite his strong feelings, after many hours of talking and cajoling, he accepted my decision.

It was a testament to Gus's excellent disposition that my once-a-month weekend duty was soon an accepted part of our family routine.

Gus cared for the girls while I was away, even doing their hair for them. He was a great father and a supportive husband. And I needed his support, because the challenges I faced while in uniform, especially in those early days, were many.

My sister Robbie, the one we called Cat, had moved to New York City not long after Gus and I made our home there. Cat was a beautiful, kind-hearted person who loved people, loved the cosmopolitan life and New York seemed the perfect place for her. She always wore the latest fashions, going to parties and night clubs, mixing and mingling with a hip crowd of people. Unfortunately, she also liked to drink, something she surely inherited from our father. She sometimes dabbled with other drugs, but alcohol was her drug of choice. The most troubling thing about Cat and her drinking was that, like our father, alcohol made her angry and sometimes violent. And then the violence often led to her getting arrested and spending time in jail. The most serious time came with a felony assault charge stemming from a fight she had in a bar. She had pulled a knife on someone but, thankfully, was prevented from using it. Gus and I ended up paying for a lawyer for her and Gus went to court with her several times, offering support and following her case. In the end, the evidence against her was too much. She received a two-year prison sentence in Bedford Women's Prison in Westchester County, New York.

I wrote to her and visited her in prison while I was pregnant with Ellen. It was painful to see my sister in those circumstances, but there was little I could do about it. Once Cat was out of prison, she went to a halfway house, tried to get her life back together and was successful for a while. She met a man named Mitchell, and the two of them were together for some time.

In the early days, she would visit with us, sometimes during the summer, taking our niece Lisa and the girls out to go shopping and exploring the city. On one shopping trip, she bought the girls platform shoes. All of them felt grown up, like they had the latest styles. The girls loved Aunt Cat. She was the beautiful aunt who liked to have fun, the one who knew the latest music, dressed in the latest clothes and was up on the latest trends.

When Cat learned that she was pregnant, she became determined to stay clean and to give up the drugs and alcohol, but by this point the damage had already been done. Her son, who was named Mitchell after his father, was born a small, sickly little boy with developmental disabilities. Cat eventually left Mitch's father in New York while she and her son returned to Aliquippa to live with our mother. Sadly, when Mitch was only three, he died.

When Cat called me to help her bury her child, I told Gus I didn't think I could do it. "It's just too sad."

"You have to do it, Judy," he said. "Death is part of life. You have to help your sister and I'll talk you through everything."

It was the first funeral I had to help arrange. Burying my nephew broke my heart, seeing my sister's devastation. And I hadn't anticipated all the decisions one had to make for a funeral. Open casket at the wake, closed during the service, death certificates from the undertaker, obituaries and programs, photos and mementoes, flowers, who would speak, who wouldn't speak, where people would sit, what happened at the graveside. I would call Gus and discuss each decision I had to make. Later, I would remember his calm, deep voice over the phone as we discussed each thing that came up. I knew exactly how he felt, what his choices were and why he chose the way he did.

And as difficult as the planning of little Mitchell's funeral arrangements were, it was only a preview of the funerals I would later have to plan. When the time came, I would replay those phone conversations Gus and I had and have the comfort of knowing exactly what he wanted.

BACK IN UNIFORM

One Friday a month, I packed my duffle bag and left for a weekend of drill duty at the Manhattan Armory or Camp Smith in upstate New York near the West Point campus. The first time I attended a drill weekend, it had been almost seven years since I had worn a uniform, but it was surprisingly easy to don the fatigues, black combat boots and soft cap to become a soldier again.

I was assigned to a clerk position with the 7th Regiment, 42nd Infantry Division and worked for Warrant Officer Bernie Hayes, the officer in charge of personnel for the unit. I spent my duty weekend typing forms, handling administrative work for the people in the unit and compiling reports. One thing that hadn't changed since I served as a WAC was the amount of paperwork necessary to get anything done in the military. It was fairly routine work but enjoyable.

In those days, very few women were in uniform. The National Guard was notoriously a white-male-dominated organization. In my first days, I was the only black female in the unit and only one of three women reporting for duty in the Regiment. On our trips to Camp Smith, a camping trailer was the makeshift barracks for all three of the women at the camp. The Guard didn't have any other facilities for us.

Aside from now serving alongside men, the biggest difference from my time as a WAC was that, in addition to my office duties, I had to learn and maintain soldier skills. For the first time, I was required to learn things like how to set up a defensive parameter, fields of fire and to qualify with a weapon. As a WAC, we weren't trained to use weapons, but as a member of the National Guard, I was required to qualify with an M16 annually.

My first time on the weapons range was intimidating. We'd been given a few hours of classroom training, lectures on how the weapon worked, instructions on how to aim by lining up a good sight picture, what the targets would look like and what was expected of us. But classroom training is one thing. Actually holding the weapon, loading it with live ammunition, moving the selector switch from safe to semi-automatic and firing it down range was something completely new and different for me. As part of the training, they taught us never to call an M16, or any weapon issued to us, a gun.

"Guns are for hunting and for fun," the instructor said. "The Army issues you a weapon for killing. A weapon requires your respect. A weapon is not a toy."

Gus, of course, had carried and used a weapon in Vietnam. I wasn't sure how he felt about my opportunity to fire a weapon for the first time. Knowing that he had used a weapon in combat might be why I had been reluctant to share with him just how excited I was for my first trip to the range.

The procedures on a weapons range are very precise, very rigid to ensure the safety of everyone involved, especially when there are people like me around who had never held a weapon before. Instructors are constantly watching, constantly vigilant to ensure you keep your weapon pointed down range, that every round is accounted for, that no one pulls a trigger or makes a move until they are told to do so. Each person is assigned a spotter and a firing lane. Instructors, several of them, walk their areas to ensure everything is operating properly. You spend a great deal of time zeroing your weapon, basically adjusting the firing sights to ensure the weapon is calibrated for you, and during the entire time, the range control officer issues instructions, usually over a megaphone of some sort.

Finally, the actual qualification portion of the task begins.

"Lanes on the right, ready?"

They wait to see the green ready signal from the spotter.

"Right is ready. Lanes on the left, ready?"

Again they wait for the signal.

"Left is ready. Firing line is ready. Firers, lock and load your three-round magazine."

I slipped the magazine into the weapon and pulled back on the charging handle, which moved one round from the magazine into the firing chamber.

"Firers, place your weapon on semi, watch your lanes and commence firing."

Everything I'd learned in the classroom went through my head as I sighted down the weapon, tried to find a proper sight picture. Finally I squeezed the trigger.

Unlike what you might expect, an M16 doesn't have much of a kick. It's not like a shotgun that bucks back and can hurt your shoulder if you don't hold it properly. Pull the trigger on an M16 and it will jump only slightly, no more than a gentle nudge on your shoulder. Despite the lack of kick, and the earplugs we wore, the weapon is loud, much louder than I was prepared for. When you're aiming at your target, your cheek against the stock, one eye closed, the sound of your own breathing echoing around inside your helmet, you feel a tension as you wait for the loud report, hoping the rounds go where you want them to go.

After firing my rounds and walking down with my spotter to see how I'd done, I couldn't help but smile to see the holes in the target mostly where I wanted them to be. I don't remember what my final score was, but it was enough to earn me a sharpshooter badge, meaning I hit between thirty and thirty-five targets out of forty. Not bad for my first time around.

Perhaps it's my time in the military that guides my thinking when it comes to gun control laws. The weapon I used was a weapon, not a gun. The target I shot at were silhouettes of humans to represent the torso of the enemy. I never thought of a weapon as anything other than a device intended to kill people, not as something to be used for sport or recreation.

When I became a general officer, I was issued a pistol, as was tradition. It was the first and only weapon I have ever owned and it still sits in the box it came in, not because I don't appreciate the gift, but because I've never felt the need to keep a mechanism of death at my disposal. While I can understand how some people may feel the need, I've never felt so fearful that I needed to keep a gun in my purse or ready to grab in my home—and that's after living in cities like San Francisco, New York and Washington, D.C., as well as traveling through a good portion of the United States.

I swore to protect and defend the constitution of the United States, including the second amendment. That said—I don't understand the need for individual citizens to own high-capacity magazines and automatic assault weapons. I also don't see why there should be problems with background checks and weapons registration, or to recognize the role that violence and mental illness play in the tragic mass killings our country has faced. There is no single answer to stop gun violence in America. I can only say that I was taught respect for firearms. There must be a way for us to keep the basic tenets of the second amendment while having sensible laws to reduce the number of illegal weapons on the street.

Weapons-training was just one new skill I learned while in uniform. I actually learned a lot of new things during those first months in the Army National Guard. Perhaps the learning curve is what made it so easy for me to grow accustomed to regularly putting on a uniform again—

that excitement to learn and do new things was motivation enough to make the monthly trips to see what would happen next. While my being away for weekend duty was sometimes difficult on Gus and the girls, I like to think that we managed the juggling act in a way that had the least impact on the girls.

Things became easier in the balance between being a wife, a mom, a student and a soldier when I finally graduated from Hunter College with a degree in Psychology and Education. It was 1976 and earning my degree had been a long and demanding challenge. I had left my hometown and joined the WACs with the goal of getting an education, because I knew that a degree would lead to bigger and better things. Those efforts had finally paid off.

Armed with my bachelor's degree, I went looking for a new job and found one as a management assistant at an agency on Wall Street that recruited health professionals. I worked in the personnel department, a high-powered, fast-paced job that demanded non-stop attention all day and sometimes long into the evening. I became personnel director after only a year, and the responsibilities increased along with the salary. My boss often called me at home to let me know that a meeting was starting early the next day or to warn me that I would need to attend a cocktail hour with board members the next evening. It was that kind of job.

Each day during the week, I donned a business suit, took the subway to Wall Street and set about the work of running a personnel department with a few people working for me, a long list of responsibilities and executives demanding flawless work. At the time, it was my dream job. Without a doubt, one of the best parts of that job was that my boss was very understanding when it came time for me to take a two-week military leave to attend my first National Guard summer camp.

That first year, everyone in the 42nd ID (short for Infantry Division) left the city on buses, jeeps and other military vehicles to convoy to Fort Drum, New York. Over the course of the summer training, I was tasked to complete several reports for the captain in charge of the S1 shop (personnel department). He told me what needed to be done, and I gathered the information, compiled the data and wrote the reports. Once he told me what was required, the work was fairly straightforward and I didn't need to consult with him about it. I was aware that once the report was done, he would have to brief it to the commander, so I did what I was accustomed to doing—took the job seriously and did the best work I could.

When the report was complete, the captain checked it over, deemed it ready to present, and then attended the briefing with the commander and his staff. Not that I expected it, but the captain never thanked me or told me that I had done a good job. He simply took the work and presented it to the unit leadership and that was the last I heard of the matter, until a few days later.

I was sitting in the office with the captain, when the commander came in.

"Great job on those reports," the lieutenant colonel said. The captain jumped up and shook the hand that was offered. "Thank you, sir."

"Very good job," the commander said. "I was impressed with your briefing and the work you put together."

"Thank you, sir," the captain said.

They went back and forth like that for about fifteen minutes, standing right in front of my desk, congratulating each other on the great job, ignoring me, ignoring that I had done all of the work. The captain never acknowledged that I was even there and never introduced me to the commander. Even after the commander left, he didn't thank me for the contribution I made to the shower of praise he had received.

I probably shouldn't have been surprised, but I was. The incident nudged me into considering a different avenue for my military career. I had earned my degree and several people had asked me why I hadn't considered becoming an officer. I was a proud enlisted soldier. I was a specialist, an E5, and knew promotion to E6, staff sergeant, was very near in my future. I liked the rank on my collar and hadn't thought being an officer was something I needed to pursue. Not until that day.

The main obstacle I saw to pursuing a commission was that I didn't want to take more time away from my family to go through the training. It would mean several months away from home. I wasn't ready to leave my girls and my husband to attend the Officer Candidate School.

In the Army, a warrant officer is addressed with the title of Mister, and Mr. Hayes had been good to me in the early days of my military career. He'd been my first supervisor since I'd returned to active duty and had been a kind but intimidating leader. I decided to discuss my alternatives with him. The broody, grey-headed Irishman usually had a cigarette dangling from the corner of his mouth, but his frightening, gruff exterior actually hid a kind and empathetic soul. He didn't mince words.

"You don't have to go to OCS," he said.

"I don't?"

"No. Get a direct commission."

"How can I do that?"

Shaking his head at me like I was an idiot, he took the cigarette out of his mouth and flicked off the inch-long ash. He counted off the reasons on his nicotine-stained fingers while squinting at me through the smoke.

"You just earned your degree. You're prior enlisted. You have extensive experience in the civilian world. Submit proof of all of that in your paperwork, you get commissioned."

"How does it work?"

He sat me down and went through the process with me, step-by-step.

"That's all I have to do?"

"Yep. Now go get started and quit cluttering up my office."

As an administrative clerk, I knew how to research and prepare personnel actions. I figured out what paperwork was needed and began to assemble the required documents. A direct commission is typically awarded to civilians with special skills—doctors, lawyers, highly skilled professionals whose training and experience can take the place of a three-month officer course or a four-year service academy.

Mr. Hayes said it was not only my education that would help with a direct commission, but my experience on Wall Street working in personnel. I was applying for a direct commission in the Adjutant General's Corps, the military branch in charge of personnel and administrative actions; the branch that perfectly fit the skills I had been building upon since I first left home back in 1964.

Part of the requirement was that I submit three letters of recommendation attesting to my skills and abilities. Two professors from Hunter College wrote letters for me, and a New York Health Commissioner on the board of the Wall Street agency where I worked wrote one as well. Once I started assembling the paperwork, it became clear that I had the education and practical experience to qualify for the commission. Still, I was careful and thorough, and made sure everything was in perfect order.

My direct commission was approved the very first time I submitted it. They even allowed me to skip the rank of second lieutenant because of my education and I became a first lieutenant in the Army National Guard

Needless to say, my commission surprised some people. A brigade commander of the 42nd Infantry Division, Colonel Erlich, had never had a woman on his command staff, let alone a black woman. In June, 1976, I became the first female African-American first lieutenant assigned to the 2nd Brigade, 42nd Infantry Division at the New York Armory. And it quickly became apparent that not only was this change something they weren't prepared for, but the transition would be more painful for some of the people involved than for others.

AN OFFICER AND A LADY

As an enlisted person, I had been an administrative clerk with the added responsibility of being the Equal Employment Opportunity specialist. Once commissioned, I became the assistant to the S1, the officer in charge of personnel actions for the 2nd Infantry Brigade, and a member of the Brigade commander's staff. I was also designated to be the EEO officer of the brigade charged with assisting anyone who had a complaint.

To fulfill my duties as the EEO officer, I was sent to school, which, at the time, was called the Defense Race Relations School and is now called the Defense Equal Opportunity Management Institute, at Patrick Air Force Base in Florida, where people from all branches of service are sent for EEO training. I spent hours in a classroom learning about discrimination—how to identify it, how to correct it, how to report it. I also learned how to counsel and advise people who feel they have been discriminated against and how to train others to prevent the behavior. Since I was about to begin my career in the white-male-dominated officer corps of the National Guard, I learned skills that would prepare me for the challenges and obstacles I would face in the years to come. That trip to Patrick Air Force Base was just the first in what would become a frequent destination throughout my military career. I would return to DEOMI several times over the years for refresher courses and, eventually, I would be invited to be an adjunct faculty member at the school, teaching students about Equal Employment concerns and diversity.

Improving diversity in the National Guard ranks would become a major part of my military profession. When I started with the Army National Guard it was so entrenched in being white and male, the idea of diversity was laughable. Like any minority or woman in the '70s, I expected to encounter discrimination, especially among my uniformed colleagues. I also expected to be the only woman in the room most of the time and the only black woman every time.

Still, during that first trip to EEO training, I couldn't know what a major impact the school and the training would have on my career. I like to think that I played a role in some of the changes and improvements that have taken place in terms of diversity and discrimination in the Army National Guard since that first trip. But at the time, as a young lieutenant, I had no idea what the future held.

Staff officers were required to attend meetings every Tuesday evening at the New York Armory. The meetings began at seven in the evening and sometimes lasted up to three hours. They were attended by the command staff and headed by Colonel Erlich, the Brigade commander. We discussed upcoming training and planned the weekend drill taskings. The meetings were mandatory, and between those weekly meetings and my job on Wall Street, Gus worried that neither of us were spending enough time with the girls.

"Something's got to give," he told me more than once.

What he meant was that, as the mother of the family, I would have to make some kind of change. There was no doubt that our life was hectic. With my new rank I added another layer of responsibility to the personal and professional responsibilities I already carried, but I enjoyed the challenges of the fast-paced lifestyle and the demands of being an officer. When I showed Gus the difference in pay I was making between a specialist's and a lieutenant's grade, he was impressed. The difference was significant. Still, he wasn't sure the pace and long hours we were both putting in were worth the time away from each other and the girls.

When he wasn't working as a hospital administrator, Gus was a busy community activist, helping people write grant proposals, volunteering for various fund-raising efforts, and just generally getting out and doing things for the community. On most Saturday afternoons, he spent a few hours working up a sweat with a weekend basketball league. He also enjoyed playing a few dollars in the local numbers pool now and then (just like the weekly lottery players do now).

Bottom line—we both had full schedules. But Gus, like most men in that era, expected *me* to make changes to *my* schedule to accommodate the family needs. He wasn't as willing to make the same changes to his own schedule. I was able to convince him to give the new schedule some time for us both to get accustomed to it and, in the meantime, I did my best to hide the fact that it took an almost superhuman effort to get the whole family's morning routine precisely timed so that we all got to where we needed to be, and on time!

Get up, get dressed, get everyone fed, get Helene on her bus, get Ellen to her school, get back on a subway or, if the timing was too far off, get in a cab and make a hectic dash for Wall Street. There were days when I was grabbing Ellen by the hand and running with her into school so that I could get back in the waiting cab and be on my way to work. On Sundays, I would make meals ahead of time to last the week—meatloaf, casseroles, lasagna, anything I could think of that we could heat up during the week, because family sit-down dinners were a requirement in our household. In the evenings, I picked up Ellen from the sitter, hit the grocery store if I needed to, rushed home to get dinner on the table, sometimes just in time to welcome Gus home with a smile. I tried my best to make it seem effortless, as if I had it all under control. I succeeded most of the time. There were times when I had to ask Gus to pick up the girls, but that was rare. Usually, my calm, I-can-do-anything attitude would keep Gus convinced that everything was possible.

And convincing Gus was the main goal. Yes, I wanted to make sure the long list of daily tasks required to keep the family running were accomplished each day, but to have the freedom to do the things I wanted to do, to have a career and serve in the guard, I had to keep my husband happy. Eventually, he grew accustomed to my schedule and the demands of my new rank and supported me as much as he could.

One of the things we had to get used to was the new requirement that I attend weekly command staff meetings at the National Guard Armory on Park Avenue. I wasn't the first black officer to attend the meetings, but I was the only woman.

There I was, sitting in a room surrounded by white men. It was how my career in the National Guard started, and it was how it would always be. Over the course of my career, each time I entered a new room with a new group of white men, there would be a period of adjustment. My attendance usually made the men uncomfortable and they would have to figure out how I would fit, how they would treat me, what changes I might force on them. They would test, probe, and observe, waiting to see what would happen, see if they had to change their behaviors to accommodate me.

The pattern became familiar. The careful speech, the silence and nervous fidgets, the shifting glances as they checked with each other, silently communicating when one of them came too close to an assumed affront or insult. It always amazed me how a roomful of grown men would suddenly change into a bunch of nervous little boys as soon as I walked in.

In those first staff meetings, Colonel Erlich would discuss some issue he wasn't happy about. "This damn training calendar," he would say and then turn to me and say, "Excuse me." "That report doesn't mean shit!" … "Excuse me."

Or "What God damn idiot did that?" … "Excuse me."

Each time he turned to me to excuse himself, everyone in the room would look at me and shift uncomfortably. After several meetings like this, I grew tired of the unwanted attention.

"I'm tired of this shit!" he said. "Excuse me."

"Excuse me, sir," I said. "But, shit, sir. If you're going to keep excusing yourself every time you cuss, we'll never get the hell out of here."

He stared at me for a long second. Then he chuckled. The other men laughed nervously.

"Okay, Lieutenant. I like that," he said. And we went on with the meeting. After that, the men became a little more relaxed around me, but it was clear I would never be accepted as one of the guys. Not that I wanted to be. My DEOMI training had prepared me for the methods some used to draw attention to the person in the room who doesn't fit, to mark that person as not part of the group. By accepting the cuss words now and then, I had taken that tool away from him. I still wasn't ready to toss my own sensibilities aside to be accepted into the group. If they were uncomfortable, they needed to get over it because I wasn't going anywhere.

We held the meetings in the commander's office, everyone sitting around his table or lined up on his leather sofa. There was a bathroom in the office and when they needed to, the men quietly excused themselves and went into the colonel's bathroom. One evening, I needed to use the restroom. Instead of leaving the room and going downstairs to the only female-designated one in the building, I walked toward the colonel's bathroom. Before I could go inside, the colonel spoke up. "You'll be the first woman to ever use that bathroom. We had it all fixed up, for when Queen Elizabeth was coming to visit, and then she never used it. So, you'll be the first female to go in there."

I paused in the doorway. Everyone was staring at me again. His game seemed to be to find out how many ways he could attract attention to the fact that I was a woman, not one of them. *Different.*

"Sir, how do you expect me to go in there and pee now?" I said. Of course everyone laughed. Part of my job seemed to be to make some kind of joke that would relieve the uncomfortable situation others caused at my expense.

Despite the occasional uncomfortable situation, I enjoyed my weekend duty, the annual training periods, the challenges and the demands. The Army National Guard quickly became a vital part of my life. Yes, it was time-consuming and difficult; no, I certainly did not want to give it up. But that balancing act was teetering on a fine point. When a new requirement in my civilian job came along that included occasional travel, I watched my tower of demands come tumbling down. Gus had had enough.

"The girls deserve more of our attention," he said. "And I miss you. I want to spend more time with you."

Ellen was enrolled in a Catholic elementary school by this time, and Helene was enrolled in a school program for children with special needs. The girls were both doing well, but I understood what Gus meant. Between our jobs, our extracurricular activities and my guard duty, we weren't spending as much time together as we wanted to. I had resisted any suggestion to change our routine because I knew Gus felt the change would have to come from me, and I wasn't willing to give anything up.

My opinion at that time was that Gus had stretched himself too thin and he should be the one to slow down. People were constantly asking him to serve on one committee or another, to help someone work through some problem or another. It wasn't unusual for him to accompany some single mother to court when her child was in trouble. It wasn't unusual for him to stop some young person on the street and, using his finely honed negotiation skills, convince the kid of the error of his or her ways. It also wasn't unusual for him to walk down the street, his briefcase in one hand, stopping every few feet and picking up trash along the way with the other hand.

Everyone in the neighborhood knew Gus and everyone wanted a piece of his time. Community group meetings, fund-raising activities, helping people find jobs, get training, contacting some agency or another—there was a never-ending stream of people looking for help and Gus never said no.

During one of her visits to the city, Gus's sister came to me, just as frustrated as I was. "You have to tell Gus that he is now a husband and a father," she said. "Tell him to stop hanging his shingle as if he's available to help everyone with their problems. He needs to be home, taking care of his own family."

As much as I agreed with her, telling Gus to stop would be like telling a dolphin not to leap. Sure, you might be able to train them to stop doing it, but you would lose all that beauty as a result. If someone needed help, it was simply Gus's nature to do whatever he could to help.

For several months, we had long discussions about our lack of quality time together as a family. There were times when I couldn't sleep, tossing and turning over the choices Gus wanted me to make. His salary was almost double what I made, and community activism was in his blood. Besides, he was doing great work. If someone was going to make a change, it would have to be me. That knowledge didn't make the decision any easier because I didn't want to give up anything.

Eventually, I began to consider teaching as an alternative to my job on Wall Street. My degree was in education and I had spent a semester as a student teacher before graduating. I always thought I would teach until the job offer on Wall Street came along. While that job paid well and offered more career potential, teaching would offer regular hours, a couple months off during the summer and much less stress, or so I thought.

After weeks and months of soul searching, I finally decided that, to keep peace in the family, I would apply for a teaching job. And so I left Wall Street and began teaching at Edgar Allan Poe, an elementary public school in the South Bronx. It was a difficult decision, one I made reluctantly. But taking the job meant I never missed a dinner again. I got to spend more time with the girls, and we were able to take family vacations together. I sometimes feel there was some divine intervention in making that choice, because it meant more precious time with my husband when we needed it the most.

TEACHING AND TRAINING OTHERS

Right around the time I decided to switch gears in my civilian job and start teaching, my immediate supervisor and mentor in the Army National guard, Major Phil Friedman, recommended that I consider a position as a Training, Advising and Counseling officer (referred to as a TAC) at the Empire State Military Academy (ESMA). The academy is where the Army National Guard held their Officer Candidate School—where OCS students learned how to become officers. TAC officers are like the commissioned officer equivalent of a Drill Instructor. Hard, disciplined, mean. Ready to push candidates to their limits. Major Friedman thought I was too soft-spoken and he figured a TAC position would harden me a bit, put some authority in my voice. I would serve as a TAC during a two-week annual training period then for a year's worth of weekend drills. After a year, the class of trainees would graduate.

Before I left for my first two-week annual training period as a TAC, my commander pulled me aside. "Now remember—they're all going to be watching you to see how you handle this."

That was something I already knew. Joe Public could go in there and be just another TAC. This was the first year in the history of ESMA that female TACs would be assigned. I would be one of three women to breach the all-male cadre. I knew everyone would be curious to see how we would handle the situation—and how I would approach teaching mostly white men and women. I was accustomed to the scrutiny my every move and decision would usually undergo and knew a satisfactory performance wouldn't be enough. I had to outperform their expectations or the whole endeavor would be considered a failure.

I agreed to take on the task knowing I had what it took for the job, but that didn't mean I wasn't nervous. Figuring I could watch and learn, I arrived to find a completely different situation than I had imagined.

I reported to my company commander, Lieutenant Colonel Ron Tipa. It was a brief meeting. I don't remember much of what he said, but I would run into Lieutenant Colonel Tipa much more often, later in my career. At that first meeting, as I looked around the room, I realized that all of the other TACs were second lieutenants. As they introduced themselves, I learned some were experienced and had taught or trained cadets before, but I outranked them. I was a first lieutenant. It finally dawned on me that, despite my lack of experience, despite the fact that I'd only been commissioned a year earlier—and a direct commission at that—I would be in charge. My heart rate tripped up a notch.

Colonel Tipa directed most of his instruction to me as I grew more and more nervous about the situation. I listened and tried my best not to look as intimidated as I felt. The last thing I needed to do was to reveal how panicked I felt.

Colonel Tipa finished his instruction and dismissed us all.

I felt I had to confront the situation head-on and try to figure out how to make it work. We hadn't even met our officer candidates yet and I already felt the assignment was running away from me. So I gathered the rest of the TAC officers in my company who were younger and far more experienced than I was in the environment. I had to be honest with them and admit it was my first time as a TAC.

"Don't worry about a thing, ma'am," my company TACs said to me. "We'll help you make this a success."

And they did. It was just as important to them that we succeed as it was to me. They told me each step of the way what would happen next, what I needed to say, exactly how to proceed from one event to the next.

On that first day, they gave me some tips to prepare me for the first meeting with the OCS candidates. I stood in front of the formation of new officer candidates, my fatigues pressed to crisp perfection, my black combat boots polished to a high-gloss shine, my helmet strapped tightly to my chin, worn low on my forehead, leaving my eyes in shadow. My web belt and harness fit snugly; my canteens, ammunition and first-aid pouches hung exactly where they were supposed to be.

The OCS candidates stood at attention, probably more nervous than I was. It was time for me to perform. I walked the row of cadets at a slow pace, standing close enough to knock them in the forehead with the stiff brim of my helmet if I needed to. I stopped in front of the first trainee. Are you ready for this training, soldier?"

"Sir, yes sir!" he responded.

"Sir? Do I look like a man to you, soldier?"

"No, sir! I mean, no, ma'am!"

"Drop and give me ten," I said.

And the trainee hit the dirt to pump out some crisp pushups while I counted loudly, grateful for his early mistake, which gave me an opportunity to exercise my authority right away.

Over the next three weeks, I was grateful for those nervous trainees. They made plenty of mistakes and offered opportunity after opportunity for me to correct them. As I corrected them, I gained confidence. I yelled at them. I questioned them. I tripped them up and tore them down. They expected harsh treatment and I was ready to give it to them. They needed to fear me just enough to be motivated to succeed, but more than fear, I needed to earn their respect. Their respect for me would motivate them to excel. We got them up in the early hours of the morning, marched them to classes for training, marched them back in the evening and put them to bed at night. We were like drill sergeants and we weren't easy on them.

I shared a trailer with the two other female TACs. Part of our responsibility was to make sure the female trainees from all of the companies got up on time and turned lights out on time. After we were there for just over a week, I was deep in the field with my cadets, when I received a message that the commandant wanted to see me. The ESMA commandant was a full-bird colonel and I couldn't understand why he would want to see me—wanted to see me bad enough to send a helicopter out to the field training site to get me. I ran to the chopper, strapped myself in and wondered what the heck all the drama was about.

I reported to him in his office, surprised at how uncomfortable he seemed to be. I couldn't help but wonder if something was wrong with Gus or the girls.

"Ah, Lieutenant Cleckley. We had to fly several females back from the field by chopper because they are complaining of bad menstrual cramps. We'd like you to go speak to them and see what can be done about this."

It sounded like group hysterics to me. How could several women be suffering crippling cramps at the same time? I wasn't, however, going to voice my doubts in front of the commandant.

"Yes, Sir," I said. "I'll check into it."

I went to the barracks and found three women lying on their cots, all moaning and groaning like the most pathetic things I'd ever seen. To say that I was angry would be putting it mildly. I walked into the room and they all continued to lay there.

"Ma'am," they mumbled.

"I just left the Commandant's office. He sent me here to check on you. What is going on?" I controlled my desire to scream at them.

"Ma'am, we just have bad cramps and…"

"Get up!" I hadn't planned what I would say, but I wasn't going to let them talk to me like I didn't understand what was going on. "I said get up!"

They scrambled up and stood at attention, still giving me pathetic looks.

I paced in front of them.

"First of all, you are all OCS candidates, and you are going to have periods for the rest of your life! I have a company of men out there who are engaged in important training, and I get called back here for this?"

They looked straight ahead, but I had their attention.

"You want to be officers? You want to be treated like those men? Get your asses out of here and get back in that field! Do you understand me? DO YOU?"

"Ma'am, yes, ma'am!"

I did an about-face and went directly to the operations office.

"You need to get the chopper ready to take those candidates back to the field."

"But what about…"

"They are fine. They're ready to go back to the field."

I wondered if the whole incident had been a test for me. Was the commandant sitting back and watching to see how I would handle the ridiculous situation? If it was a test, they weren't done with me yet. After the second week of training, I was called to the commandant's office yet again. It was rare for someone of my rank ever to be called to his office and this was my second appearance there. I couldn't imagine what it was about this time.

When I reported to his office, he was sitting at his big desk, with the chief of staff and the command sergeant major standing behind him. He asked me to take a seat. He was uncomfortable again. "Lieutenant, as you know, the male officers live in the rooms at the officers' club. One of the female TACs has been seen drinking with several other officers. While there's nothing wrong with that, sometimes she has been seen going into this officer's room."

He shifted uncomfortably. The chief of staff and the sergeant major weren't looking at me, and I had a feeling what was going to come next.

"As I said, she has been visiting this officer's room and they, ah, get amorous. This female, well, she makes a lot of noise… if you know what I mean. And, ah, lieutenant, we need someone to talk to her. We would like you to talk to her, because frankly, we think she's giving women in uniform a bad reputation."

I thought about the request and knew they weren't going about this the right way. My DEOMI training kicked in again. I was already seeing red. To say that her actions were affecting the reputations of ALL women in the military was discrimination. They were looking for excuses to blame women, to claim that we didn't fit into this training situation. If she was getting loud while being amorous, then someone else must have been with her, making her loud, but these officers obviously didn't care what role the man was playing in this sordid affair.

"Sir, have you spoken with her company commander?"

The colonel cleared his throat. "No, we thought it would be best if you talked to her."

"Well, sir, I think it would be best if you talked to her company commander. I'm not in her chain of command. And by the way, sir, has anyone spoken to the man involved? Who is going to talk to him?"

The colonel shifted nervously, glancing quickly at the two men standing behind him who hadn't said a word.

"Okay, lieutenant, thank you. Thank you. We'll take it from here."

I stood, went to attention and saluted. The colonel saluted back and I left. I knew I had put them on the spot, but I was shocked. If the colonel received the complaint, chances were the man involved in the affair outranked the lieutenant. He could have been a captain, a major or even a lieutenant colonel, someone who was senior to the second lieutenant and, in all probability, someone who was married. If blame was going to be placed somewhere, it should have gone to the ranking officer in the engagement. Instead, they said the female was giving women in the military a bad reputation? I couldn't believe their nerve.

Later, I told the female involved that there were some rumors going around and she needed to be careful. She denied sleeping around, but I expected her to do that. Still, I wanted her to know that people were talking. What she did with the information was up to her.

I've spent many hours wondering about both of those incidents and still don't understand how to categorize them. Was it sexism? Was it simple ignorance about how to treat women? It was the first time women TAC officers were at the academy, but did that mean the whole military chain of command needed to go out the window? It was clear that we were seen as women first, officers second and soldiers last. The rules of the game somehow didn't apply to us—not in training, not in the chain of command and not in the command's eyes in terms of the automatic respect our rank and uniform should have received.

These men were hardened, experienced, high-ranking leaders. I had been an officer only a short time, but it was long enough to give me a hint that there were men in the Army who were clueless when it came to working and training with women. If in just this short two-week exercise I could face two ridiculous discriminatory and sexist situations, then surely there would be more to come.

Still, the whole experience of being a TAC officer at the academy had been worth it. I learned more about myself as a leader, and gained confidence about my own capabilities. Despite the higher set of standards I faced, I believe my tenure there was a success. Major Friedman, a dear friend who is retired now and living in Florida, was right to recommend that I take on the TAC job. Perhaps he made the suggestion because, being an officer of Jewish heritage, he could relate to the discrimination I might face and the possible barriers some people would throw in my way for whatever reason, be it my race or my sex. Whatever his reasons, his advice was helpful at the time and now, as my accountant and great personal friend, I still take his advice and guidance on things both financial and personal, very seriously.

Teaching children was far different from teaching cadets, but some of the skills I learned at the academy came in handy when I taught kindergarten my first year at Edgar Allan Poe Elementary. My second year there, I was teaching second grade. As the kids grew older, so did the discipline problems. I quickly gained the reputation as a teacher who could handle the problem children. Mrs. Cleckley didn't accept any messing around in her classroom. Gus warned me what would happen: "You better be careful—you're going to develop the reputation as the teacher who can handle *all* the discipline problems."

At the time, I didn't pay much attention, but soon his prediction came true. By my third year, I was teaching fifth grade hold-overs, the kids who should have moved on to sixth grade but didn't. Not a day went by that something significant didn't happen. These kids knew more about the "street" than I would ever know, and I had my hands full. I had a classroom full of kids who had to be watched constantly. I arrived to class early enough to write everything on the board I needed to write for the day, because I didn't dare turn my back on them for one second. I broke up fights, sometimes falling to my knees while jumping in the middle of one altercation or another; I confiscated knives and other weapons and I ducked as kids threw desks. There were times when they literally tried to kill each other. I wonder now, if I were teaching today, would I have ended up in jail for getting physical with some of those kids? The answer is probably...*yes*.

Teaching was always eventful and Gus heard every detail. He would come home from work and I would be waiting for him, bursting to tell him about the latest incident.

"You won't believe what happened today," I'd say, following him into the bedroom.

"Give me a minute, honey. At least let me take my jacket off."

I would tell him about how the principal had called me over the intercom. "Mrs. Cleckley, lock your door, right now!" I had received intercom calls like that before and I knew that I couldn't hesitate. I obeyed the order as soon as I heard it, rushing across the room and throwing the bolt lock on the door just as the mother of one of my students began kicking and beating on the door, screaming at the top of her lungs. She claimed her son had stolen her food stamps and she was out for blood. Armed police officers were close behind, trying to restrain the woman but with little effect. The kid, frightened to death, was trying to hide from his mother while all the commotion was going on. When I heard what she was accusing him of, his earlier behavior became clear. I glanced at my desk drawer where several packages of cookies and candy were stashed out of sight. I had confiscated the contraband from him earlier, after I caught him sharing the goodies with other students in class! I didn't know what was more shocking—that a child had used stolen food stamps to buy cookies and candy, or that a mother would want her own child arrested for it.

That wasn't the first time police were in my classroom and definitely would not be the last. One day, the police brought two students to me after they were caught skipping school. Evidently they decided they would rather go to the Bronx Zoo instead of coming to class. They weren't just truant, however. While at the zoo, they'd somehow started a fire. I couldn't understand why the police brought them back to my classroom instead of taking them to juvenile jail.

As that first year with the fifth graders progressed, students began to have arguments over who would get to clean the board for me. Eventually, I was able to turn my back on them, for a few seconds at a time, after having taught them what behaviors were unacceptable with me. I even took them on field trips, something unheard of for my group of unruly students. Even something as simple as taking them to Central Park, located only five subway stops away from the school, was a big deal. It was shocking to learn that some of them had never been there before. On one trip we visited the Museum of Natural History and another time I took them on a tour of the National Guard Armory where I drilled, telling them about my duties in uniform, what sorts of things we did during a drill weekend. Most of them were fascinated, having never been exposed to the military before.

I learned so much from them; just as I'm sure they learned a lot from me. Mostly, I learned that young people need discipline. If they don't get it, and are left to their own devices, the only possible result is chaos. They learned that rewards can come through good order and discipline.

As difficult as the job was, going into teaching was the perfect answer to the balance my family needed between Gus's job, my military duty and the care my daughters required. Helene was wearing glasses now. Her small face partially hidden behind the large, thick lenses, but they corrected some of her vision problems and she constantly expressed wonder at the world around her. She was doing well in school, talking up a storm, making friends and attending an annual summer camp that became a permanent social event she still looks forward to every year, even now as an adult.

My daughter Ellen displayed early signs of brilliance, reading and comprehending well beyond her age, discussing what she had learned, asking probing questions. It was clear she shared her father's inquisitive nature.

My teaching job meant that I was home from school in plenty of time to have dinner on the table, ready for our family meals together. While I was away for my military duties, Gus had time alone with the girls, which he obviously enjoyed. My annual, two-week summer training periods became their special time together, time he looked forward to. And the extra pay was an added bonus.

In 1978 it was still odd for a woman to be an officer in the National Guard. People were always surprised when they learned what I did on some weekends, but there was something about the job that I simply enjoyed. I loved wearing the uniform, loved being part of my unit. I couldn't really articulate it, but, eventually, Gus understood my devotion to the role.

"Honey, I am so glad you joined the military," he said to me one day. "I know it makes you happy and it's worked out for the best." He hugged me and added, "I still wish you had discussed it with me first, but it was the right thing to do."

For three years, my lighter work schedule brought our family closer together. My teaching job remained challenging, but fulfilling. Gus was doing well with his career and still played basketball every Saturday with a close group of friends. We were invited out to dinners, parties and other events, sometimes going to see shows and special events that came to town. The girls were thriving, doing well in school, and rarely misbehaving. We were happy.

Soon, all of that changed.

GUSTAVUS

Gus came home from his usual Saturday basketball game and found me relaxing in the bedroom. He was sweaty and smiling. I playfully struggled against his attempt to wrap me in a damp bear hug, my struggles futile against his need to mark me with his manly perspiration.

It was a bright Saturday afternoon in October. I don't remember what I had been doing before he came home. My only memory is what he said next. "Honey, look at this. What do you think this is?"

He cocked his foot on the edge of the bed and pointed to a large lump on the inside of his thigh that poked out just beneath the edge of his shorts. It was about the size of a ping pong ball, round and hard. He poked it, his brow wrinkling as he stared at it, then he looked at me.

"I don't know, but you better get that checked out right away," I said. "How long has it been there?"

He shrugged but it was clear from the size of it that, if he had been ignoring the lump, it couldn't be ignored any longer. I worried about what the lump could be. Gus was a lively, healthy man and the thought of a serious illness seemed impossible.

On Friday night, a week later, Gus came home from work a little early. He had a bottle of champagne, fresh scallops and shrimp he picked up from a local fish market.

"What a treat," I said. "What's going on?"

"Tonight, we're going to celebrate life." He beamed his infectious smile and I liked the idea. Our life had been exceptionally fulfilling lately. I was scheduled to attend my weekend drill the next day and wouldn't be back home until late Sunday night, so it felt right to make a special night of it. We cooked the meal together, including the girls in the preparation. I had become a pretty decent cook by this time and while we often ate fancy meals at home, the fresh seafood was a luxury. We had a lovely family dinner filled with chatter from the girls about their day, Gus joking and teasing. When the girls went to bed and Gus and I were cleaning up, he said he needed to talk to me.

He sat me down and took my hands between his. "Honey, the results of the biopsy came in today. It's cancer."

And just like that, my world stopped turning for a moment. I found it hard to breathe.

"It's okay, baby. I'm going to get it treated and we're going to beat this." He spoke with such confidence that my pounding heart slowed down a notch. But I had so many questions, beginning with, "What kind of cancer is it?"

"It's lymphoma. They say it's stage three."

Knowing what kind didn't help. I knew only one thing about cancer—cancer kills. I began to sob. Gus held me, but I couldn't slow the speed of my thoughts, my mind leaping to the worst-case scenarios. Then I thought about having to put my uniform on to leave for the weekend. I simply couldn't face it.

"I'm not going to drill tomorrow," I said.

"Oh, yes, you are," he insisted.

"No, I can't!"

"You're going to go to drill and the girls and I are going into the office tomorrow. Everything is going to be fine."

Every moment I spent packing, I worried about my husband. I hated to leave him, but I understood his need for us to act normal, as if the earth hadn't suddenly shifted under our feet. Leaving for duty early the next morning to go to Camp Smith, I felt as if I were trudging through molasses. I was heavy with worry and somber with thoughts of what was to come. But somehow I managed to just put one foot in front of the other and do what was expected of me.

I had been assigned to conduct a class with a captain in the unit and we were busy arranging desks in preparation for the session, when a colonel stepped into the room.

"Hey, Captain Anderson," he said to the officer, then, turning to me, he said, "Hey, sweetheart," and turned to leave.

I froze. Needless to say, the colonel had no idea that I was in no mood for the affront.

"Excuse me, sir," I said. "My name is not Sweetheart."

The colonel stopped and turned slowly to look at me. Captain Anderson stared at me in shock, his face flaming red.

"Excuse me?" the colonel said.

"I said my name is not Sweetheart, sir."

"Pardon me, lieutenant. But I didn't see your name."

"You don't have to see my name, sir. You can obviously see my rank. I am not a sweetheart."

The colonel just stood there, regarding me from head to toe as if committing my image to memory. Finally, after several seconds of us staring at each other, he nodded. "Okay." And he left.

As soon as he was out of ear shot, Captain Anderson sputtered, "What is wrong with you, lieutenant? He was only trying to be nice. You can't talk to a colonel like that!"

"He wasn't trying to be nice. If he could recognize you, he could recognize me as the officer that I am, too. We're both in our fatigues and our ranks are clearly displayed."

"But he's a colonel," Anderson said. "He could go back and report you."

"He won't report me. He won't tell anyone because he knows he was wrong."

Calling a junior officer sweetheart had several different connotations that would negatively reflect on the officer's record. I was sure the colonel was just as aware of the potential consequences as I was. The man wasn't going to report a thing and, in fact, he never did.

That weekend, my mind was so heavy with thoughts of Gus that I couldn't have cared less if the man reported me to the world. I was in no mood to take his slight. I've often been told that I have balls, which I've always found to be an ironic compliment, considering it's usually given after my response to a sexist insult. Balls or no, I don't believe insults like that are made innocently. The person usually understands exactly what he is doing and, like most folks engaged in sexist behavior, he is only surprised to be called on it.

By the time my drill weekend was over, I was extra happy to be reunited with Gus and the girls. It had only been two days, but it had felt like a lifetime. That evening, we sat down to dinner like we had so many nights before. I attempted to appear calm, to act as if nothing was out of the ordinary, but I doubt I pulled it off. I felt tired and sad and kept looking at Gus. The girls didn't seem to notice the tension and Gus acted as he did on most nights, like an attentive father.

After the meal, Gus told the girls the news. He put Ellen on his knee as he spoke to both of them. "I want you girls to know that Daddy has a disease. Daddy has cancer. It's not a good disease, but Daddy is going to be fine."

"Daddy, you're sick?" Ellen asked.

"Yes, but I'm going to be just fine. We're going to remove the bad thing, and I'll be just fine."

Gus had always been an optimist. His diagnosis didn't change that aspect of his nature. This was 1980 and for several months, he *was* fine. He continued his hospital administration work at Montefiore Medical Center and they referred him to Sloan-Kettering Cancer Center in Manhattan for his treatments. Sloan-Kettering is an institution known for its state-of-the-art therapies.

From the moment he told me the diagnosis, I took books from the library, reading everything I could find about lymphoma, the treatments and the symptoms of the disease. I'd sit up in bed, reading the heavy texts. He would climb in bed next to me and try to take the books away from me.

"Put that down," he'd say.

"I'm trying to read, honey."

"You don't need to know all that stuff." He'd hug me, trying to take my mind off what couldn't be forgotten.

I watched him constantly to see if I could anticipate symptoms. Every moment of every day, my mind reeled with worry despite the fact that he appeared healthy and normal. And then he was admitted to the hospital for his first chemo therapy treatment. My brave husband had signed up to try an experimental therapy. The chemo cocktail he received was a new mix they hoped would reduce the tumor and the side effects. As he lay in bed waiting for treatment, Gus laughed and joked with the nurses. I was a worrier, so I spent both days with him in the hospital. I tried to keep a brave face, to have the balls so many people said I had, but it was rough. I was nervous, frightened, my stomach tied in knots. Much of the time I felt as if I were in a fog, finding it hard to stay focused on a conversation, hard to think of anything but that my husband was sick and that I wanted everything to be alright.

Several friends came to give support, visiting during the couple of days he was admitted. Later, they told me that every time I left the room, he asked them to keep an eye on me. It made me realize that as much as I was worried for him, he was worried for me, and I wanted to take that burden from him. I worked harder to be stoic, to stay strong. That's what Gus needed from me.

As strong as I tried to be, it was impossible to stop myself from wondering how life would continue if the worst happened. My husband had always enjoyed living the high life, treating us to dinners at Tavern on the Green, taking cabs when the subway wouldn't do, and wearing the nicest clothes and shoes. He constantly had his nose buried in some non-fiction book about Gandhi, or Malcolm X, treatises about helping the urban poor or succeeding against terrible odds. His little surprises, his unfailing need to help others, his laugh and his steady support were the foundation on which our family and our life were built. He was a big man who filled our lives with so much joy and optimism that losing him was unthinkable. The only thing I could do was ensure he stayed focused on recovery and healing, make sure he took his medications, kept his appointments and, above all, relaxed and didn't get stressed about me and the girls.

After a month, a second round of chemo was scheduled. This time, it wasn't an overnight treatment but several hours in the hospital on a Friday afternoon as an out-patient. Throughout this time, for the three and a half months he was treated, he continued to work, to fulfill all of his community obligations, even to play his Saturday basketball games. When he began to lose his hair after the first treatment, he chose to shave his head and he was a very handsome bald man. He didn't lose weight, never really looked sick and seemed the same man he was before the diagnosis. It was almost enough to make me believe that the doctors were all wrong. There was nothing wrong with my Gustavus.

After the second treatment on that Friday night, he was to call the doctors every seven hours to report how he felt. There seemed to be few side effects. Since he was doing so well, he encouraged me to stick to my schedule to attend my DEOMI training in Delaware. I took the train and spent Friday and Saturday night at the Hilton in Delaware, surrounded by EEO officers from every service, learning about new policies and guidelines for my military job. I called Gus Saturday night to see how he was doing.

"I feel great," he said, and he told me what the girls had been up to.

I still worried, but it was good to hear that his spirits were up and they were all having a nice time together.

The seminar I attended was a full schedule of long hours sitting in a conference center. That, combined with the train travel, wore me out. Sunday, I came home to find a note from Gus and dinner waiting for me. He had taken the girls to Madison Square Garden to see a Knicks game. They came home a few hours later, excited but exhausted and ready for bed.

"How are you doing," I asked him.

"Woman, would you stop worrying? I'm fine." He gave me a big hug and kiss.

The following Monday afternoon, I was still exhausted from my hectic weekend. My students had been particularly rambunctious that day and were getting on my nerves. I hadn't taken a day off in a long time and it was clear I needed one. Before I left school, I strategically placed my lesson plan in the open for the next day, someplace where a substitute would easily find it. I planned to play hooky from school and, as bad as my kids could get, I figured anyone called in to take my place might need a little help.

Gus was working late that Monday night and he came home after eleven, after attending a community meeting with the nuns from Ellen's school. I was in a deep sleep by the time he tiptoed in our bedroom, but he forgot himself and flicked the light off. I woke up immediately—still petrified of the dark.

"Gus! Honey, it's so late." I looked at the clock, still groggy from waking up. "You have to take care of yourself."

"I'm fine, honey. I'm going to live until I die. I just got back from my meeting with the sisters. We had a good meeting and I feel just fine."

"Okay, but come to bed. You have to get up in the morning."

"I'm going to have a sandwich and listen to some jazz and then I'll come to bed."

He went down the hall and I must have gone right back to sleep because I woke the next morning snuggled in his arms. He pulled me close and whispered, "Let's stay home today."

I almost purred with happiness. "We've been together so long, we're thinking alike," I said. "I already set out a lesson plan for a substitute today."

"Yeah," he said, excited as a little kid. "Let's get the girls off to school, and we'll just spend some time in bed, and later we can have some of my special chili."

Gus went into the kitchen to take the chili he had made out of the freezer. When he came back to bed, he was smiling. We had to get up soon to get the girls off to school, so we lay on our sides, Gus spooning me as we talked. He leaned over and kissed my cheek, sucked in a deep breath and went totally limp, his head flopping away from me.

I thought he was playing around. His arm was heavy on me, and I could barely move.

"Gus, what are you doing?" I laughed.

But he didn't move. Suddenly, the whole room was in a vacuum of silence, my heart already racing from his abrupt unnatural stillness. I shifted out from under his arm, grabbed his face and turned it toward me. His eyes were rolled back, his mouth slack.

My heart froze in panic.

"Gus! Gus!" I screamed and then ran to the bathroom and put towels under the cold tap. I put the wet towels on his face but there was absolutely no change. By this time, I was simply screaming his name over and over again while dialing 911. I sputtered and stumbled and the operator told me to calm down. Her command reminded me of my military training. I took a deep breath.

"I'm calm," I said, and gave them our address. "My husband was just talking to me. Now he's gasping for air, and his eyes are rolled back in his head." At some point, I must have told her that he worked as a hospital administrator.

"Which hospital?"

"Montefiore."

"Hang on, ma'am. We'll have people there right away."

I hung up and rushed to the intercom to warn the doorman that an ambulance was on the way. "Ma'am, the police are already here...," the doorman said.

"Send them up!"

The girls had wandered out of their bedrooms, frightened by my panic. Ellen jumped up and down, screaming and crying, "Mommy, Mommy!"

"Go get Anita," I told them.

The girls tore out of the apartment and up the stairs to Anita's place, leaving the apartment door open. Neighbors from across the hall could hear me screaming. One of my neighbors, a respiratory therapist, came into the apartment and turned Gus onto his back, removed the pillows from the bed and gave him mouth-to-mouth. Then several more neighbors were in the apartment, curious, wanting to help, all buzzing about with little effect. The girls came back with Anita, who helped with the CPR, while another neighbor took the girls back up to Anita's apartment. I was so grateful the girls were spared the trauma of watching what was happening to their father.

Eleven minutes after I made the 911 call, the ambulance techs were in the room. They continued CPR and used a bag to force air into Gus's lungs, but nothing changed. They used a defibrillator, quickly spreading gel onto the paddles and placing them on his chest. Watching his body jerk from the shock was awful. The smell of burned hair and flesh filled the room. The electrical charge left ugly brown burn marks on his chest.

"Get her out of the room," one of the techs said, but there was no way I was going to leave. I was crying and calling his name over and over, but I felt eerily calm, as if I were watching myself going through this, watching my life fall apart.

"Please, honey. Please wake up," I begged.

As they worked on him, I kept pulling on his big toe which I knew was sensitive; a touch that would normally make him wince in pain, hoping it would wake him, bring him back to me. I watched everything going on, but I never once thought he was going to die. Not like this. Not so quickly. Not when we had such a pleasant and peaceful day planned.

I kept thinking he was going to be upset with all of these people in our house. How was I going to explain it to him? There I was in my pajamas, while all of our neighbors and several strangers moved around our apartment, their low whispers creating a hum that seemed to increase as the seconds ticked on. Everyone in the building knew my husband and they had all seen or heard the commotion. In no time, a large crowd had formed in and outside our apartment, everyone asking what was wrong with Mr. Cleckley.

The medical team worked hastily for thirty minutes or more. When nothing changed, their movements slowed down. There simply wasn't a need to move rapidly anymore. The monitor they had connected to him was still beeping, though.

"What are you doing?" I demanded. "You can't stop!"

"Ma'am, we're very sorry. He's gone."

"But it's still beeping. You can't stop. He can't be dead."

But my Gus was gone... and for a long while, I felt dead, too.

A WIDOW

The first person I called was Gus's brother in West Virginia. Frank is a lawyer and a very calm man. When he answered the phone, all I could say was that Gus was gone. He didn't ask any questions. "I'll be right there," he said.

Once I made the call, I mentally checked out. I couldn't fathom what had just happened. We had been talking. We had been laughing together. Less than an hour before, I had been in his big, warm arms, feeling loved and cherished by him, looking forward to playing hooky together. My big, strong, handsome man could not be gone.

I felt frozen in shock and could barely move, as a whirlwind of activity swirled around me. At first, there were so many people in the apartment, buzzing around and whispering, everyone afraid to say anything to me. Slowly the neighbors and gawkers trickled away, many of them in business suits, having stopped to investigate the commotion on their way to work. As the buzz of activity died down, the reality of my loss settled around me, heavier and heavier. I felt incapable of carrying the load. All I could do was sit and stare, breathe in, breathe out.

One neighbor sat with me until Frank arrived, but I have very little memory of what anyone said or did. The clocks ticked as time moved on, the noise from the street drifted up into the apartment, whispered conversations floated around me and I sat in my bubble of shock and grief.

The girls stayed in Anita's apartment until their uncle Frank retrieved them several hours later. He must have dropped whatever he'd been doing and driven straight to the airport because he walked into my apartment three hours after I made the call.

Frank shepherded me though those terrible days and helped me make scores of decisions that otherwise would have been too confusing. Through quiet conversations and extreme patience, he helped coordinate every step I made. We knew we would have to hold two separate celebrations of Gus's life. The first, a large memorial service in New York to accommodate two to three hundred people so that Gus's friends, colleagues and all of the people touched by his community work would have a chance to pay their respects. The second service would be held in Gus's hometown of West Virginia. Planning the separate events, informing everyone, making one decision after another, was all-consuming.

Between the planning and fretting over every detail, the well wishers arrived. For several days, the doorbell rang incessantly. People brought food and flowers, and I was surprised by the number of people who brought money. I later learned that this was something people did, especially for a young widow with children. At the time, I felt overwhelmed by the number of people who wanted to help financially. People like the friends who played in Gus's regular, Saturday basketball game. They were just a group of guys who spent a few hours on Saturdays, working off steam. When Gus died, the men brought money and, later, organized a tournament in his honor. They had t-shirts made that said The Gustavus Cleckley Basketball Tournament and for two years they held the event to raise funds that went toward Ellen's college tuition. Another group of people in the neighborhood, the ones who played in the local numbers pool Gus participated in, also made a gift of money. I didn't know them very well but recognized the faces of the people Gus would stop and talk to, discussing the latest picks and winners. They quietly presented their gift with whispered condolences and sentiments of shock that he would go so quickly and unexpectedly. They handed over neatly stacked bills in several denominations wrapped in a brown paper lunch bag, some of it probably the winnings of that day.

I was particularly touched by the staff of Montefiore Hospital dedicating a bench outside the building with a small brass plaque proclaiming the bench in Gus's name.

The memorial in New York was so well attended the funeral home was standing room only, with representatives from Montefiore and several other hospitals, all of the various charity groups and community organizations he donated time to, and so very many friends. We had planned for hundreds and they came in droves. I was gratified by such an outpouring of support, proud that Gus had left such an indelible mark on so many people's lives.

As soon as the New York services were completed, we shipped his body to West Virginia and held another funeral for his hometown. All of the pallbearers were high school and college friends, including Hal Greer, a former NBA All Star with the Philadelphia 76ers.

We spent four days in West Virginia, surrounded by Gus's family, my family and friends who had come from all over to attend. So many people shared their memories of Gus, their appreciation of his friendship and their good wishes for me and the girls, the days in his hometown helped me realize just how much my husband had been loved and respected.

Throughout these days, there were times when I felt as if Gus was speaking directly to me, to tell me what he wanted for each service. I remembered the phone calls I had made to him while I planned my nephew's funeral, the late-night conversations we had had when he told me, step-by-step, what he would do, what choices he would make. I could almost hear his voice as he talked about those funeral plans, death certificates, flowers, eulogies. Little Mitchell's arrangements had been a practice run for me, a rehearsal for my husband's passing. Now, as I made these arrangements, it felt as if he was by my side ensuring everything went as he wished.

When the services were over, when the thank-you cards had been sent, the out-of-town visitors gone home, the girls and I got on a plane and returned to New York. We were alone now. And I had to figure out how to cope.

Frank came to New York and spent a week with us, helping me straighten out our financial affairs. I will always be grateful for his help at that terrible time.

My girlfriends, Hannah and Charlene, surrounded me and the girls with love in the way that only true girlfriends can. They stood by me throughout my grief. On many nights they sat with me and simply listened while I talked about my husband, my soul mate and friend.

Three weeks after Gus's death, the principal at Edgar Allan Poe called and offered his condolences. Then he revealed the real purpose of his call: "Mrs. Cleckley, we were wondering when you are planning to come back to school. You know, the substitutes simply cannot handle your class as well as you can. I don't want to rush you. But we could really use your help."

I couldn't answer him. I was grieving and didn't have any idea when that would change. I simply didn't know when I would have the energy to face my classroom again. Gus had been the one I turned to when the stress from those wild kids became too much for me. Who would be my sounding board now? Who would help me sort through the problems I faced each day in the classroom?

I knew I had to go back to work. Gus had left us a nice life insurance policy, but that money wouldn't last long—not in New York City, not with two girls to raise. Helene was sixteen years old and attended a special school where the staff took great care of her. There was no way I would compromise on that. Seven-year-old Ellen-Lizette attended an academically challenging private Catholic school and was thriving in that environment. I couldn't compromise her education, either. The realities of my situation were becoming clear: my teaching salary, even when combined with my National Guard wages, wouldn't adequately pay the bills and provide for my girls; and the stress of my classroom, coupled with trying to raise the girls on my own, wasn't what I wanted in the long term.

After a month, I did go back to my classroom, but by then, teaching had lost its luster. It was simply too difficult for me to stay as focused as I needed to be to keep charge of a classroom full of demanding pre-teens. The stress of the classroom, combined with the need to deal with my day-to-day issues left me feeling miserable, weighted down with loneliness and grief. And over the following weeks, I came to realize that, given our financial situation, I would eventually have to make some life-changing choices. But my thinking was so rattled I could barely decide what to have for dinner, let alone figure out where we would live or what I would do with my career. The absence of Gus was like a tangible void, one I brushed up against every moment of every day. Sometimes it would wash over me like a cold breeze. Other times, missing him slammed me in the chest, the memory brought on by a smell, a song, an expression someone used that would remind me of him.

The evenings at home were the worst. I kept expecting to hear his key in the door, expected to come around the corner and see him, his glasses perched on his nose, his forehead wrinkled as he concentrated on a book he was reading. The apartment was too quiet, too still, even with me and the girls in it. It was as if we were holding our breaths, waiting for Daddy to come home, but he never would. Not anymore.

Amidst all of this emotion, I was expected to figure out what to do with my life, with my daughters lives, sort out Gus's finances, his life insurance, the benefits from his job—all those things the living are expected to sort out when their loved ones die. The responsibility almost crushed me.

Much of it I simply didn't deal with. I left his things on his dresser exactly where he had neatly placed them when he undressed the night before he died. His wallet, his glasses, his change, his watch—everything remained right where he left them for months. His clothes stayed folded in his drawers, suits and shirts hanging in his closet. Tapes he'd listened to still sat in the tape deck. Books he'd been reading stayed marked where he'd left them, never to be finished. If I couldn't deal with these everyday things, how could I make decisions that would affect the rest of my life and my daughters' lives as well?

But... the living do keep on living. We find a way to push on, to get up each day, eat, work, breathe. The days ticked on and weeks went by and then one day I found myself laughing over something and I realized how different the laughter felt from how I'd been feeling and I thought, maybe the worst had passed. The crushing feeling wasn't so crushing anymore, the tears still came but they weren't as debilitating as they once were and the hollow feeling that was my heart started to fill again with the things life would allow. And eventually, I knew it was time to make some decisions.

At the top of the list was where we would live—where we could *afford* to live. I love New York, but it's one of the most expensive cities in the world. I thought moving somewhere less expensive would help. Of course, the first place I considered was San Francisco. Gus and I still had a lot of friends there and I loved the city, but living in California wouldn't be much cheaper than living in New York. It was very clear that I either had to make more money, or I had to move, sooner rather than later. Those thoughts occupied most of my thinking through months of indecision. Each time I felt I was close to a solution, I changed my mind again.

It seems the most profound changes happen when your life is in the greatest turmoil.

About six months after Gus died, I reported to duty at the Armory. My brigade commander asked to see me. He sat me down and we had a conversation that changed my life once again.

"Why don't you consider going fulltime active duty in the Guard," he said.

My first thought was, no way! I would never consider such a thing. But after a moment, I realized my experiences as a WAC would be very different from the way life would be now in the modern Active Guard. I was an officer for one thing, no longer an entry-level enlisted person. Most importantly, I wouldn't have to leave my children behind. We would have full medical coverage, a housing allowance and many other privileges that would help me make ends meet. I was a Captain by this time. A fulltime captain's salary wouldn't make us rich, but all the added benefits would mean we would be doing fairly well.

Still, I hadn't been a fulltime soldier for almost eleven years and I hesitated.

"The universities and colleges are short of ROTC teachers right now," the commander said. "How would you feel about teaching ROTC cadets at a university somewhere?"

I pictured the orderly, disciplined, interested and more mature students I could expect in a Reserve Officer Training Corps program. Then I pictured my classroom in the Bronx. Needless to say, I was intrigued with his suggestion.

"Think about it," he said. "Weigh the pros and cons and tell me what you think."

So that's what I did. The more I thought about it, the longer the pro list became. As a fulltime soldier, the housing allowance alone would be a major plus. While I didn't know where we would live, if I went on active duty, I knew that taking the weight of rent off my shoulders would be a massive relief. Teaching students at the university level was also appealing. Plus, if I taught at a university, I could take evening classes and work on a graduate degree. There were benefits available to help pay for Helene's special-needs training. I was a captain, but down the road I could look forward to further advancement, something that wasn't necessarily possible in the New York City public school system.

On the flip side, there were very few cons, far as I could see. And then I thought back to the day when Gus hugged me and said, "Honey, I'm so glad you quit Wall Street."

The decision to quit Wall Street was one I was led to reluctantly, one my husband and I argued about for many hours, one I would eventually realize was a good decision. It also seemed to be a decision I was fated to make. When I quit my fast-paced job for teaching, I had no idea how precious those extra days and hours with my husband would become. I had no idea that my experience in the classroom would provide an opportunity to start a new career in the military and support my family. I had no idea it would eventually lead to the extraordinary achievements that came about later in my military career.

Still, it took me a long time to decide to go fulltime in the Guard. For one thing, I couldn't just make the jump, I had to apply and be accepted for the fulltime job. And in order to apply, I first had to complete the Advanced Officer Course. I also wanted a safety net, just in case I regretted my decision.

I disappointed Mr. Titlebaum when I requested a leave of absence from the school system for a year, but he reluctantly granted my request. Then I set to work pulling my application packet together.

At the time, the Officer Advanced Course was a long process of correspondence courses that most people took a year to complete. I was determined to get it done in six months. Once I completed the course, I could immediately submit my packet for the active duty position. The packet is basically a file of information providing my training, education and experience in a series of required forms. There are strict regulations outlining what an application packet holds and detailed instructions explaining exactly how everything should be put together. My application was for a three-year commitment. At the end of that commitment, I could stay on active duty or return to civilian life. Knowing that I could change my mind if things didn't work out eased some of my anxiety about the decision. I simply didn't know if I wanted to make a career of being a soldier, and there was always the chance the Guard could deny the request.

Finishing the Officer Advance Course became my fulltime job. Each morning the girls left for school and I sat down at my desk to study. The correspondence course program was a series of booklets that contained the training and a final test. As I completed each booklet, I sent it in and waited to receive the next booklet. I hunkered down and got it done. In six months, I had completed the program.

Next I had to submit my request to go on active duty. I submitted my packet just before Christmas, 1982, and after the New Year, I received notice that I had been accepted to go on active duty. I was to report June 1st to my new duty station in Hampton, Virginia. I would go from teaching fifth graders to teaching ROTC cadets at Hampton University, a historically black college.

It was time to begin preparing myself and my children for this major change in our lives.

HELENE

Although Helene never seemed fully behind the idea of the move away from New York, she never voiced any objections, either. Then one day her social worker and some of her program officials asked if I would come in to meet with them.

"Mrs. Cleckley, we're wondering if you've looked into programs for Helene in Virginia," the social worker said. "You see, Helene has told us that she doesn't want to leave New York."

She hadn't said anything of the sort to me.

"You must understand. Helene has been coming here since she was seven years old. Even for a normal child, this kind of disruption would be severe. For Helene, well, it's very upsetting for her. Also, you have to consider that we have a unique program here. We're concerned that you won't be able to find a comparable program for her in Virginia."

It is difficult to explain the bright star that is my oldest daughter. Visually impaired she may be, but her view of life is clearer than most people with full sight will ever grasp. She knows what she likes, knows what she wants, and once her mind is made up, it is difficult to sway her. She is very much like me in her stubbornness. While she may have difficulty making her point in a direct way, she had always let me know exactly where she stood on a particular topic. Until now.

I left the meeting stunned and hurt by the notion that my daughter felt she couldn't talk to me about her desire to stay in New York. I decided I needed to sit down with her for a talk. For the uninitiated, it is difficult to tell that Helene has a problem with her sight. She will look in your direction, but she doesn't maintain eye contact. Her gaze will wander over your face, the room and then return to whatever she is focused on at the time—rarely sitting still, she is usually listening to music, compiling a list of the songs she is recording on a tape, drawing a picture with colored pencils and stickers or putting a puzzle together. Conversation takes a backseat to whatever activity she is engaged in at the time.

That evening when I walked into her room, she sat at her desk, her music blaring the latest R&B tune she was obsessed with. She loved music and kept it at a constant, ear-splitting volume.

"Turn your music down for a minute, honey. I want to talk to you."

She didn't need me to say anything else. She knew what I wanted to talk to her about.

Helene's usual way of talking was to use a litany of words that traveled a twisted route to her point. Touching on topics here and there that seemed to make little connection to the subject at hand, she would always circle around to the main message. Her message to me that night was that she loved New York, couldn't imagine living anywhere else, and she simply and stubbornly did not want to leave. She stated her desire and then turned away from me, her shoulders hunched around her ears in a signature gesture that meant there could be no further discussion.

Just as Helene had a special and unique way of going through life, her approach to the loss of her father and the changes in her world was special, too. She loved New York, her school, her teachers, our apartment, the life we once had. She didn't want any more changes. The problem was that she hadn't given me any sign that she had objections to the course I was planning. During our discussion, I never lost sight of the fact that she grieved for Gus as much as I did. They had been very close. He was the only father she had ever known, and losing him along with moving away from her friends was a difficulty I had anticipated, but not to the extent she felt it.

"I take the subway to get around. I love the subway. I like going to the corner store on my own. I am independent here. There won't be any programs for me in Virginia. How do you know that there will be anything for me to do? I'll be bored there. I can't stand to be bored. I want to live my life in New York." She went on like that for a while, listing all of the reasons why life anywhere else would be unacceptable. Helene was eighteen at the time, and skilled at stubbornly defending her position

She was adamant. The way she rattled off all of the reasons she should have her way and the obvious time she had spent preparing her arguments meant she had practiced her speech. She had probably mumbled it to herself, repeating the argument over and over to herself in preparation for the squabble she knew she would face with me. I felt outgunned.

She'd displayed that same stubbornness each year when it was time for her to attend summer camp. Since she was seven, Helene had been attending a camp in upstate New York for visually impaired children. As she grew up, she graduated to a summer camp for young adults and she never missed a year. Even now, she spends two weeks at the camp each year, with daily activities, art projects, water sports, all the things you associate with a summer camp, surrounded by other blind and special needs young adults. She insists on going because it is the highlight of her year, the time when she can reconnect with the other campers and counselors and be herself without worry. When it comes to summer camp, nothing can get in the way of Helene's attendance and she tends to be very vocal about what she wants.

If I said to her, "Helene, Oprah Winfrey is going to lend us her private plane so we can go anywhere in the world," I could predict what Helene would say: "Is that during my camp time, Mother? Because if it is, I can't go."

Ever since the first year she attended, our family has known that it is simply forbidden to plan an activity that conflicts with Helene's summer camp. And now I recognized the stubbornness she usually reserved for her summer camp in her argument against our proposed move to Virginia.

Most eighteen-year-olds would be busy thinking about graduating high school, starting college, living on their own for the first time in their lives. Helene wasn't ready for that independence, not at that time. Her circumstances wouldn't allow for it. With her glasses, she could see well enough to read and to get around, but the light and circumstances have to be just right or her vision is dangerously bad. She would hold onto my arm when we walked together, with me guiding her a bit, drawing her attention to upcoming curbs and steps. She was perfectly capable of cooking a microwave meal for herself, but only after I taught her to wear an oven mitt when she removed her meals so she wouldn't burn herself.

Helene is determined not to let her learning disability get in the way of what she wants to do in life, but at that time, she wasn't ready to live alone. Gus had always tried to prepare me for the time when Helene would want to leave home, but in my mind, we hadn't reached that point yet. I wasn't ready to allow her to live on her own.

"I can take care of myself if someone will help me," Helene insisted. "Why can't you let me stay here?"

Later, in another discussion at the school, Helene's point was reinforced. "Mrs. Cleckley, we think you need to consider the possibility of allowing her to stay in the city."

Hearing one of her teachers siding with Helene made me wonder if I was just being overprotective. Was I preventing her from doing something that might be good for her? Would moving her have a more negative effect on her than allowing her to try to go it on her own?

After hearing Helene say for the twentieth time that she wanted to stay, I didn't have any choice but to begin to consider how we could make it work. I must have driven my friends crazy with my need to discuss the problem. Eventually, the idea of finding someone to be a live-in caregiver came up.

I hadn't planned on giving up the New York apartment. It was a beautiful and spacious three-bedroom apartment in the city and, while it was too expensive for us on an elementary school teacher's salary, I had calculated that we could afford to keep it with my military pay, at least for a while. I had three years to make a decision about staying on active duty. I intended to keep the apartment for a while, so I could return to it if things didn't work out as I planned.

So I found a suitable caregiver who came highly recommended, someone we had known for many years. She was in her early twenties, a person Helene was comfortable with, and, while I hated the idea of being separated from my daughter, I felt leaving her in the apartment where she was most comfortable, along with a responsible caretaker, was the best option. We decided to give the arrangement a try for six months. I visited often, hopping on a plane and staying with them in the apartment for weekends at a time. I could catch a People's Express flight for thirty-five dollars, round trip, so almost every other weekend I was able to spend time with Helene.

Things went well at first. Reports from her teachers were good; Helene's room and the apartment were tidy and neat. More importantly, Helene seemed proud of her ability to live "on her own" and thrive. Several months later, however, it became clear that the situation was deteriorating. I received disturbing phone calls from friends living in the building that there were frequent unfamiliar visitors to the apartment. Then, on my last visit, I found the apartment messy, Helene's room not as orderly as it normally was and, worse, I learned that the caregiver had allowed another couple to live in the apartment. I was shocked at the turn of events.

The more I thought about it, the more I realized Helene would never tell me that anything was wrong. She didn't want to leave the city, so she would keep her mouth shut for fear that I would drag her to Virginia with me. I had trusted the young caregiver to do the right thing by Helene. Evidently, that trust had been misplaced.

When I realized other people had been living in the apartment, I immediately severed the arrangement with the caregiver. I told her that she and her friends had to move out immediately because I was giving up the apartment. I knew Helene would still have the same objections to moving to Virginia, so I consulted with friends and spoke to the nuns at Ellen's school for advice. Many of the nuns had grown to know our family very well, through Ellen's attendance at their school, but also from the community work Gus had done with them. They were familiar with our family situation and, since my husband's death, had been very supportive.

The nuns offered to allow Helene to move into the convent with them. The nuns already knew and respected my daughter. I welcomed the idea and so did Helene. I packed up Helene's belongings, moved her into the convent and was surprised at how quickly she settled in. She stayed on as a permanent resident and lived with the nuns for several months until we all agreed that she was ready to live on her own again.

Helene was twenty when she moved out of the convent. The nuns and I found her a studio apartment and arranged for a home attendant to come each day to spend several hours with her, cooking, cleaning and generally ensuring she was okay. They went grocery shopping together and the attendant made sure I received all the receipts. While Helene was capable of taking care of her own day-to-day needs, I paid the bills and handled all of her finances. During the day, Helene would spend time at the Jewish Guild for the Blind, a kind of adult daycare that kept her busy, interested and making friends. She is very social and loves to spend time with friends.

She had been living in her studio apartment for two years when a one-bedroom apartment in our old building became available. The familiar building offered Helene a beautiful, large apartment, with the same doorman and many of the same neighbors we had while Gus was alive. Everyone in the building knew her and watched out for her. She was very happy there.

Helene's attraction to the city stemmed from her desire for independence. Although she hadn't mastered the whole subway system, she could use it to navigate through her small sphere of the world and that gave her the perception, at least, that she could go where she wanted. She could pop down to the store on the corner to buy a candy bar or get herself from her apartment to her programs without waiting for someone to drive her. The subway allowed her to keep herself busy.

"I like to stay busy, to feel alive," she would say.

But the city changed. Over the years, it became more dangerous to ride the subway and, while Helene's perception of the transit system hadn't changed, I grew increasingly uncomfortable with her traveling anywhere alone. When medical problems repeatedly became an issue, I knew it was no longer possible to allow her to take public transit alone.

Helene had suffered from petit mal seizures before, but they started to become more frequent: she would black out and then not realize what had happened to her. Her home health aide and the workers in her programs informed me of the increase in frequency of the seizures. That alarming news led to several visits to a neurologist and changes in medication, but the seizures didn't stop completely. They were mild but unpredictable, and frightening. The seizures combined with the increasing danger of the New York City subway, and soon I had to tell Helene she couldn't ride public transportation alone any longer. She fought the decision, not wanting to give up her perceived independence, but the decision had to be made.

She remained in New York for twenty years until I moved Helene to Virginia. Every year, no matter what else is going on in the world or her life, she still goes away for two weeks to be with her friends at camp.

Nothing will get in the way of that.

To this day, she still loves New York. Alicia Keys is one of her favorite artists, I suspect mostly because of her hit song "New York." Each day, Helene boards the van that takes her to her adult daycare program where everyone knows her name and where she keeps active. Her puzzles, her drawing and her stereo, which she keeps running constantly with everything from the latest pop to the old school standards, all keep her busy.

"I like to stay busy and feeling alive."

PART TWO

MILITARY LIFE

CHANGES

For the greater part of my adult life, I lived in either San Francisco or New York, both cities known for their robust commuter systems. Now, for the first time in my life I needed a car. But first I had to learn to drive. I hoped it would be a little like a variation on the Sinatra song: *If you can drive in New York, you can drive anywhere.*

I enlisted the help of a good friend who lived in our apartment building, Hanna Stephens, to drive me to my first lesson.

It didn't go very well.

"Turn here," the instructor said, his eyes wide and knuckles white. "Slow down! Check your mirrors. You don't need both feet to drive. Use your right foot. Your *right* foot."

His shouted instructions were confusing. The tires squealed; the New York drivers were unafraid to use their horns, even at a car that had "student driver" emblazoned on the side. The instructor was thrown forward and back in his seat while I braked, accelerated and braked again. Half the time I couldn't decide whether to stop or go. Eventually, I became good enough to pass the driving test, but for a long time, I wasn't comfortable behind the wheel.

Once I had my license, the next step was to buy a car. Hanna went with me to Brooklyn where I found a reasonably priced new sedan. I bought the car, but I was too nervous to drive it off the lot.

"You can do this," Hanna said.

"No, I can't. I need the instructor to tell me what to do!"

Hanna laughed, but only because she didn't realize I was serious. I tried to smile, to pretend I wasn't petrified as I got behind the wheel. My foot flew between the brake pedal and the gas, my palms sweating and my knuckles white, and we stuttered our way home from Brooklyn. I believe prayer and divine intervention are the only reasons we made it back to my apartment building alive. I parked the car in the garage and left it there until we were ready to move.

As horrible as I was at driving, planning to move my household and my girls was a far greater challenge. Ellen seemed excited about the prospect of going to a new place. I knew she would miss her friends so I spoke about the move like it would be a great new adventure. I was sure that, in time, she and I would be able to make a good home for ourselves in Virginia.

I had already decided to leave most of the furniture in the apartment for Helene. The government movers came and quickly and efficiently packed everything we wanted to take. It was the first of several times I would work with movers, supervising their packing, filling out the inventories, numbering every item loaded into the truck, completing the insurance forms, and watching as our life was incased in bubble wrap and sealed into boxes. Ellen's white princess bedroom set and my bedroom set, the same bed I had shared with my husband, were the only large items we took. It was only the first of several government moves I would make in my career and it was definitely the most difficult.

How could I leave the apartment and go somewhere else without Gus? I felt as if I was leaving him behind, saying goodbye to him and the life we had made together in New York. There were so many things to do for the move, I just had to stay busy and focused on the goal so that I wouldn't wallow in the memories of him. I knew in my heart that my decision to move was the right one. Leaving still hurt. There wasn't much I could do about that but push through it.

It was June, 1983 and I don't know what I was more anxious about—the new life we were beginning, or leaving Helene behind. As it turned out, I was much more anxious than either of the girls. Ellen was excited about going away with Mom and starting a new life. Helene was excited about staying in the city she loved so much and trying to live life more independently, without Mom. It was a complete change to our lives, but my daughters were resilient.

My friend Hanna drove with us to Virginia. When I say drove with us, what I really mean is that she drove us. I was already so nervous about the big move I didn't need the stress of driving for the first time on an extended road trip. We made the seven-hour drive without mishap and checked into the hotel on the base in Hampton. Hanna stayed with us that first night and flew back to New York the next day.

After that, Ellen and I were on our own.

Wanting to ease my way into the driving thing, I had asked the realtor I was working with to find us a house no more than three miles from the University. He found a cute little home on a corner lot with a large backyard. Shortly after we moved in, Ellen and I both started going to school. Ellen's school bus picked her up right in front of the house and delivered her to the elementary school she attended, and I put on my uniform, got in my new car and started working fulltime as a soldier.

When I put on a uniform for the first time and served as a WAC in the '60s, the decision had been made out of a desperate attempt to provide for Helene, to ensure that I could get an education and to give us a new life. When I joined the Army National Guard in the late '70s, that decision had been about finding something interesting to do with my time, something challenging that I could take pride in. Although the decision to become a fulltime soldier again was about caring for my family, it was also an attempt to fill the void left by my Gus's death. I had been a single parent before I met him, but that earlier experience of raising a child alone didn't make things any easier the second time around. In my head, Gus was my constant companion throughout the move. I asked him often if I was doing the right thing, wondering how he would have reacted to the choices I made. I like to think he would have been proud of me.

Slipping back into wearing a uniform every day had been easier than I anticipated. Even driving, after a few days, became less stressful. I no longer hesitated when Ellen asked me to take her to a nearby mall. My almost weekly flights back and forth to New York were draining, but I enjoyed going to the city, seeing old friends and spending time with Helene.

Still, every day I was reminded that Gus wasn't with me.

I knew early on that my decision to go on active duty was the right one. The move was working out for the best. Ellen and I loved our little house and it wasn't long before the house was filled with her and her new friends laughing and enjoying themselves. We lived comfortably with my salary and benefits, and I slept peacefully knowing both girls were happy with their lives. I even enjoyed the eager college ROTC students I taught—a pleasant change from the belligerent fifth graders I was accustomed to—and had very few problems in the classroom.

Things should have been perfect. But they weren't.

My years at Hampton University exposed me to the most blatant sexual harassment of my career.

A SCHOOL OF HIGHER LEARNING

Hampton University in Hampton, Virginia is included in the Historically Black Colleges and Universities listed in the Higher Education Act of 1965. It was instituted near the end of the Civil War to provide higher education for former slaves. The alumni list includes Booker T. Washington and other notable black scholars. With all of the firsts that happened at the storied university—in most recent times, students from Hampton were the first in Virginia to stage a lunch counter sit-in—including a woman in the ROTC cadre should not have been a big deal in 1983.

But it was.

I was the first female professor to teach military science and the first Army National Guard member to serve at the university. I taught freshmen as an assistant professor. I also served as the S1, the personnel manager for the ROTC department.

Dr. William Harvey, the president of the university, made a great fuss about my addition to the department. He crowed about my being the first woman in the department and went out of his way to ensure everyone knew what a ground-breaking move it was. The campus newsletter ran a story about my assignment, lauding the arrival of the first woman in the department.

This was 1983. What had taken them so long?

Dr. Harvey invited me to his office for tea and told me how difficult it was to get me there. "The National Guard Bureau was a little hesitant to assign a female to the Reserve Officer Training Program here," Dr. Harvey said. "You are the first woman, but we're glad to have you."

My arrival, it seemed, was welcomed by everyone at Hampton University except some of the people I would be working with. The head of the ROTC department was a full-bird colonel. The rest of the instructors were captains. I was a captain, too, but all of the other professors had dates of rank earlier than mine, which meant they out-ranked me. The lack of status didn't bother me. I had been the junior-ranking person in a new group before. I had also been the only woman in a unit before. None of that was new. The only new dynamic was that all of the officers I was working with were African-American, save one white captain.

I arrived eager to begin teaching, excited about starting a career in academics, thrilled to no longer be the lone black person in the room. It didn't take long, however, to realize that these men weren't as excited about having a woman in their ranks as Dr. Harvey had been.

My years of teaching in the Bronx gave me the experience I needed to control just about any unruly classroom. Lucky for me, I rarely needed that experience at the university. It was refreshing to spend a majority of my time teaching instead of meting out discipline. I respected the inquisitive nature of my students and they respected me. Soon, I felt very comfortable with them and I know they enjoyed being in my classroom. Many of them told me as much.

These were the future leaders of the Army. They were all African-American and many of them were young women, at a time when seeing a black officer, male or female, was still a rare occasion. My ROTC students represented an exciting future of great possibility and I wanted to do right by them.

The classroom was the easy part. What went on outside the classroom between some of the male instructors and their young, female students was disturbing. The officers in the ROTC program were married men, but a few seemed to regard their classrooms as appropriate places to find romance. In short order, I began to hear rumors of impropriety and to see the evidence for myself.

Having knowledge that colleagues are engaging in infidelity is further complicated when you're acquainted with their wives. The faculty and their spouses sometimes had social gatherings at their homes, so I knew and liked their wives. The men would be outside at the barbecue grill, while I sat inside with the women, preparing side dishes or just standing around talking. These women became my friends. We'd have long conversations about our children, about our likes and dislikes, all the things women discuss—kids, shopping, houses, work. As military spouses, they were accustomed to meeting new people as part of the nomadic nature of the military, so they welcomed me into their group quickly. But I wasn't one of them. I wasn't the spouse of their husband's new co-worker. I was the new co-worker. I worked with their husbands every day, probably spent more time with their husbands than they did.

Still, there was no way I could be the one to tell them that their husbands were being inappropriate with eighteen- and nineteen-year-old college students. The situation was untenable.

One day, I talked to several of the female students and asked, "Why are you messing around with these married men?"

They exchanged nervous glances with each other. At first I thought they would just deny everything, but one of them finally spoke up. "You have to understand, ma'am, they're captains. And they control our grades. I want to make the military my career."

"What you are doing has nothing to do with grades and your career!" But it was like I spoke a foreign language. They told me they didn't feel forced into accepting or condoning certain behaviors and denied being told their grades would be affected, but I suspected better grades, along with the novelty of being wooed by their male instructors drove them to participate in the inappropriate behavior. I spoke to them about self-respect, about professionalism and about what their actions could mean for the rest of their military careers.

"Is this how you expect things to work when it comes time for promotions? Imagine what would happen if, years from now, people say that you slept your way to the top?"

My words didn't get through to them, not at that moment anyway. I hoped they would consider what I had said and I offered to be available to them at any time if they wanted to talk to me about it.

After that conversation, however, it occurred to me that I had been speaking to the wrong people. The women were too young to understand the ramifications of their actions. So I made it clear to the other professors that I had objections to the way they had been acting and expressed my opinion that, at least in appearance, the relationships seemed inappropriate.

They didn't feel I had a right to my opinion.

One day, I walked into my office to find that several of my pictures, awards and diplomas had been removed from the walls and put on the floor. Of course, no one knew how, when, why or who had done it. The message seemed to be that I didn't have a right to be in my office; that I should leave. But I wasn't going anywhere.

Another day, I walked by several captains standing around schmoozing. One of them stopped me and said, "Tell me, why do you have an ass like a white woman?" He had a sly smile on his face.

"Excuse me?"

"You know, it's not like a sister's ass. It's flat like a white woman's ass."

The other officers grinned and chuckled, all of them acting like juvenile bullies.

"You shouldn't be looking there in the first place," I said and walked away, my head up and my back straight.

The slights, disparaging words, outright rudeness continued and increased. I had become friendly with Dorothy Barnes, the Professor of Military Science's (PMS) secretary who helped me navigate my way through the university bureaucracy. According to her, the other officers were jealous of my ease with the students, of the way the students enjoyed being in my classes and with the way their parents were praising my classes to the commander. The hoopla over my arrival hadn't helped the situation. None of the other officers had been invited to tea with the university president, nor had the campus newsletter given their arrival front page status. I was a threat to their comfortable kingdom.

"Those students love you," Dorothy said. "And the other teachers can't stand that."

I wasn't sure their actions were about jealousy, but I tried not to let their attitudes get to me. I wasn't always successful. One day, when I returned to my office after lunch, I passed the conference room and saw the cadre assembled. I hadn't been notified, but when I saw everyone else in the room and realized the deputy was holding a staff meeting, I entered and sat down.

"I didn't realize there was a meeting," I said.

"Come in, come in," the deputy commander said.

No one else acknowledged my arrival. When the meeting was over and everyone else had left, I confronted him. "Excuse me, sir. I was never told you were holding a staff meeting today."

"You don't have to be invited to every meeting I hold, Captain," he said.

"But sir, if you're having a meeting with the academic staff, I am part of that staff. Why would I be excluded?"

"Again, I don't have to invite you to anything. Who do you think you are to demand to be invited to the meetings I hold?"

He continued on like that for a bit, obviously not happy about being confronted. The longer he explained himself, the angrier he became. It wasn't long before he started throwing rude and impertinent remarks at me. The words he used were unprofessional and personally insulting. The lieutenant colonel was in charge of the other professors, all captains, who had been insulting and berating me from day one. This man was the Deputy Professor of Military Science, the Deputy PMO. Negative treatment from him was confirmation that he tacitly agreed with the way the men treated me. It pushed me over the edge.

I leaned towards him and pointed my index finger in his face like a dagger.

"You need to go home and look in the mirror and try to see what you are doing here," I said. "You are being very rude and very ugly, and I don't understand where all this hostility is coming from."

The more I talked, the more worked up I became. By this time, I was leaning so far over him that my finger was almost touching his nose. It was at that moment that Dorothy knocked on the door and stepped into the room.

"Excuse me, Captain Cleckley. You have a phone call from Colonel Pierson, the Army National Guard advisor at Fort Monroe."

I didn't want to walk away from the confrontation, but I knew I needed to before I said or did something that would get me into real trouble. It wasn't in my nature to lose my temper or respond to insults with a raised voice. Volatility never brings clarity to a situation, especially when the person you've confronted is your boss. So I took a deep breath, stood up, straightened my uniform and followed Dorothy out of the office. As I left, I noticed several of the other officers had been standing outside the door, listening. I went into my office and Dorothy followed me.

"You don't have a phone call," she said. "I needed to get you out of there before you stepped over the line and got yourself into trouble."

She was so right. I was grateful for her help, but still so furious at the lieutenant colonel for his insults that my hands were shaking.

"I think you better sit down and gather yourself," she said.

That was easier said than done.

A few days later, the deputy apologized to me, saying he had overlooked telling me about the meeting. He said he should have just admitted the mistake instead of saying he didn't have to include me. I accepted his apology, thinking Dorothy probably had a hand in forcing the apology.

I later learned that many of the students, both male and female, had been making their own observations of the treatment I was receiving from the faculty. Evidently, some of the students had complained to their parents about it. When parents spoke up on my behalf to the professor of military science, wondering why the female officer in the ROTC program was receiving such treatment, the colonel decided the negativity had gone too far. He called the cadre together and gave them a stern warning. "Leave Captain Cleckley alone!"

The negative behavior stopped for a time, but the men still found ways to make my life unpleasant. No matter how badly they treated me, however, I was determined to stay. To do otherwise would only mean they'd won. My original assignment was to serve on active duty for at least three years. After that, I could choose to extend my service for another year or go back to civilian life. Despite the harassment and bullying, one thing was clear: I loved being in uniform. Ellen and I were doing well in Virginia and Helene was getting along in New York in her studio apartment. I grieved for Gus every day. It still angered me that he had been taken from me before he was even forty years old. I knew in my heart that I had lost my soul mate and would never find another man to fill his shoes, but I had to carry on. The military suited me, setting aside the battles I faced with my colleagues at Hampton.

I decided to stay on active duty.

As diligent as my colleagues were about harassing me, they were just as diligent in tracking their promotions. Each week they anxiously checked the latest edition of the *Army Times* newspaper, where promotion announcements were made, listed in groups by the year of most recent date of rank. Getting promoted to major was an obsession for many of them. Since they all outranked me, I didn't pay much attention to the announcements. I figured my turn would come after some of them were promoted.

That wasn't the case.

After two years at Hampton, I was notified that I would be promoted to major long before any of my colleagues. The men were so angry about my advancement they had to be ordered by the colonel to attend my promotion ceremony. My mother, my brother Mickey and his wife Susan came to Hampton to participate in the ceremony and watch the gold oak leaves get pinned to my collars. Of course my daughters were both there and, following military tradition, I threw a party at my house.

Since they were ordered to go, all of the officers from the program came, but they didn't seem to enjoy themselves much. Their wives, however, were very proud of my accomplishment. Shortly after my promotion, I decided that staying at Hampton was a lost cause. I had been there just over two years, but they all hated me. I had never filed a formal complaint against any of them, although I could have. And even though I did my job and tried to stay out of their way, the environment was toxic and exhausting.

Five months after my promotion, in June 1985, I was offered a position at Fort Eustis, as the Reserve Componant advisor to the Army Training Support Center. It was a position normally held by a lieutenant colonel, but evidently my background in teaching and my performance at Hampton was enough to make the leadership in Washington believe that I could handle the position, even though I was a newly pinned major. Since Fort Eustis was just up the road from Hampton, I didn't need to move and Ellen didn't have to change schools. It was a perfect assignment for me at the time. I accepted it gladly.

It amazes me to this day that an institution of higher learning, one that was born from the fight for freedom and equal rights for blacks, would be the location where I would face such discriminatory behavior, not from whites, but from fellow black officers. If I had to find something positive about the experience, it would be learning that losing your temper is the wrong way to deal with conflict. I learned that I could work with anyone, whether they liked me or not, and that it was better to remain calm than to bring volatility into the work place. I also found a new lifelong friendship in Mrs. Dorothy Barnes, the secretary who stopped me from stepping over the line.

In my new assignment, I was once again the only woman and once again the only black officer in my department. This time, however, the climate was much different and so were my experiences.

A CALL FROM BOBBIE

Late one night, several months before I left Hampton University for good, my sister Bobbie called and woke me from a deep sleep.

"Daddy died," she said.

"Oh, I'm sorry to hear that. I'll pray for him." I didn't feel sad or shocked, any of the usual feelings someone would have hearing the news their father had died. I wasn't interested in the details of his death, immediately making the assumption that his alcoholism had something to do with it. He had been my father in biology only. Unfazed, I hung up the phone and rolled over to go back to sleep.

A few minutes later, I sat up in bed wide awake. I called Bobbie back.

"We're going to the funeral," I told her.

"We are?"

"Yes. I'll take some time off and meet you in Baltimore. Get all the details and let me know."

While I couldn't have articulated exactly what I was thinking at the time, I was in near panic to ensure we would be at that funeral. Mother had never divorced Robert Jeter, remaining his wife even though she had no idea where he was through most of the marriage. He had basically abandoned her and us five children. He had spent most of the rare times they were together in a drunken stupor. Mother was getting older and slowing down now. She had little to show for the years she had devoted to raising his children. I was resolved that my mother was going to get the social security death benefits she deserved. I would need a copy of his death certificate to file for the benefits and the only way to get it was to go to his funeral and advocate for my mother's rights.

I knew how to file for the benefits, having gone through it when Gus died. It wasn't a lot of money, but it could make a big difference for my mother. I personally found the idea of going to the funeral distasteful. I had met my father's side of the family when I was young, but had little contact with them over the years. It was time to get reacquainted.

Bobbie had maintained some communication with our father's family. She had always sought his affection and attention. Even when we were children and she had helped keep his secrets, she seemed to accept him for the drunk that he was. She grieved his loss. I didn't understand it, but that's how it was.

Ellen, Bobbie and I met up in Baltimore and we drove together to the funeral in Philadelphia. Ellen had always been curious about her grandfather's family. Being light-skinned, she wondered where her coloring came from. I had told her about her grandfather, that he and his siblings were also very light-skinned. There was talk that my paternal great-grandfather had been of mixed race and that his mother had a child by a white man she worked for. Ellen was naturally curious about that history and interested in meeting the extended family.

For me, the funeral was surreal. I remember walking up to the casket and looking down at my father, feeling very little. Memories rushed back and they weren't pleasant ones. He was gone, but his passing would have little impact on me and my family. I took my daughter's hand and said, "Ellen, meet your grandfather."

After the funeral services, my aunt held a small reception at her home. My father's family welcomed us warmly. We were introduced to aunts, uncles and some cousins we had never met before. Several of them commented they wished I had worn my uniform. I thought that was rather strange, as if they wanted to show me off, or satisfy their own curiosity about my career.

I kept my eye out for the funeral director and as soon as I saw him alone, I approached him and explained who I was. "Would it be possible for me to get a copy of his death certificate?"

"Certainly, please follow me."

Within minutes, I had my father's death certificate in my hands. We politely said our goodbyes and left. I had what I had come for and I never had contact with my father's family again.

Two weeks after the funeral, I went to the Social Security office with my mother's marriage license and my father's death certificate and filed the proper paperwork. Not long after that, my mother began receiving the Social Security checks she deserved. From that time until she died, she received a check each month. They were the only reliable and steady financial support she had ever received as a result of her relationship with Robert Jeter. My brother Larry had only been a year old when my father left for the last time. She managed to raise five children without much help from anyone. She deserved every penny of that money.

In truth, I have no regrets that my daughters never knew their grandfather. The example they had of a man's role in a family was their father's, a faithful, hardworking, community-minded man who loved his family and stood by us to the end of his days.

MAKING THE CHOICE PERMANENT

Leaving Hampton University was like taking a deep breath of fresh air. I didn't realize how much the hostile work environment affected me until I left it behind. A lot of people seemed to have known what I faced every day at work—the students, the students' parents, the other faculty and even my active duty career advisor knew things were in a bad way, but no one seemed to know what to do about it. Finally, my career advisor guided me in the right direction.

Several months after I left the university, I began to get phone calls from investigators with the Inspector General's office, asking me about harassment in the ROTC program. They weren't looking for information about my experiences; they were assigned cases that some of the parents and female students still in the program brought against the faculty. I was glad that some of the women had finally found the courage to step forward to stop the harassing behavior of their instructors. Of course by now, none of the former cadre members are associated with the military. At least one of them was eventually forced to resign his military career. I take no pleasure in the knowledge.

While my time at Hampton often presented challenges, I'm still proud of the work I did there. Many of the students made the military their career and I enjoyed monitoring their progress through the ranks and have kept in touch with several of them. I was recently invited to the Pentagon to witness a promotion of one of my former students to full colonel. He acknowledged my contribution to his career during his acceptance speech at the ceremony.

Another student, Colonel Anthony Reyes who is now retired, invited me to his promotion ceremony at the Women's War Memorial at Arlington Cemetery. During his acceptance speech he said, "General Cleckley was one of my professors when I was going through the ROTC program. She was one of the kindest professors I've ever had. I learned many things from her." Then he paused and turned to me and said, "General Cleckley, how do you like me now?" He displayed the silver eagles on his collar while the audience roared with laughter.

I would miss students like Reyes when I left the ROTC classroom behind and took the position at Fort Eustis. The move to Fort Eustis meant I had permanently changed my career direction from teacher to management. There would be no going back to the New York school system. Once again, the military, which always seemed willing to become a part of my life at those moments when I was most desperate to care for my family, provided the solution to what felt like insurmountable problems. Even though my new job wouldn't be in the familiar world of a classroom, by this time I'd learned to be flexible, to enjoy change and to know, no matter what, I could handle just about any challenge.

Once again, I was the most junior person in the office, serving alongside a group of lieutenant colonels and, more in keeping with the situation I usually expected in the Army, they were all white and male. The new job was one meant for a lieutenant colonel, and here I was, stepping into the job as a brand new major. But the job was made easier by the respect I received from my fellow officers. I traveled a great deal, which meant I had to stay organized and do a lot of planning to ensure all of Ellen and Helene's needs were taken care of. The officers and staff were always respectful and never made me feel uncomfortable in the all-male office.

When I reported to the Army Training Support Center at Fort Eustis, my commander, a West Point graduate, was a stickler for military protocol and traditions, uniform exactness, physical training. A hard charging colonel, he led us through our assessments of military training across the country. I represented the Army National Guard and the Army Reserve, and was responsible for pointing out the positive and negative issues I found with non-commissioned officer (NCO) training for those forces.

My work concentrated on NCOES training, the non-commissioned officer education academies, where progressive leadership skills are taught to NCOs from specialist E4 through the sergeant major academy at Fort Bliss in El Paso, Texas. I traveled from training base to training base, touring the facilities, observing the training, listening to students and cadre, looking for ways to improve the programs for the unique conditions of the reserve forces.

Unlike active duty service members, training for reserve and National Guard forces was restricted to one weekend a month and two to three weeks each year. Anything outside of those times required special orders as well as time away from home and civilian jobs. As soldiers move up in the ranks, the training they require increases, resulting in more instances in which they need to be placed on temporary duty orders to complete the required training. Part of my job was to ensure that the best use of time was employed to reach the training objectives. I even inspected the warehouse where all of the Army correspondence courses were held. I was familiar with the correspondence courses because I had completed scores of the booklets while taking the advanced officer's course.

In addition to my job assignment in training assessments, we had soldier duties that went along with the job by virtue of being at Fort Eustis. Our West Point-trained commander insisted we hold physical training (PT) every day. On Mondays, the entire command went on a joint run. I had been participating in PT while on active duty, but at Fort Eustis, PT training was taken to a higher level. By the time I left there, I could do seventy-five pushups and had obtained the maximum score of three hundred on the annual PT tests several times.

Our commander enforced not only a strict PT schedule, but insisted on following the military tradition of hosting command parties for the officers on his staff. Although there wasn't a strict schedule for them, eventually every officer was expected to host one of the parties and invite the officers and their spouses to their home. Military protocol is often sticky. There are regulations and field manuals written on whom to invite when, where people should sit, who gets various levels of treatment—the list goes on and on. I knew when it came time for me to be the party host, I couldn't screw it up.

I was lucky to have a nice corner home with a big back yard, the perfect location to accommodate all of the guests. I rented party tables, arranged for some catered food and the weather was perfect. The party went over well.

An important aspect of the party culture was the role a spouse plays in an officer's career. Everyone knew I was a widow raising two girls. Hosting the party was a challenge to do on my own, and I was constantly reminded of the role Gus would have played (and enjoyed!) had he been alive. His loss still left me breathless at times. During the planning and then experiencing the party and its success, I felt Gus watching over me.

When I first decided to go on active duty, a colonel I worked for advised me to continue to wear my wedding band and to never forget the spouses of the men I reported to and the one I worked for. I didn't understand the advice at the time, but while at the Training Support Center, when there were so many required social functions, I realized that even though I sometimes traveled with their husbands, the spouses never considered me a threat. I don't know if I was deemed non-threatening because I wore my wedding band or because I was African-American. Either way, the wives weren't jealous of the time I spent with their husbands and that was fine by me.

My time as a training advisor went by quickly. I traveled a great deal, saw several different military bases and, for the first time, had to purchase the expensive dress blue and dress mess uniforms which I was required to wear to several black-tie social events. Dress blues and whites have to be purchased and they aren't cheap. Add the custom tailoring and the special medals and the uniform is a large investment. But I ended up using it frequently.

In general, my time at Fort Eustis gave me the opportunity to become more familiar with military protocol, to see and observe the details of the breadth of military training and expertise around the country and to understand more fully the roles and responsibilities of an active duty military officer. I did everything required of me, both on the job and socially.

After almost three years at the Training Support Center, I hoped that my stay would be extended for another year. I enjoyed the job and liked living in Virginia. But my desire for an extension wasn't going to happen.

"We need you here at the Bureau," my career advisor said.

Colonel Howard Bowie had been managing my career since I moved to Fort Eustis. His job was to match an officer's skills and experience with the right job. Colonel Bowie believed my next job should be at the National Guard Bureau, the headquarters for the nationwide National Guard organization.

"We need you to take on the job of Branch Chief in one of our divisions." He pointed out that I would be the first woman and first African-American in the Active Guard and Reserve (AGR) to ever hold the position of Branch Chief of Federal Recognition. I would be in charge of the federal recognition of promotions, officer records and waivers for the fifty-four states and territories of the Army National Guard— an awesome responsibility. To say that I was a little hesitant would be putting it mildly.

A NEW SIGNATURE BLOCK

"You can do this, Julia," Colonel Bowie insisted.

I wasn't convinced that I was ready to take on the responsibility. The position of Chief of the Military Personnel Management Branch of the Army National Guard required that I supervise a large staff of NCOs, a couple of officers and civilians. Thirty people all together. A lieutenant colonel was supposed to be in the slot and I was only a major. It was always good to be in a position that required a higher rank, because a promotion was more likely to happen when the time came around, but the higher rank also meant greater responsibility. I was intimidated by the challenge, but grateful that the people who selected me for the job thought I could handle it.

"It's a very diverse group, but you'll get them whipped into shape," he said. "You'll need to report by June."

The June deadline only gave me a few months to make arrangements to pack up my home, find a new place to live and a new school for Ellen. In the Army, it's called a Permanent Change of Station or PCS move. This would be our second PCS move but for a shorter distance, just up the road a few hours to Springfield, Virginia. PCS moves are always hectic since they mean a long list of things to do, and very little time to do them.

During this hectic time, I sent Ellen to visit my brother-in-law, Frank and his family, and asked Bobbie if our mother could stay with her in

Ohio temporarily until we got settled. My mom had been having some health issues and I knew the upheaval of the move wouldn't be good for her. Once Ellen and I were settled, I fully expected my mother to rejoin us in Springfield.

With Ellen and my mother gone, I was able to supervise the final step in the move, when the government movers come to the house to pack your things. Everything is wrapped, labeled, packed and shipped to your next duty station. We'd done it once before when we moved from New York. That move, still in the shadow of Gus's death, felt as if it had been a lifetime ago. This new move was more exciting to me, more filled with possibilities and not so burdened with the sorrow of our loss.

We were excited about our new home in Springfield. When Ellen and my mother returned, I thought we would soon settle in, but it was not to be.

It became clear that my mother wasn't happy. After a few months, she began to talk about returning to Aliquippa, the town she considered home.

I had always wanted to buy my mother a home of her own and her desire to go back to Aliquippa seemed like the perfect opportunity to make that dream come true. Six months later, we were able to find her a small home in a great neighborhood, only minutes from my brother Mickey and his wife Susan.

My mother lived there for several years and was always proud of her home. I visited her every month to make sure she was doing well, that she made it to her various doctor appointments, received her social security checks, paid her bills and generally cared for herself. And each year, the girls and I spent the holidays with her.

My first day on the job at the Bureau, I wanted to get right to work but the public affairs staff had their own ideas. They wanted to send out press releases announcing my arrival at the Bureau in another attempt to point out my historic appointment.

"This is news, ma'am," they said. "You're the first woman to ever be assigned as a branch chief of Army personnel at the bureau, not to mention the first African-American to have the job."

While it might have been news to the public, it wasn't news to me. I begged them not to do it. I knew from my experience at Hampton University that even a little publicity could generate a lot of resentment, and I didn't want to have that kind of pressure on me when I was about to step into such a challenging position. Besides, it was 1987. It seemed odd to me to want to crow about the first African-American woman to hold the job of Branch Chief at such a late date. It was another clear sign of just how white and male the National Guard Bureau was at the time. To issue press releases that drew attention to that fact didn't seem prudent. I turned down the offers of press coverage. It was a decision I never regretted.

As Branch Chief, I was in charge of federal recognition like awards and promotions, while managing thirty civilians from General Schedule or GS level 6 employees, all the way up to GS-12, as well as several NCOs. My deputy, Rod Kleinfelter, had served in the department for many years and had been the acting chief until my arrival. He could have been resentful that after so many months of doing the job, he was now losing his position of authority—but he wasn't. I trusted him immensely and still keep in touch with him. He openly shared his knowledge and kept me straight during the three years I served in the department. I owe much of my success in that job to Rod's help and loyalty.

With my staff's help, my task was to assess promotion packets and awards from each of the fifty-four states and territories of the Army National Guard. Promotions were awarded by the states, but my office had to provide a federal level of recognition for the promotion to be finalized.

I knew from the first day that managing my employees was going to be a big part of the challenges I faced. Desks were covered in stacks of files, piles of work that sometimes didn't get done. Later, I would find that some of my employees had exercised their positions of power by conveniently losing files. If you pissed one of them off, records would suddenly disappear. Some of the missing files were hidden above the ceiling tiles hanging over their heads! The entire staff felt overworked. *Disgruntled* isn't a strong enough word to describe the attitude I found when I first arrived.

I had had my first taste of managing people while serving as a WAC. Managing a classroom of troubled unruly kids while a teacher at one of the toughest schools in the Bronx, certainly added to my job experience. Now, having to manage a large but somewhat overwhelmed staff of military *and* civilian employees was definitely daunting. As a manager, my belief was: if you give your employees everything they need to succeed, failure is not an option. And then, as an employee, if you work hard, do your best, stay honest and true to your position, I will back you up, move you up, do whatever I can to help further your career and your ability to do good work.

The civilians working in the office had seen military chiefs come and go over the years. Every two years, a new officer was placed in the job, some new guy who would have his own ideas about how to run things. Two or three years later, he would leave and yet another new guy would come along. The civilians were accustomed to this regularly scheduled change in leadership. I'm sure most of them thought they had seen it all, but of all the officers who rotated in and out of the office, they hadn't ever seen anyone like me. Some of them went to Rod with complaints, but that was okay. I knew I could never please all of them. There would always be a few unhappy employees no matter what I did. The goal was to have as few unhappy employees as possible.

I began by making little changes at first, but they were changes that made it clear I cared about my employees' well being, was ready to listen to their challenges and complaints, and wanted to do what I could to help them get the job done. The first change, and it was a minor one, was to start having monthly birthday recognitions. I cleared it through the civilian personnel office to allow my employees to take their birthdays off. I would give them personalized birthday cards and include a certificate they could use for a day off on their birthday or a day of their choosing. I even held 'town hall' type meetings during which staff members were invited to air their complaints, speak their minds about both positive and negative issues in the office.

I made the small changes mostly to recognize them as people, to show gratitude for the hard work they did and to acknowledge that the roles they played were important. In return, there was a firm understanding that people would do their jobs—records would no longer be hidden in the ceiling, all phone calls would be returned, and all personnel actions would be completed. I didn't have to threaten them with disciplinary action; they learned quickly that I wasn't afraid to take steps to correct bad behavior when necessary. In a multitude of ways, I let my employees know that I was at least willing to consider their issues, even if there wasn't much I could do to completely fix the problems.

My boss, a full-bird colonel, trusted my decisions and always went to bat for me when there were complaints. Like him, it was important to me that I could trust my employees and that they could trust me.

A major part of our duties in the office had to do with granting waivers. If someone wasn't quite qualified to get into the guard, to get a promotion or attend some school, our office would assess their given qualifications and decide whether or not to allow them to move forward with their plans. A waiver could be granted to someone who was perhaps too old to join, or didn't quite make the weight requirements. Perhaps they were applying for a school that required a prerequisite they didn't have, or required that they hold a particular career position. Long-established Army regulations gave strict parameters for what could or could not constitute a waiver-able issue. Applicants' packets were submitted to our office from National Guard units around the country, and we would either grant or deny the promotion or waiver or award they were applying for, based on the regulations. Eventually, I became expert at finding the Army regulations that applied, understanding what could or could not be allowed, and making decisions. In the interim, I relied on the civilian experts in the office to make recommendations.

There were many times when, after analyzing the packets submitted, I would have to deny the requests. Denying a request was never easy because we knew that someone's hopes and dreams were affected. To deny a waiver could mean the requester wouldn't get into the school he or she wanted or would be denied a hoped-for promotion or even the ability to become a soldier in the Army National Guard. Because of the nature of many of the waiver requests, they were endorsed by the two-star General Officer from the state or territory. General Officers are never happy to learn that their requests are denied. Each packet, granted or not, required a memorandum with an explanation of the ruling, bearing my signature as Major Julia J. Cleckley.

For months, most of the denials I signed resulted in phone calls of one kind or another. Some people would call me directly, looking for further clarification. Others, especially the field grade officers senior to me, would often call my boss directly to complain or question my decisions. Almost weekly I was called into my colonel's office to explain why, despite some senior leader's wish, I had denied a request. The people in my branch were very knowledgeable and we never denied a request unless there were Army regulations to back up our decisions. Still, the weekly calls into my boss's office to explain myself grew tiresome.

"Julia, you've got people out there upset again," he would say.

I would show him the regulation, show him the law, and explain my thinking and the validity of our decision.

Sometimes the requests for waivers were unforgettable.

"No sir, we can't grant a waiver to this person who has a felony weapons charge on their record," I said. "I realize the general has friends in the Pentagon, but someone who was caught carrying an illegal weapon will not get my wavier to join the Army National Guard."

On another occasion, I said, "Look, sir, they are requesting a waiver for this chaplain who, several years ago, flashed his neighbor and was arrested! Is that really the kind of chaplain we need in the National Guard?"

"So, you don't think we should reconsider this?"

"No, we cannot, sir. Not under my watch are we going to allow this person to become a soldier in the Guard."

It generally wasn't hard to convince my boss that we had done the right thing. He would go back and explain my decisions to the person kicking up a fuss. Lucky for me, my boss trusted my decisions, which were rarely reversed. Still, the time and effort I spent explaining myself were wasteful. Then one day I had an epiphany. I had been signing each waiver denial as Major Julia J. Cleckley. Maybe changing my signature block would alleviate some of the problems. I began to sign the memoranda with Major J. J. Cleckley, Chief, Federal Recognition.

Miraculously, the complaints and the weekly visits to my boss's office dwindled to nothing. Evidently the senior leaders from the states had felt perfectly comfortable questioning a female officer about her decisions. When I changed my signature to J. J. they weren't so quick to question my decisions because they didn't know that I was a woman.

"What's going on around here?" the colonel asked a few weeks later. "I don't get any of the calls I used to get. Are you approving everybody now or something? How come I'm not getting any more angry phone calls?"

I explained my new strategy.

"That's very smart, Julia. Very clever."

Throughout my career, starting as Branch Chief on through to Division Chief, and even when I became the G1, I was required to make trips to state offices to provide briefings or give speeches. When I took trips like that, I sometimes took employees along and many times those employees were male and white. We would go into an office and the staff people we visited would direct their comments to the white men who accompanied me.

"We really appreciate the work you do at the bureau," they might say.

The men traveling with me would correct the mistake, pointing to me and explaining that I was the person who signed the packet.

"Oh! You're J. J. Cleckley?" they would say, full of surprise.

No matter how predictable their reaction, it was always a shocking confirmation of what I suspected all along. The experience taught me that no matter what you do, how much evidence, direction or experience you might have, if you're a woman, some people will feel justified in questioning your decisions. It's unfortunate that it takes a unisex signature block to get some things done. But it was a lesson I only needed to learn once. I continue to sign my name that way to this day.

My newly adjusted signature block helped smooth operations in my department, which was a good thing because by this time I was eligible for promotion from major to lieutenant colonel. There was only one promotable position in the Personnel branch and two soldiers eligible for it. I was one of them. I knew that I had all of the required schooling under my belt and had received excellent annual reviews in my Officer Evaluation Reports. My date of rank was earlier than many of the other majors up for promotion, and I was in charge of the largest branch with the most responsibility over any of the other majors in the running. So it was a shock when the only lieutenant colonel promotion available at the time was given to someone else.

Almost as soon as the announcement was made, there were murmurs from others that subtle racism was involved in the decision. The officer promoted was a white male, with a date of rank several months later then mine, who was in charge of a much smaller branch than mine. It wasn't a surprise that the news caused tongues to wag. Eventually the officer in charge of making the decision came to me to explain. The colonel pointed out several reasons why the decision had been made, reasons I'd already heard as possibilities from others, mostly having to do with the types of jobs the officer had held before, specifically combat arms-type positions which I, by the simple fact that I am a woman, would never be able to hold. Nothing about the promotion or the personnel position the officer held at the time had anything to do with combat, but that didn't deter the promotion board.

The combat arms argument would come up again at a crucial moment later in my career, but at the time it didn't sway me. I was still left with the impression that, had the choice been between two white men, the one with my background and experience would clearly have been the choice.

That was the moment in my career when I learned the value of patience. My personal policy had always been to do the best job I could without thought of reward or recognition, but at some point you have to acknowledge the times when recognition and promotion are deserved. It was and still is a common view among my generation of African-Americans that just getting the job done is never good enough. You always have to do more than the next guy, excel at what you do because you are always working from the position of a deficit. Unless you excel, unless your efforts aren't clearly above and beyond those your efforts are compared to, you will never get the promotion, never be the one to get the reward. I felt at the time, at least in the Army National Guard, that when held side by side, if all things are equal, the choice almost certainly will go to the white male.

The reward for doing good work should come with the knowledge that you didn't let the challenge get the best of you. I've always mentored people using that philosophy and continue to believe it to this day. When I didn't get the promotion, I didn't whine and complain about it, but my patience was taxed knowing that it would be at least a year before another opportunity for promotion would come around. Throughout that year, I kept my focus on my job. I wouldn't sit back and relax out of frustration or spite.

The officer who received the promotion was a friend of mine and even he was surprised by the decision. I never let it get in the way of that friendship.

"Julia, I'm sorry," he said to me. "I don't know why they made that decision."

"Don't worry about it. My chance will come along in time."

And I knew that to be true. My training and experience had already made me eligible for promotion. More time would only mean the *next* time a promotion opportunity came around there would be no question about my eligibility.

Just as the whole promotion controversy was dying down, the end of my three-year assignment rolled around. My new assignment would take me to another position in the Pentagon. Word quickly spread about my departure and where I would be going. Shortly after that, I was sitting in my office when I saw my secretary, Mrs. Kerry Ashford, crying and talking to a huddle of people. I asked Rod, my deputy, what was going on. Mrs. Ashford was obviously very upset.

Rod stepped into my office, closed the door and explained what had happened.

"Tell her to come see me," I said.

Mrs. Ashford came into my office, but it took a great deal of coaxing for her to finally explain that she had overhead an elevator conversation. "He said, I'm glad the black bitch is leaving," she said between her sobs. "I turned to him and said, 'Don't you call Major Cleckley that!'" She was obviously very disturbed by the name calling.

"Don't worry about things like that," I said.

"It's not right. He's just terrible to say such a thing."

"It's okay, Mrs. Ashford. Don't worry yourself about it."

The next day, the man who made the comment came to my office. I assume he'd figured out that I would eventually hear about his comment. He stood sheepishly in my doorway.

"Excuse me, Major Cleckley," he said, "may I talk to you for a minute?"

"You know what? Right now, I'd just like you to know that I'm black and I'm proud, and today, I'm a bitch. So get away from my door."

He stood there for a long moment, a blank expression on his face.

"Get away from my door," I said.

He left.

The most interesting thing about this story is that, just four months after going to a different job in the Pentagon, and more than a year after the name-calling incident, I was promoted to lieutenant colonel. That same person who'd called me a 'black bitch' came to my promotion ceremony. He even shook my hand, a big smile on his face. "Congratulations, ma'am," he said. And through the years he has been at every one of my promotion ceremonies and even attended my retirement ceremony.

Along with a room full of well wishers, my thirty civilian and military employees came to the Pentagon to attend my promotion. I'm sure I hadn't made all of them happy, but I believe that by the time I left for my next position, they were a happier, more efficient team than the one I found on my arrival.

Three years as a branch chief taught me important lessons about leading people, avoiding conflict, Army rules and regulations, and how to get things done without having my authority challenged. These were good lessons to learn. They helped prepare me for the challenges ahead in my military career.

CAREER MOVES AND SUCCESS

My next job as the Guard and Reserve Advisor for the Deputy Chief of Staff for Personnel, the DCSPER, or DESper as we pronounced it, would present the sort of challenges expected of a staff position at the Pentagon, but by this time, I was better prepared. I still hadn't been promoted, however, so going into the job as a major meant that I was again serving in a position normally filled by someone above my rank.

"You're going to have to mend some fences, clean up some of these backed-up files before you can really get started, Major Cleckley," my new boss said. "I have to be honest with you—you have an uphill job ahead of you. It will be a challenge, but I believe you're up to the task."

I was accustomed to cleaning up messes while garnering the professional help and friendship of others along the way. You ask for favors, and then you return those gestures when favors are asked of you. It was never easy, but no one person can clean up serious problems. You have to get others to help, to buy into your needs by providing their assistance, knowing that you have to be ready to return the favor when the time comes. One of my co-workers in the office, LTC Ronald L. Horne, a very sharp Regular Army Officer, took me under his wing to guide and inform me of how things worked in our section. He had been assigned there for a while and he provided good sound advice and mentoring during my tour in that office. He became and still remains a good and loyal friend.

My first day on the job at the Pentagon, no one was there to hand the job over to me, to give me any insight into the position, to explain the ins and outs or provide any sort of hand off. I walked in to find a pile of phone messages the previous person never bothered to return, stacks of ignored files that had been sitting around for months, and a mountain of paperwork that would only grow taller unless someone tackled it.

Evidently the previous advisor had been allowed to do next to nothing for three years. He sat in that office, often not returning phone calls, sometimes aggravating people, turning people away who needed his help, and no one bothered to correct the situation. Something told me that, as a black woman in that position, I would never have been allowed to neglect my professional responsibilities to such an extent. Every day, I needed to prove myself. Apparently, the man who held the job before me didn't feel similarly responsible.

Several people were quick to point out the previous guy's lack of professionalism. It was frustrating that so many people could point out what he had done wrong, but nobody had ever taken the initiative to correct the problem while he was there. He was allowed to move on to his next assignment, still in the military, still wearing the uniform, only now he was someone else's problem.

As much as we may not want to admit it, Active Guard and Reserve officers always have something to prove to our Active Duty counterparts. The Active Army consistently approaches Reserve and Guard members with some skepticism, believing that we're only part-time soldiers, without the skills or discipline to perform as well as our Active counterparts. From the look of the office I stepped into, the previous advisor played right into those negative expectations and shattered relationships with his undisciplined, unprofessional, shoddy work.

The biggest fence I had to mend was with the Undersecretary for Personnel. My predecessor's reputation for unresponsiveness had reached the upper strata of the Pentagon and I knew I had to make every effort to win back their respect. As soon as I could, I made an appointment to visit with him, introduce myself, and let him know that I intended to make improvements as soon as possible.

I didn't know it at the time, but I wouldn't have long to learn the finer points of my position. I arrived at DCSPER in late 1989. By August 1990, President George H. W. Bush began calling up Reserve and Guard soldiers for the first Gulf War, the mission called Desert Storm.

For previous conflicts, Reserve forces had been just that—kept in reserve and only called up when the Active force needed to be replenished. By the time the first Gulf War kicked off, war plans and strategies had completely changed. Reserve and National Guard units were now expected to play an integral part in any conflict. No longer waiting on the sidelines, thousands of Guard and Reserve soldiers were called up immediately to complete the unit structures of their active-duty partners. For years, we had planned, trained and equipped our Reserve to play that role, and now it was time to see if our new strategy for waging war would work.

The Gulf War provided a test of those plans. Could the Guard and Reserve respond to the task when called upon? Could we mobilize and equip thousands of troops, not just from active-duty military bases, but from small towns and cities across the country? What would happen when Reserve and Guard soldiers left their fulltime jobs to put on uniforms for a deployment that would go on for months at a time? We had planned and trained for this call-up. Would it work?

When the call-up started, it was my job to report on the status of deployments throughout the process to the Army Pentagon staff. My reports included information about which Reserve and National Guard units were notified of mobilization, what stage their call-up was in, how many people they would be moving and a long list of other details. I began working an overnight shift while we moved to twenty-four-hour operations. I worked 5 p.m. to 7 a.m. at the Pentagon. During each overnight shift, I pulled together all the numbers I needed for my daily reports. The information was constantly changing while tens of thousands of men and women and all of their equipment were readied and shipped to their duty locations. It was a huge amount of information to track and report to the planners.

My promotion to lieutenant colonel had finally come just before the war, and it came at a good time. Every morning, at the end of my shift, I had to brief the DCSPER in the Battle Update Brief or the BUB. Briefing a three-star general can be intimidating, especially if you don't have the rank to back up your position. Briefing general officers was just part of the job, but briefing as a lieutenant colonel made things a little easier. Still, it was vital that the information I provided was clear and accurate. I soon grew accustomed to regularly briefing generals.

In addition to my overnight shift, I had to monitor the daily work that came across my desk. Technically, after I briefed at the BUB, I was off duty, but during the war, I was often at my other desk until nine or ten in the morning, only to be required to come back again by five in the evening.

One meeting I was required to attend occurred weekly. At this meeting, the room was full of general officers. As a lieutenant colonel, I was one of the lower-ranking people in the room.

The thing to bear in mind is that military meetings, like most things in the service, have several universal similarities, no matter where you go. First, there is the importance of seating. The principle players sit in designated seats around a large conference table or briefing room. The highest-ranking person, the one everyone directs their information to, sits in the most central location, the most prominent seat. Others take up additional seating scattered around the room. The additional seating, often called the back row, is for generals' aides, deputies, lower-ranking people, observers and others who would not brief but have some interest in the meeting. These people are sometimes called back-seaters. Having "a seat at the table" in this situation has exactly the connotation of the euphemism—you have a significant role to play in the gathering.

The second thing about military meetings that is universal is Power Point. Every meeting is conducted using Power Point slides or some other form of graphic slide display, often so filled with arrows, symbols, graphs, pyramids, bursts of color and usually such tiny font that, even when displayed on massive screens, they are impossible to read or understand. At times it seems as if the goal is to make slides as incomprehensible as possible, making it a game to see if everyone will look at the ridiculous jumble of information and pretend they understand what it means.

In this particular meeting, representatives from every Army staff office attended to brief the Army leadership. The Chief of Staff of the Army, the Vice Chief and a cascade of other stars had their designated seats at the table. This meeting was so large it was usually standing room only. We each had a slide with our issues listed. We were required to provide a status update and the senior-ranking officer would decide whether or not the matter or the issue was closed or if further updates and information on the topic were needed. As matters were resolved, they were removed from the slide.

For weeks, I had been attending these meetings, the only female in the room, and every week, one particular pesky issue continued to show up on the National Guard slide. It had something to do with a bright idea someone had to change an administrative requirement during a unit's deployment. I don't remember all of the details, but it was something that would have been difficult to accomplish while in peacetime and was now nearly impossible to accomplish in the middle of a war while deployments were going on. Still, the idea had ended up on my slide and each week I asked the people in charge of the matter for the latest update. Each week they reported the same thing: they were doing research or they were discussing the best way forward, basically telling me that nothing further had been done. Each week I repeated what they told me to the generals in the room, knowing the action wasn't moving forward and not having any power or influence to make it change. The matter stayed open and I continued to report the same status. It was getting old and, frankly, seemed like a waste of my time.

One day at one of those meetings, I must have been extra-tired. The ten-hour shifts were getting to me. My work in the office was piling up and I was exhausted. When the same pesky issue appeared on the slide again, the generals called on me to explain.

"National Guard," one of them said.

I couldn't stand to give them the same update anymore. "Sir," I said. "This matter will never get resolved, so this baby is closed."

The room fell silent for several seconds. There were a few surprised expressions, while others kept their poker faces on. I was tired of briefing the same item each week and I knew it would just keep showing up until someone made the decision to take it off. So, I made the decision.

"Okay," the general said. "It's closed."

There were murmurs in the corners as everyone whispered their surprise. They had all seen the matter come up on my slide every week, so they must have known my frustration. After the meeting a couple of the officers approached me.

"I can't believe you told him it was closed," one of them said. "You've got balls."

It wasn't the first time someone said I had those parts of the male anatomy. Considering that I was usually the only woman in the room, I could see why they might want to ensure that I was more like them than I appeared.

In any case, the item was removed from my slide and that was the last I saw of it.

As wars go, the first Gulf War was short, with actual combat only lasting a matter of weeks before the Iraqi forces fled from Kuwait and abandoned their occupation. We spent much more time mobilizing people to go and bringing people and equipment back than any of the time spent at actual warfare.

Still, it was enough time to learn that our strategy for the Reserve forces, while not perfect, would work. The deployment of Army Reserve and National Guard troops was, however, a very real strain on the jobs and families of those soldiers who were sent to war. Some soldiers came home to find their jobs gone and they were forced to pursue help through the Soldiers and Sailors Relief Act to get their jobs back. Others returned to find their marriages broken, their civilian lives in tatters, and their worldview changed forever. But those things always happen when soldiers are deployed. They are the fallout of war.

I recall that during the initial call-ups, some Reserve and National Guard troops refused to report for duty, claiming, among other things, they hadn't joined the Army to go to war. They'd joined for the tuition assistance and never expected to be called on to deploy to an actual war zone. It seemed a ridiculous notion at the time, that anyone would become a soldier, train for combat and then think the nation would never call on him or her to perform the expected duty. But at the time, we'd been at peace for a couple of decades. We'd grown accustomed to thinking about the military as a place to gain training and experience, to garner the benefits of tuition assistance. The call-up to Desert Storm changed that thinking.

And now, after a dozen years of war on two different fronts, no one would join the military today without understanding the very real probability that they could be called on to deploy to a war zone. Even as the Afghanistan and Iraqi deployments draw to a close, the war on terror still rages and there's no telling when and if the military will be called on again to ship troops someplace overseas.

Part of a soldier's uniform is the unit patch worn on the left shoulder sleeve. As a soldier moves from one unit to the next, the unit patch is replaced to show their current assignment. When a soldier deploys to a war zone, the unit they deployed with becomes a permanent part of their uniform. Combat patches are worn on the right sleeve, a permanent symbol that the soldier has been to war. When I worked at the Pentagon, the right sleeve patch was rare. Now, to see a solider with a naked right sleeve is rare. That says a great deal about the way the military has changed from the peacetime service I knew, to the wartime service of today. Soldiers can choose not to wear the combat patch but most do wear it.

Soon after becoming a lieutenant colonel, I began to get requests to serve on promotion boards to determine which officers had the qualifications to be recommended for elevation. I was the only black, female, field grade officer at the Army National Guard Bureau, and since each of the boards needed to maintain a certain level of diversity, my services were frequently required. I served on National Guard boards for states across the country and our territories like Guam and Puerto Rico. I also served on Department of the Army boards as the Reserve representative and saw firsthand how Active Duty board members sometimes passed over Guard and Reserve officers because they didn't understand issues germane to Reserve service or because the Reserve or Guard member hadn't prepared their packets according to Active Army standards. Serving on all of those boards taught me invaluable information about how the system worked. One thing became crystal clear to me: the packet submitted for any board has to be flawless, Officer Evaluation Reports have to be stellar, and recommendations have to come from the highest-ranking people available in order to meet the minimum eligibility criteria.

All the things I learned about the board system I passed on to others, not only to help minority officers but to help *all* National Guard and Reserve officers as they competed for promotions alongside our active-duty counterparts. I simply wanted the process to be fair. I hated to hear about people who missed out on opportunities because of a clerical error or because someone else had managed to circumvent the system. Later in my career, I was able to make changes that affected the entire Guard by implementing training to improve reporting procedures.

The training and experience on the boards also helped me personally. I knew that if I was ever going to get promoted to full-bird colonel, I needed a vital bit of training that wouldn't be easy to get. I had already earned a graduate degree by this time, but what I really wanted to do was go to the Army War College. Ellen had just started her first year at Cornell University and Helene was doing well on her own, so it was a good time to attend. But first, I needed to submit an application packet and get recommendations and approvals from several people. Even if every document was in perfect order, the competition would be tough. Officers selected for the War College were those most likely to get promoted, those most likely to continue in their careers and those with support from someone high up in their chain of command. When it came to competition for seats at the War College, it wasn't unusual for people to let mentors and influential friends know they had applied and were counting on their help to be selected. Having the best packet or the best experience didn't guarantee your application would be approved, however.

I relied on all the knowledge I had amassed about selection boards and used it to develop my own packet. I made some calls and located the Department and the Army National Guard civilian who assembled the boards and told him my intentions.

"It sounds like you have all of the necessary qualifications," he said. "I think you'll be the only woman applying in this round."

He advised me not to talk too much about my intentions with anyone. Since I was working at the Pentagon, I could get endorsements from my active-duty supervisors in the building for my packet.

"The active army officers you work for can approve and sign your documents," he said. "I'd just keep quiet about it."

I knew endorsements along with good Officer Evaluation Reports would carry clout with the people making the selections. It was another example of the different way in which Reserve and Army National Guard soldiers were viewed in the military culture. Despite the fact that I worked fulltime in uniform and had the same training and experience, being an active National Guard officer was sometimes perceived as inferior to my active-duty officer colleagues. That difference in status is a strange part of the military culture that seems impossible to change.

"Wait until close to the deadline to submit the paperwork. That way, it won't get lost," he advised. 'Lost paperwork' was an excuse often used to keep people from getting what they wanted, be it a promotion or new assignment. He understood the things that could go wrong, the missteps others had made, so I followed his advice to the letter.

After everything was stamped and approved by the people I worked for, I hand-delivered the packet, driving it to Edgewood, Maryland, and walking it into the office where the boards were held. I truly believed that if some members of the Bureau had known that my packet was waiting to go before the board, my application would have been waylaid. Even after I submitted the packet, I worried that all my maneuvering wasn't enough. I may have been a bit paranoid, but I envisioned the possibility that should it come down to a decision between me and someone else with powerful backing, I would lose out. Perhaps someone with a grudge would say something negative to the people on the selection committee. Perhaps someone would think the black female officer shouldn't take a seat from a white male officer. Perhaps, like the time I didn't get the promotion I felt I deserved, someone would think that an officer from a combat arms branch was more deserving of a seat than I was. In truth, the process was so political that I was prepared for just about anything to happen.

Paranoid or not, my efforts and precautions paid off. I was selected and was granted my request for the prestigious school.

The Army War College is at Carlisle Barracks in Pennsylvania. A class of students will either attend the resident course in Pennsylvania or, if they already have a graduate degree, they can request to attend a fellowship program earned at a qualifying university. I was accepted into the fellowship program and was slated to attend Tufts University School of War and Diplomacy in Boston.

Critical thinking, strategic leadership and planning, complex problem-solving are just some of the lofty goals of the War College. Notable Army leaders throughout history have attended the college, and now there I was, sitting amongst the latest class.

For the first two weeks, everyone selected reported to the Carlisle Barracks campus for orientation. The orientation also included a trip to the Pentagon, where we received several briefings and presentations.

Of course, going to the Pentagon wasn't a big deal for me. I had worked in the building for a couple years and knew my way around the halls of the twenty-nine-acre building. The multiple rings and floors of the massive structure are like a warren where thousands of workers burrow around each day. "The Puzzle Palace," as it is sometimes called, has that nickname for a reason. One could work there for months and still get lost in it. I'd grown accustomed to the mostly windowless halls, the confusing jumble of offices and stairwells. For many in the group, however, their first trip to the building was significant.

For me the presentations we received that day were more interesting than the tour. One in particular was very memorable: General Colin Powell spoke to us. He was chairman of the Joint Chiefs of Staff at the time and came to a large auditorium where we were all assembled. Powell was an inspiration, talking about his experiences, the need to set goals and achieve them.

I was one of only three women in the class and, of course, the other women were both white. I was sitting on the end of a row. When General

Powell finished speaking, everyone stood as he made his way out of the auditorium. When he walked near me, he looked at me and stopped. Then he reached out and shook my hand.

"Congratulations," he said smiling.

In that one word and simple gesture, he made it clear that he understood how difficult it must have been for me to have the opportunity to be sitting in that room. It was only one word, a very brief encounter, but I'll never forget it. Of course, I was treated like a celebrity for the rest of the day. People asked me if I knew him, assuming that was the reason he shook my hand. I understood why he had extended the gesture, but I kept that to myself.

After the orientation period, all of us fellows were sent off to the various universities where we had been assigned. I had put most of my things in storage and took the minimum amount of stuff with me to Boston. I found a one-bedroom apartment in the city and, for a year starting in July, 1992, I attended the Fletcher School for Law and Diplomacy at Tufts University.

There were three other fellows at Tuffs and we all shared an office. As fellows, we didn't have many assignments to complete but we each were responsible for completion of a study due at the end of the year. The topic of the study had to be submitted and approved by professors at Tufts as well as the faculty at Carlisle Barracks. In addition to the study, early in the first semester, I was asked to arrange and coordinate transportation for a class trip. It took months of paperwork, phone calls and logistical arrangements, but I was finally able to secure a National Guard plane to transport the entire class on the trip.

For two weeks, we traveled from Boston to Ankara and Istanbul, Turkey, followed by Qatar and finally to Israel. Our professors had arranged for a full schedule of cultural seminars, meetings and presentations. We met with diplomats, dignitaries and world leaders. One student's father was a sheik who greeted us in Qatar and treated us all to suites at the Sheraton Doha. One of my treasures from that experience is a picture of me standing with Menachem Begin.

I enjoyed my nine-month fellowship very much. The experience was eye-opening; I learned so much and met so many great people. I even tried to make my stay at the university permanent.

"I think we need to have an Army National Guard person here at Tuffs University to greet incoming students and ease their way into the fellowship program," I said to the assignment officer at the Bureau.

"Give it up, Julia," he said. "We need you back here in Washington."

I laugh at that lame attempt now, but at the time, I really hoped to stay. I was only disappointed for a short time. War College was meant for people who had bigger and better things in store for them and I was ready for those challenges.

QUALIFIED BUT UNWANTED

The three other officers in the fellowship program with me had orders for their next assignments long before I did. After several months of limbo—no solid news about where I would be going—I was finally told that my next assignment would be Chief of Inspections and Analysis, Office of the Army National Guard Inspector General. I was a little disappointed. I had hoped for a job that required a colonel. The position was for a lieutenant colonel, which was my rank at the time, and would mean I wouldn't see promotion to colonel anytime soon. Despite that disappointment, the job was in the Pentagon, which meant I could stay in the house I still owned in Springfield, Virginia. The more I thought about it, the more appealing the job became, so I mentally prepared myself for what was ahead.

One day, the soldier I was meant to replace in the Inspector General's office called me to say there might be a problem with my getting the job promised to me. "Julia, word is that the Army Inspector General thinks the job should go to an officer with combat-arms experience."

"But *you're* not combat arms," I said.

"I know, Julia. But I thought I should give you a heads-up on that. And remember. You didn't hear it from me."

Combat arms referred to Infantry, Armor, Special Forces or some other combat-related branch. It was a clever but transparent move. By making combat arms a qualifier, they would not only limit who would qualify for the job, they would guarantee that the job would go to a man since women were not allowed in combat-arms branches. This barrier had come up before in my career, preventing me from getting the promotion I felt I deserved. It was a common halt to a woman's military career, whether officer or enlisted. Women were barred from combat jobs, and in many areas, forward progression required that there be some combat-arms training or experience to qualify for certain positions. In some cases, the qualification of combat arms wasn't *needed* to do the job, but the qualifier was used to weed out people, even if the position was purely administrative. Most significantly, unless a woman was in the medical branch, it was nearly impossible to achieve anything higher than a one- or two-star position. By barring women from serving in combat arms, the military didn't just create a glass ceiling; it erected a solid wall that announced in bright, flashing neon lights: Your Career Stops Here!

It wasn't until 2008 that the first woman was promoted to be a four-star general in the history of the U.S. military. General Anne Dunwoody, who was the commander of Army Material Command at the time of her promotion, retired from the military in 2012, and at the time of writing this book, no other female four-star has replaced her in the Army's highest ranks. Janet Wolfenbarger became a four-star general in the U.S. Air Force in 2012.

Still, the combat-arms barrier was a tough one to crack. Secretary Panetta, just prior to stepping down as Secretary of Defense, finally shattered that barrier by opening all combat-arms positions to women. At the writing of this book, the Army hasn't figured out how they will make the change work, but the fact that the barrier has been removed, that all opportunities are now available for women is a fantastic change.

I would not have wanted to be infantry or armor or any of the other combat-arms positions, but I'm sure there are many women out there who not only want to serve in those capacities but are fully capable of doing so. At least now there is the possibility of equity, the opportunity to reach the highest goals imaginable. I find it exciting and I look forward to seeing what the future holds for women in the Army and other services.

But while I was at Tufts University, waiting for news of my next assignment, the combat-arms barrier was still firmly in place and it appeared, at least from where I was sitting at the time, that the all-male qualifier was being used to prevent me from getting a job I was otherwise fully qualified for. I was sure that my personnel file, which included my education and experience, had already been passed around my soon-to-be new office. I instinctively knew that the Army Inspector General my colleague mentioned wasn't the one who came up with the new requirement. I figured the lieutenant colonels and colonels around him, the men I would be working with should I get the job, had decided they didn't want a woman, especially a black woman, in their midst.

What a senior leader wants usually gets done, but the phone call from my friend wasn't official word. His warning prompted me to start making phone calls to the Tours office at the Bureau to check on the status of my new assignment. But no one there would give me a definitive answer. I got "I don't know what the holdup is" from everyone.

The logistics of the delay in assignment became worrisome. The fellowship was drawing to a close and I needed to make arrangements to move out of my apartment in Boston and give the tenants who were renting my house in Virginia adequate notice that they had to leave. Ellen was finishing her second year at Cornell and I needed to pick her up and bring her home. But none of those plans could be made final until official orders were issued to book government movers and to start the ball rolling. I didn't have much time left to make any of those things happen. By this time, all of the other fellows in the program had orders to their new assignments and their new duty locations. Thirty days before the end of the program, I was still waiting for orders. On top of all of the personal logistics, I knew that if I was going to the Inspector

General's office, I would need to attend the three-week IG school at Fort Belvoir, Virginia. Time was running out. I had little choice. I couldn't wait any longer for the Tours/Assignments office, where assignments are managed, to issue my orders.

I waited until a Sunday and called the company commander I had served with while a tactical training officer at the officer candidate school in New York. Colonel Ron Tipa was now the Army National Guard G1, the chief in charge of personnel. The people at the Tours office were subordinate to Colonel Tipa. Since the Tours office was unable to give me any answers, I figured Colonel Tipa could.

I purposely made the call on a Sunday afternoon. I wanted him at home and relaxed, away from the pressures of the office. Once I had him on the phone, I gave him the whole rundown. The rumors about combat arms, the lack of information from the people at Tours, the run-around I had been getting and my feeling that the combat-arms requirement was only meant to eliminate my eligibility.

"Sir, they're just not giving me any answers. The bureau has spent a lot of money sending me to War College and I'm more than qualified for this job. If I learn that the IG has made this new requirement for combat arms because they don't want a female to have this job, I will bust the Army wide open."

He said a lot of things aimed at reassuring me that bigotry and misogyny were not the intention. He had to say those things. No one, including me, wanted to believe that the new requirements were set up specifically to exclude Julia J. Cleckley. He couldn't ignore, however, that, even if it wasn't intentional, the move appeared to be discriminatory. I think Ron Tipa had heard enough about me to understand that I would stir up a shit storm of trouble, if forced.

By the end of the phone call, I had done all I could. Now I just had to wait and see if my efforts would have any result. I didn't have to wait long.

The very next day, people from the Tours office called me.

"What did you do? Why did you call the G1?"

"I'm only three weeks away from a PCS move. I needed to get some answers and I wasn't getting any."

Once again, the person on the phone marveled at my maneuver, saying I had those all-important portions of male anatomy. He told me people were upset that I had gone over their heads, but I expected that. Apparently, Colonel Tipa went to his rater, the Director of the Army Guard, a general officer, and explained the issue to him. That general personally went to the two-star Inspector General and told him that I was the officer they were getting and to stop putting up roadblocks to the assignment.

I was fairly sure that the rapid response to my call didn't happen simply because Colonel Tipa wanted to help another New York National Guard Soldier. Although I never had to voice the possibility of sexism, Colonel Tipa and his boss knew that the appearance of discrimination was so evident they needed to fix the problem and fix it immediately. They knew I wasn't joking about going all the way with my charges. Considering how vulnerable they appeared, they had no choice but to clean up the mess.

Shortly after that, my orders were issued and I was able to start making the plans I needed to make my transition back to Virginia and enroll in the Inspector General course at Fort Belvoir. I spent the next three weeks scrambling to get everything done in time. I barely made it. Government movers didn't come to pack my belongings until two days before I was scheduled to start the Inspector General School at Fort Belvoir. All of my things were cleared out of my Boston apartment and the next morning, long before the sun came up, I got in my car, which was loaded to the roof with suitcases and boxes, and drove to Fort Belvoir. By the time I arrived, I was twelve minutes late for the first class.

If I hadn't been proactive, I could have been in limbo for months.

It was frustrating that I had to call in a favor, but I was glad that I had.

Arriving in the IG office, having knowledge of the efforts expended to keep me out, was awkward. It was also empowering. Proving myself had been part of every job I had held in the military. This time I knew in advance that I wasn't wanted and would have to prove myself to officers who had already seen my qualifications, knew my experience and background, and still judged me unfit.

I was ready to show them how wrong they were, but family issues arose that took priority.

While I'd been away at War College, I'd been unable to make my monthly visits to my mother and her situation back in Aliquippa had begun to change. She was still living in her home, but my brother Mickey and his wife Susan were growing worried about her.

"She won't let us in," Mickey said when he called me one night. "I don't know what's going on with her."

When I called her, I would have to let the phone ring and ring until she was forced to answer. She simply didn't want to be bothered.

"Hello!" she would say, frustration in her voice.

"Mom, you have to let Mickey and Susan in. They just want to check to make sure you're okay."

"I'm fine. I don't need anyone to check on me."

"Mom, you have to let them in. They want to help you."

My siblings reported that she spent her time sitting on her porch, smoking and refusing to be bothered by anyone. She was going through menopause and it made her irritable and completely uncooperative. She was also diabetic, had high blood pressure, and refused to quit smoking. She frequently contracted infections of one kind or another, colds, strep throat or some other illness that sapped her energy and left her listless.

These reports were difficult to hear while I was in school in Boston, but I felt helpless to do anything. I often asked my siblings, who lived just over an hour away from her, to help take care of her, to run errands for her. But they had lives of their own, responsibilities and commitments that demanded their attention. Many times they couldn't help and were resentful about being asked. Care for Mom became a huge friction point for the family, but something had to be done.

As soon as I was finished with school and was able to visit her, I saw right away that things weren't going well. Since the months I'd last seen her, she had lost weight and seemed to be deteriorating. I called a family meeting, getting everyone together to discuss what to do.

"Mom's health is failing and she's not going to get better. I want her to come live with me in Virginia," I announced.

"She's never going to agree to that," Mickey said.

"I know," I said. "That's why I need your help. I'll tell her that she's just coming for a visit. I need you all to be here, to help me get her in the car."

It was dishonest, but I knew it was the only way she would agree to come with me. Ellen came along and helped us convince Mom that she needed to come to Virginia to visit with us. We managed to get her in the car that day, but even after we had her comfortably settled in my house, she never stopped saying she wanted to go home. Despite that constant struggle with her, I was glad I insisted on the move. After staying with us for about three weeks, she had a stroke.

We were in the kitchen, and I watched her slowly slump down, her face going strangely slack. When I spoke to her, she tried to respond, to tell me she was okay, but it was clear that she wasn't. Ellen and I rushed her to the hospital. Her long, slow recovery began almost immediately. She didn't lose her speech or her ability to get around, but Ellen and I had our hands full keeping her away from her cigarettes and on a serious diet regimen to control her diabetes.

It was important to get my mother on stable ground because my new job in the IG office at the Pentagon would require me to be away from home more often. My roles as Chief of Inspections and the Reserve component representative required me to inspect arms rooms—the secure space in which weapons and ammunition is stored to ensure compliance with the strict security requirements, and to inspect training at Active Army, Reserve and National Guard bases to be sure they were fulfilling all the necessary requirements for the Reserve and National Guard troops. I had a staff of three and worked closely with the Active Army Inspector General's officers, often traveling with them from base to base. Most of those IG officers were colonels and lieutenant colonels, all were men, and more than likely the very men who had tried to keep me out of their all-male club.

When we were required to go on trips, I put on my combat boots, strapped on my helmet and protective gear and ate dust as we traveled over vast Army training areas to inspect everything from training methods to equipment and instruction. We flew around in Black Hawk helicopters, drove over rough terrain in Humvees, and slogged through fields and mud. It was hard work, but nothing I hadn't done before. I had personally trained in the field, trained officer candidates and taught ROTC cadets. I knew what it took to make men and women into soldiers. I never once complained.

It quickly became apparent why some of the officers had tried to prevent me from becoming a member of their team. We spent days at a time on the road. Traveling with a group like that meant sharing meals together. They would meet in hotel restaurants and follow their meals with a cigar at the bar, the kind of male bonding one would expect from a group of soldiers away from home. They tested me often, trying to see how the female would react to their sometimes inappropriate behavior. Would I complain about going to the field? Would I whine about working late? Would I give them a hard time about their harsh language, their drinking, their disgusting cigar smoke? These men, the lieutenant colonels and colonels I was traveling with, had heard a woman was coming and panicked. Their fraternity was in jeopardy. Making combat arms a requirement would have sealed their boys' club from female entry, but I had put a stop to their plan.

For several months I went on every trip, proving that I was willing to get dirty, willing to do what needed to be done. I went to dinner with them and sometimes stayed for a glass of wine, but never overindulged. I have never been much of a drinker and wasn't about to change that to gain their approval. They were always respectful, treated me like a lady and fellow officer and, over time, they let me know that, despite their initial objections, I had been accepted into their club. After a while, I felt that I had accomplished what I had set out to do and didn't need to prove myself anymore. I began to stay home more often and sent one of the three officers who worked for me (males) on the trips.

Six months into the job, the Army National Guard held a promotion recommendation board. I knew my packet was being considered since I was eligible to be promoted to colonel. Once the board was held, Colonel Tipa stopped by the office and told me I had done well.

"You're in the top five," he said.

Still, months went by. I couldn't get promoted until I was targeted for a colonel's position and I was told that they couldn't find the right job for me at the time. It was suggested that I become an instructor at DEOMI, the Equal Employment Opportunity School in Florida, but the acting director of the guard said he didn't want my talents 'wasted' teaching in a school. Every job that was suggested for me was rejected by someone as being not the right fit, at least that's what the G1 told me.

I was patient. Colonel Tipa told me I had been in the top five so I was sure the promotion would come in time. Still, the rumors kept flying about where my next assignment would be and I was growing restless. People I knew would stop by my office and tell me their promotions were approved. When I say people, I mean men.

"Julia, my promotion is approved. My state is preparing it to go for senate approval."

"Great. Good for you," I would say, wondering what was happening with my career, since many of the men promoted ahead of me hadn't been to the War College.

One day, after nine months in my job, a female colonel I knew, who had served on my recommendation board, stopped by my office. Because she had served on the board, she was prohibited from speaking to me about specifics concerning the results of the board, but she seemed angry about something and did some of her venting in my office.

"Julia, when is your paperwork going in for promotion?" she asked me.

"I don't know." I explained what Colonel Tipa told me. She was shocked.

"You were number two on that board! If I were you, I would march right over to the director's office today and ask him what is going on."

The more she talked, the more I learned why she was feeling angry. She thought things were progressing unfairly and felt the need to share her knowledge. She told me about one lieutenant colonel who had come out in twenty-first place on the board and hadn't been to the War College. "He's already got a new assignment and his promotion packet is in," she said.

It was a good question, but I wasn't quite ready to raise an alarm. I waited and watched and hoped things would sort themselves out. They didn't. And so I was faced with a dilemma. I had information that I shouldn't have. I had to use that information without letting anyone know how I came by it. It was a tricky situation, but if what the colonel had told me was true, I had every right to raise a stink.

So, a year after I had done it the first time, I called Colonel Tipa at home on a Sunday. He was still the G1 and had a stake in ensuring that boards and promotions were conducted fairly. If I shook the bushes too hard, the rotten apples would partially fall on his head.

After the usual pleasantries, I told him that I knew that I had come out number two on the board and that several people who had gone before the same board were already on the senate confirmation list.

"Who told you that? That information can't be discussed. That's violating the board. All of the results could be thrown out."

"I realize that, sir, but the person who told me was upset. This person felt there was a possibility that people who were less qualified were getting promoted before me."

"You need to tell me who gave you that information."

"I'm not going to tell you, sir. I just wanted you to know that this person encouraged me to discuss this issue with the director. I don't want to go to him about my promotion. I have been very patient; however, I'm not sure how much longer I can wait as I watch other people getting promoted over me."

He was well aware of the implications for his department. Several men had been promoted before from the list. I was a qualified War College graduate who had evidently done better on the board than most, not to mention that I was a DEOMI graduate and knew what equal employment opportunity steps to take, should I need to go that route.

The following Wednesday, Colonel Tipa called me. "Julia, we got the general to sign off on a job for you."

"That's great. What is it?"

"You're going to be the division chief of personnel policy. You're going to be working for me, Julia. You'll be one of my five division chiefs."

"Great. That sounds like an excellent fit." I had already held several personnel jobs, so it made perfect sense. I wondered why it hadn't been suggested earlier, but I didn't ask.

"You'll be the first black division chief," he said.

"Well, what else is new?"

I often think about how that job came to be mine. The Army had just spent thousands of dollars to send me to the War College in preparation for being a colonel. I had paid my dues in the trenches and checked all of the blocks necessary to ensure I was qualified for any job they gave me; still, the promotion and the job that went with it were withheld from me. I sometimes wonder how much longer I would have been made to wait if I hadn't made that phone call—if I hadn't threatened to expose the way I was being given the run-around.

Of course, if I hadn't been given the inside information, I never would have known what was happening. I am grateful that throughout my career, people who liked and respected me, usually called me to give me a heads-up when sketchy things were happening around me. I wonder how many qualified women, minorities and others have been in the same position and simply didn't know that they were being robbed of their opportunities. Time and again I had witnessed what happened when people watched out for their buddies, when strings were pulled and influence was used. I felt I was left with little choice but to force the issue.

MY FRIEND ELLEN

The relationship between a mother and daughter is a special one. It can start out being very close, but usually, when the daughter reaches a certain age, usually in her teens, the mother and daughter naturally grow apart. The daughter's friendships and other interests gradually become more attractive than spending time with Mom. Mom struggles with the new person that her daughter has become, the independent person who can fill her days with things that don't include Mom.

It was different for Ellen and me. We were close, even through her teenage years we spent a great deal of time together, sharing our troubles and our secrets. She was my sounding board and I was hers. She told me all about the details of her life.

Her girlfriends would sometimes complain: "Ellen, don't tell your mother this time! You tell her everything." But she would always tell me, always talk to me about what was going on in her life.

She was only seven when she lost her father. When Helene chose to stay in New York, Ellen and I made the move to Virginia together, discovering new interests, making new friends, venturing out on my new career. We talked to each other about missing Gus, about our fears and challenges. It was the same kind of relationship I had enjoyed with my own mother, so it seemed natural to me that we would be best friends.

As a little girl, Ellen was a ball of energy and never tired of trying new things. Ballet and tap dancing classes, swimming lessons, piano lessons; every activity offered at the local YWCA in New York, Ellen wanted to try it. Helene took piano and swimming lessons, too, but it was clear to Ellen that she could do things her older sister couldn't. While she never wanted to exclude Helene from her activities, she also knew she couldn't deny herself the joy of trying new things just because Helene couldn't do them.

Aside from her many interests, Ellen and I spent hundreds of Saturdays together shopping, going to the movies, visiting the zoo, walking the halls of museums, and we usually included several of her friends. I was a favorite of many of her friends' parents because I was always taking a group of kids on some adventure somewhere. I enjoyed seeing and experiencing things through Ellen's eyes, hearing her excitement over new things and new ideas.

She was a bright and eager student who read everything she could get her hands on and demonstrated early talents for art, writing and studying. I still wonder where she got the talent to draw, something that was way beyond my abilities. She could pick up pencil or pen and create beautiful sketches of anything she wished.

It didn't surprise any of us that she graduated high school with honors. Her future prospects were limitless. The military, however, never entered her mind. "Momma, with all due respect for what puts food on the table, I don't think I'll be choosing ROTC in college."

"That's okay, honey," I said. "Whatever you want is fine by me."

By the time she was ready for college, she had already decided on and rejected a long list of possible occupations, her dreams for her future constantly fired by a huge imagination. At one time or another, she wanted to be an actress, a lawyer and even a veterinarian. During high school she had worked part-time at a veterinary clinic and observed surgeries on cats and dogs and other domestic animals. She applied for and was accepted to Cornell University. At the time of her acceptance, her plan was to eventually enter Cornell's top-rated School of Veterinary Medicine. But when we visited the school and discovered that her training would include euthanizing animals, Ellen knew that occupation wasn't right for her.

"No, I could never do that!" she said.

She was full of compassion, maybe too much compassion. Euthanasia, a necessary practice for veterinarians, was a deal-breaker for her. She gave up that goal and set her sights on easing human suffering. When she told me she would change her major to human services, I worried for her. I knew how soft-hearted she could be, how much she would take on other people's troubles, how difficult it might be for her to confront the realities of life in a city's welfare system, for instance. Still, she wanted a career that would help people.

Socially, she was popular. She spent lots of time with her girlfriends, but there was a part of her social life she found wanting. During her second year at Cornell, she called me one day, angry. "Mom, I went to a party and a boy tried to talk to me. I had no idea what to say! I'm in college and I don't know how to talk to boys!"

"How is that my fault?"

"All you do is go to work and to church. You dress nicely all the time, you look great, but you never go out on dates. You didn't set a good example for me."

She was upset and I understood why. Everything she said was true. I did not date, hadn't considered including another man in my life since Gus died. But once Ellen got onto the topic, she wouldn't let it go. She took every opportunity to remind me that I was a woman, one that had been without her husband for over a decade. She insisted that her father would want me to be happy. I was happy, I explained, but her prodding had sparked some thought on my part. I began to consider the possibility that I might let another man into my life.

My thinking along those lines didn't change Ellen's feeling that she was unprepared for the college dating life. She hadn't dated at all during high school because her interests focused on school; however, her high school years hadn't been devoid of a social life. A couple of her high school friends were members of Jack and Jill, an African-American organization that mentors young people through social events and volunteer opportunities, preparing them for leadership roles as adults. While we weren't members of the organization, during her senior year in high school, Ellen sometimes went along with her friend Alexia to Jack and Jill events. Boys attended all of the dances and social events the girls participated in that year, so it wasn't as if Ellen didn't have *any* experience being around them.

Throughout her last year in high school, Alexia's mother wanted to sponsor me in joining Jack and Jill. It's a very formal organization with events for adults as well as the young people. But since Ellen was in her last year of school, and since I've never been much of a joiner, I chose not to become a member. Ellen was still able to participate in events and I knew she'd met several young men along the way.

Despite all of that, she surprised me when she decided to go stag to her prom.

"No, you're not," I told her. "This is a lifetime memory. It's too special for you to go and just hang out with your girlfriends. You have to have a date."

"Mom, I don't *have* a date," she complained.

"You're going to have pictures taken and you're not going to be standing there with your girlfriends."

"But Mom, there are three of us who don't have dates. It wouldn't be fair if I had one and they didn't."

I didn't let that stop me. I was determined to step in and correct the problem. I called a friend who knew a young man who was a freshman in college. I asked my friend if she thought he would be a good date for Ellen. I learned as much as I could about the young man, and then called him myself.

"If you're free, my daughter would like to invite you to escort her to her high school prom," I said.

"Well, of course, Mrs. Cleckley," he said without hesitation. He knew my daughter from some Jack and Jill events she attended and knew she was beautiful. He was more than happy to be her prom date.

Ellen was flabbergasted. "That is not right, Mother. You're making him take me! I don't even know him."

"You need a date for the prom and you're going to have one."

So, my hand-selected escort took Ellen to her senior prom. They went to dinner first and then to the prom held at a hotel in Crystal City, where they danced and had a good time with the rest of Ellen's classmates. In the end she was glad she had the memory of her first date, even though her mother had set it up.

There was one young man during the time she was in college whom she dated for about a year and a half, but nothing serious ever came of it. I told her to be patient, not to feel rushed. I was confident that she would eventually find the right person, just as I had found my soul mate in Gus.

Ellen concentrated on school but indulged herself in a wide variety of interests. She took acting lessons and continued her study of art and writing. She even took some classes in fashion design. During her junior year, her designs were selected to be in the annual Cornell fashion show. She created four original designs along with handbags and accessories to go with the outfits. When the designs appeared in the show, Ellen stepped out from behind her models during the finale, just like they do for high-fashion designer shows. It wasn't her major, but she enjoyed creating things. Her participation in the program was a great honor for a junior, but it was just one of her many accomplishments.

I was always proud of her achievements, but finishing her undergraduate degree was a big moment and I wanted to make it special for her.

"Do you want a car or do you want to go to Europe?" I asked her.

"I want to go to Europe!"

So I took three weeks off and the two of us went on a European trip. We made Germany our base and drove to all of the great spots to visit there like Garmisch, Heidelberg and Nuremberg. We made side trips to Switzerland and hit several places in Italy, including Venice and Vincenza. Ellen shopped for shoes, marveled at the art museums and took hundreds of pictures.

When the trip was over, she seriously set about finding her first job out of college. She found work at a group home for disabled adults in Vienna, Virginia and complained about her salary. "Mom, I graduated from an Ivy League school and I'm only making thirty-six thousand dollars a year!"

"But that's a lot for a first job, honey," I assured her.

She had been working at the group home for a year when she learned about a graduate program in education at George Washington University. She set her sights on the program, filling out applications, sitting through interviews, telephone interviews and a long approval process. Eventually she was granted a full scholarship.

I couldn't help but be proud of her. After she completed her graduate degree, and after a year of teaching at a private school in Alexandria, Virginia, she decided to relocate to my favorite place in the world, San Francisco. She lived with her godmother, Sonja, for three months before she found a job teaching special education students at a public school in the city and found great satisfaction in the work. The apartment she eventually moved into was very near Sonja's. She enjoyed her apartment, but she visited me and her grandmother constantly, using the frequent flyer miles I would transfer to her.

As much as she visited, I missed having my daughter near me even though we talked every day. Eventually, after four years, she decided to return to Virginia to live close to home. As it turned out, her decision to move back East was vitally important—more important than either of us could have predicted.

NOT THE BLACK MESSIAH

In April 1994, I slowed my busy schedule down long enough to plan and hold my promotion ceremony. The step up to colonel is a big deal. Like the step up from major to lieutenant colonel, not everyone who wants the promotion succeeds. Going from lieutenant colonel to full-bird colonel, the number of officers eligible dwindles even further. Many are passed over, opting to retire rather than wait for what will never be theirs to achieve. The weight of the accomplishment wasn't lost on me and I wanted to make the most of the moment.

The ceremony was huge, with more than four hundred guests. The promotion was another one of those historic moments and this time there was no way I could stop the public affairs machine from making a big deal out of it. *It was a very big deal.*

Both of my girls attended, along with many of the people I had worked with throughout the years. Friends and colleagues gathered to watch as Ellen and the director of the Army Guard pinned the silver wings of my new rank on the epaulets of my uniform. Naturally, I couldn't help but think about Gus and what he would have thought of my accomplishment. Losing him had been the impetus for my choice to become a fulltime soldier. I hoped that he could see what had become of his family, and that he was proud.

When the ceremony was over and the cameras stopped flashing, I went back to work. Not long after starting in the personnel division at the Bureau, I identified several problems about the military workforce and made it my mission to come up with solutions. Fairness was my watchword, one I was not shy about sharing. While researching what was happening with the reports, it wasn't long before I detected a few instances when it was clear someone wasn't getting a fair shake, and I stepped in to help them. I made a phone call or had a discussion with someone, letting it be known that my office was paying attention to the matter. In most instances, a small amount of effort ended with the desired result.

A case would start as a call from someone I knew, telling me about one of their minority soldiers who hadn't been given a seat in a class they needed while someone less qualified was given the seat. Then there were people who didn't get the promotions they felt they deserved, people who felt they were being singled out for disciplinary action, and people who wanted a transfer or new position but were denied the request. All of them were seeking help because they felt the adverse action was because of their race or sex. After I had helped a few people straighten out their problems, word spread like wildfire and I began to get phone calls with complaints from all over the country and our territories. People called me with EEO problems, with complaints about how their requests for training or promotion were handled. NCOs and officers came to me with discrimination complaints. Time and again I heard personal stories of unfair selections, missed opportunities and preferential treatment going to someone less worthy.

Before long, the calls, emails and people stopping by my office for help became overwhelming. There were times when I had a long line of people standing outside my door waiting to speak to me. My staff barely had time to get their day-to-day work done, since I was constantly giving them special projects as we researched one complaint or another.

"Ma'am, I was told to call you," the phone call would begin. Then the caller would launch into a long explanation about some discrimination, sexual harassment, or other fairness complaint. Many of the callers were female or a minority. The fact that so many people in so many different places had been told that I was the one who could help could have been taken as flattery, but what I truly felt was shock. Shock at the volume of calls, at the severity of the problems and that, of all the people in the Army National Guard, I was the only one these soldiers felt could help them.

My deputy came to me one day expressing alarm over the volume of calls and complaints. "Ma'am, the phone never stops ringing. Just when we've listened to one complaint, three more come in. We're being inundated. This can't go on."

"I agree," I said. "I can't solve everyone's problems. There's only so much we can do. I am not the black messiah of the Guard bureau."

I was frustrated. The people coming to me had genuine problems and complaints, but my office simply wasn't equipped to handle them all.

Word of what I said made it back to the director of the Army Guard.

"Julia, I heard what you said about not being the black messiah. Do you really feel that way?"

"Sir, we are being inundated with calls and complaints. I simply can't handle every EEO or discrimination concern we get. I've been charged with increasing the diversity of the force, but with that increase will come increased complaints about fair treatment."

"What do you suggest we do?" he asked.

"We need someone who is EEO-qualified at the Army Guard Bureau to listen to concerns, and refer them to the proper personnel"

Anyone familiar with the military knows that change within the services can be like watching a glacier melt, then freeze, then melt again, the process going on and on. The briefings and justifications and regulations and mountains of paperwork seemed endless, but I managed to get a few others on board with the idea and, once I had a few key people on my side, the movement to establish an EEO advisor position in the

Army National Guard Bureau took hold. Eventually, we were able to install not one but two EEO officers charged with hearing discrimination complaints and making recommendations to the proper offices for resolution. The new office helped ease those calls to my office and I could refocus my attention on my own goal for the division: to increase diversity and improve the personnel policies and evaluation process.

Even after the new office was established, I continued to serve on the Army National Guard Bureau's EEO committee and eventually headed the committee for the Army Guard Director. The committee was made up of enlisted and officer representatives from each of the regions, meeting quarterly to discuss issues and concerns. As a group, we would research problems and make recommendations for new policies or suggest new regulations. We worked with the states to improve processes and procedures, all in an attempt to improve the EEO posture of the Guard. This was no small task.

Promotions and admittance to schools were decided by review panels, a group of officers or NCOs charged with reviewing personnel packets and applications to evaluate a solder's eligibility. A requirement of all review panels is that they be diverse, with women and minorities represented. A black woman could serve to fill two requirements for diversity. As a result, I continuously received requests to serve on one panel or another, thereby "killing two birds with one stone."

While I enjoy traveling, the requests were so numerous that, under normal circumstances, I would have said no to at least a few of them. Serving on review panels can be mind-numbing and exhausting work, not to mention the fact that living out of a suitcase for weeks at a time eventually grows tedious. At the time, however, I had a very good reason for wanting to stay away from home; a reason that represented the biggest regret of my life. As a result, I accepted every opportunity my work schedule allowed to serve on the panels, traveling to every state in the union as well as Guam and Puerto Rico.

The travel gave me an excuse to avoid going home, but it also gave me great insight into how essential a properly written evaluation is to a soldier's career. Army National Guard members as well as Army Reserve members had a reputation for having inferior training and discipline, compared with active-duty soldiers. It was a frustrating legacy that had little basis in fact. Most Guard and Reserve members had been on active duty prior to switching to the part-time force, which meant their basic training and requirements were exactly the same. Still, the reputation endured, causing many reserve members to miss promotion and training opportunities and to suffer unfair comparisons to their active-duty counterparts.

Time and again, while serving on boards, I saw proof that a lack of expertise in writing NCO and officer evaluation reports was a major source of the problem when it came to assessing the suitability of one soldier over another. Many leaders simply couldn't write a decent evaluation or didn't understand the enduring importance their report would have on a service member's career.

I made it my mission to implement training objectives to improve every Guard member's skill in writing the reports. I spent several weeks and months training a corps of people and then sent them out across the country to discuss and hold seminars on the proper techniques. I spoke to groups at every opportunity, telling them that by skimping on the time they spent writing a proper evaluation, they could possibly cheat their soldiers of opportunities they deserved. Evaluation reports were not simply a required, annual review. They were documentation of what that individual had accomplished from one year to the next. Taken as a whole, they represented that person's potential. And poorly written evaluations reflected directly back on the leadership who signed off on them.

There were times when I felt like I was speaking to an empty room. NCOERs and OERs had long been a paper shuffle with everyone expecting to receive what appeared at first glance to be a glowing report, but in actuality was a litany of platitudes and code words. This battle was a difficult one, but I was determined to fight it. Eventually I saw personal evidence that some senior leaders had been listening.

While implementing these changes, I did a great deal of traveling. I was invited to speak about mentoring and diversity in the workplace at Guard events all over the country. I traveled to serve on a number of evaluation boards, for promotions, commands, for school selections and a host of other things. Teaching proper evaluation methods, ensuring the training was done properly—it all meant that I was away from home for extended periods of time.

And that was fine with me.

MY BIGGEST REGRET

I was in a profession that meant I was surrounded by men most days, but I never allowed myself to look at any of them as possible mates, nor had I allowed myself to be seen as someone dateable. I tried to stay coolly detached, being friendly and conversational, while never letting anyone into my intimate space. I was an Army officer. A professional. I never considered that I might, one day, want another man in my life, let alone that I could somehow become the object of a man's desire.

One man, someone I had been acquainted with for years, going all the way back to my early days at the New York Armory, a person who had asked me to go out with him a few times since my husband died, finally convinced me to give him a chance. Our first few dates were utterly pleasant and respectful. He had obviously planned them down to the last detail, keeping my wishes and tastes in mind. I was charmed by his attentiveness.

At first, things seemed good. It began as a long-distance relationship. He lived in New York, so for a year, we only saw each other every other weekend. Distance and time away can color everything in a positive light. When events cropped up that made me question things about his character, question the relationship, I was able to explain them away, assume the best and convince myself that I was mistaken and seeing monsters in the shadows. Then, just before we were to be married, it became clear that I had been mistaken about the true nature of the man

I was about to wed.

We were engaged and planning the details of our wedding when he confessed to something that shocked me. He reminded me of the anonymous letters I had received while I was a lieutenant at the New York Armory, letters that had disturbed me at the time and which I viewed as sexual harassment. Letters filled with inappropriate confessions of attraction to me, a married woman and mother of two.

"I wrote those letters," he confessed.

I didn't know what to say. All those years ago, when I was happily married to Gus and raising my two beautiful girls, he had held a secret attraction to me and thought anonymous letters were the appropriate way to further his cause.

"But you were married at the time," I said.

"I know, but I still loved you."

I remembered the contents of those letters. *I've watched you every day... I love the way you walk, the way you speak... I can't stop thinking about you... Just writing these words to you makes me feel better...*

They were shocking letters which, at the time, I thought were written by someone unstable. Even after I had demanded publicly to everyone at the Armory that the letters must stop, he had kept his secret—kept it for decades. He had watched me, he said, the way I raised my daughters, the relationship I had with my husband, and he wanted me for himself. "After your husband died, I wanted to take you in my arms and comfort you."

I should have taken his confession as my cue to run for the hills. I should have given the ring back, called all of my friends personally and told them the ceremony was off, but I didn't.

I hadn't even followed Ellen's advice. Early on, she had been just as charmed by him as I had been, and happy for me to have found someone special to share my life. About six months into the relationship, when we were still in a long distance association, she advised me to slow down, to take more time to get to know him. At that point, he'd begun to display traits that worried me. A moodiness that would come on unexpectedly, a tendency to pretend he didn't hear us when we spoke to him and a habit of saying disparaging things about people we knew, only to smile broadly and shake the same person's hand as if they were best of friends. That duplicity was a worrisome character flaw that I brushed off and tried to ignore.

He asked Ellen for her permission to propose to me, long before he and I had even discussed the prospect of marriage. She gave it, but she later told me she found it odd that he would ask her permission.

Despite my misgivings, we were married. And as the weeks and months of our marriage progressed, I would learn that his confession about the letters was only the beginning of many revelations that would completely change my view of the man.

I admit that my approach to dealing with the uncomfortable nature of our relationship was cowardly. My job required that I travel and I decided to take every opportunity to do so. I called my brother Larry and asked him if he would take care of Mother for a while.

"Just for a few months," I told him. "Just until my travel schedule slows down."

He agreed. When Mother was settled in a place where I knew she would be cared for, I hit the road and rarely looked back. My bags were constantly packed and ready to go. One day I overheard my deputy in the office: "I'll have to check Colonel Cleckley's schedule to see if she's available to travel at that time."

"I'll go, wherever it is!" I yelled from my office. "Schedule it. I can leave tomorrow."

On another occasion, my deputy called me in my Texas hotel and said, "They want you to go to Arizona."

Before he was even able to get the location out, I had already made up my mind.

"Okay, set it up," I commanded. "Do I have to go home first? Can you book the flight directly from here?"

There were days when I woke up and didn't know where I was. Night after night, I was in a different hotel, running to catch a flight and picking up rental cars. I called Ellen daily. She was my confidante and my rock. I'm not sure how I would have made it through my mistake without her help.

For more than a year, I lived on the road, trying to avoid going home, wanting to deny the massive mistake I had made. Eventually, I couldn't run from the truth any longer. I asked him to leave.

By this time, my nomination for promotion to brigadier general was before Congress. The last thing I wanted was a scandal. He didn't agree to the divorce immediately, but our lawyers eventually worked things out and we were divorced.

The marriage and engagement lasted about two and a half years. People who know me will obviously know the man I married, but I've purposely kept his name out of this book out of respect for his privacy. I consider his role in my world as a brief blip, a tragic misstep. I cringe at the memory of it, but like all other challenges I faced, I persevered and moved on.

EARNING THE STAR

The tall, lanky, painfully shy girl from Aliquippa could never have imagined that one day she would become a general officer in the United States Army. That timid creature didn't exist anymore. She disappeared after I put on my green uniform and entered the Women's Army Corps, serving three years of active duty during Vietnam. She became a distant memory as I rejoined the Army National Guard, earned my commission, rose through the ranks, and armed myself with training and experience, taking on one leadership role after another.

As Chief of the Personnel and Policy Division of the Army National Guard at the Bureau, I had shattered the glass ceiling in ways I never could have anticipated. Still the only woman, and the only black woman to ever hold such a position, the accomplishment couldn't be ignored. The silver wings of a full-bird colonel decorated my uniform, an achievement many of my peers never reached before they retired. At the time, I knew I wasn't done yet. There were more possibilities. More I could do, more I expected from myself. Others seemed to agree.

The Chief of the National Guard Bureau at the time was an Air Force three-star general. For a year and a half, he had been telling me, and anyone else who would listen, that he was going to nominate me for a star. He was the first African-American to hold the chief's position and he may have felt some responsibility toward ensuring other African-American officers were given opportunities. He would tell me and everyone else the nomination was imminent, but month after month went by without movement toward that goal.

One day I was called into the Army Guard Director's office for my annual Officer Evaluation Report. The director was my senior rater, the man who approved my OER. At the time, he was Major General Roger Schultz. We had an easy-going working relationship.

By this time, the Bureau had merged two divisions—Policy and Personnel Actions—into one division, and I was in charge of it. The size and complexity of these two large sections into one division, in addition to my duties with the diversity office, meant I had a lot of balls to juggle. Despite this, I tried to run my division quietly without getting Major General Schultz involved in the day-to-day problems that arose. It wasn't my way to copy him on every email or to ask him to step in to solve a problem for me unless it was something that obviously required his attention.

By this time, I had served on more promotion and evaluation boards than I could count, racking up thousands of frequent flyer miles, reading hundreds upon hundreds of promotion packets and evaluation reports. I could identify the difference between a good evaluation and one that was thrown together with little regard for the individual. I had made it my mission to train others in the proper way to write and evaluate soldiers using the system. I could easily say that, when it came to Army evaluation reports, I was an expert at them.

During my training, it had been my mission to attempt to make the OER reflect a true evaluation of performance. While training other officers, I attempted to explain that, by automatically giving everyone an Outstanding Performance rating—a top block—we were penalizing those who really were doing outstanding work and rewarding those who deserved much lower ratings. In essence, we were simply reinforcing the notion that one didn't have to do well to get promoted. One only had to not screw up too badly. The practice of giving everyone a top block rating rendered the OER a useless document.

A satisfactory rating—a two block—could be just as effective as a one block especially if the description of the performance reflected the true nature of the work done and not a bunch of empty words that were dreamed up to fill a page.

So when Major General Shultz showed me that I had received a two block rather than the top block, I was rather pleased. He had obviously listened to me. The narratives he wrote to describe my performance were excellent and, I felt, truly reflected the work I was doing.

"Thank you, sir. I think this is great."

"You're not upset that you didn't get the top block?"

"Of course not. It's the words that make the difference with this new system."

He leaned back, a bit surprised. "You know, I have to rate all of the adjutant generals in all of the fifty-four states and territories, and senior rate every senior-ranking division chief. You're the first person who has reacted this way. Most officers think that getting a two block is the end of their career. There are tears and temper tantrums, people falling on the floor."

He was laughing a bit, but I knew he was telling the truth. I had seen the same sort of reactions myself. Falsely inflated evaluations had, over the years, become part of the culture. Everyone seemed to know and accept that an evaluation wasn't a true reflection of an officer's or enlisted person's performance. Creative writers revealed truly bad performance in code words and phrases. The practice, in my opinion, reduced the evaluations from a valuable management tool to nothing more than a joke. I was determined to do my part to change that.

"I know, sir. It's unfortunate. Which is why I've made such an effort to inform the ranks about the proper way to provide evaluations. To be honest, this is the first time in a long time that I've not been given the top block, but I think what you've given me is excellent. It's obvious that you put great thought into the narrative. The words are more important than the number with this system."

He stared at me for a few long seconds.

"You know, I've been hearing the chief talk about putting you in for a star. Has he done that?"

"He calls me once in a while on the red phone and tells me he's still working on it, but nothing definitive has been done."

"I'm not only pleased with the work you're doing managing all of personnel and policies. I also applaud the progress you're making in the area of improving diversity in the Guard. And since you work directly for me, I'd like to make you a general," he said.

I hesitated for a second, trying not to get too excited about the notion. "Well, sir. I'm very flattered. I wouldn't object."

"Do you think the chief would be upset?"

"I don't know, sir, but like I said, I'm sure nothing definitive has been done by his office."

"Well, we're going to fix that right now."

While I sat there, he picked up the phone and called the adjutant general in the state of New York.

"General Fenimore? General Schultz, here. Listen, I've got Colonel Cleckley in my office. I'd like you to nominate her for a star, but the caveat is this: I want her to stay at the bureau and work for me."

In the Army National Guard, the state adjutant general or TAG is responsible for general officer nominations. At the time, the New York TAG was Major General John Fenimore. General Fenimore had to start the nomination process. General Fenimore must have agreed to General Schultz's terms because the next thing I heard was General Schultz saying, "Okay, great. We'll get that paperwork started right away."

They exchanged a few more pleasantries and Schultz hung up the phone.

"Now, Julia, you get Major Etzel in here right away. I assume he'll be the one you want working on your packet for you."

"Yes, sir."

Major Roger Etzel was my right-hand man and had been with me for several years. He was someone I counted on. I knew I could trust him with such an important responsibility.

"Well, get him in here today so we can get started on that packet. I want to get this thing rolling right away."

"Yes, sir. I'll send him down."

I left General Schultz's office feeling a bit dazed. The call to New York and putting the packet together were only the first steps on what I knew would be a long road. Generals aren't made overnight. The packet had to jump a long line of hurdles before the final vote of approval from the Senate. Still, the process had begun and I couldn't help but feel proud of the possibility that I could be promoted.

Ellen, of course, was one of the first people I told. "That's great, Mom! A general! That's fantastic."

The other person I had to tell was the man I had been married to for two years. My second husband was a retired brigadier general himself. I had learned fairly quickly that any career success I achieved rankled him. I knew he would view my nomination as some sort of threat to him and the accomplishments of his career. Retirement wasn't sitting well with him. There was every possibility that my news would make him feel inadequate because his military career was over. Most people, upon retiring from the military, find another career to pursue. He was in his early sixties, plenty of time to work in some other capacity, if he could only find something that interested him. So far that hadn't happened and he was ashamed of his lack of progress. He often assumed that I had a negative opinion of him because he wasn't working. His assumptions were ridiculous, but nothing I could say convinced him otherwise. News of my nomination would cause unwanted and unnecessary conflict, so I kept it to myself as long as I could. He knew several of my co-workers, so keeping it a secret wasn't possible, but I still held back the news. Eventually, I did tell him and he was predictably cool about it. I didn't let him ruin my joy.

As the weeks and months wore on, I feared that drama from the tension in my marriage might derail my nomination. My husband was unpredictable and sometimes volatile. He wasn't violent, but I honestly never knew what he might do next, how he might react to things I said or did. Our brief marriage needed to end, but I waited. As soon as the nomination made it through the Senate, I planned to take steps to correct the mistake I had made. In the meantime, I traveled as much as I could, avoided spending too much time with him, and hoped I could hold out until after the Senate approval process had finalized the recommendation.

While I waited for senate confirmation, I was given a new job. I went from being a division chief to being in charge of all of personnel, the G1. I was not only the first female, black or white, to serve as a division chief, I was the only black officer on the entire G-staff—the only black director in the Army Guard at the bureau. In fact, during the entire time I served as the G1, I was the only black person sitting in the weekly chief-of-staff meetings.

In addition to being the G1, I was charged with developing an office with the goal of bringing more diversity to the force. The experience I had gained over my entire active-duty career prepared me well for the position and I had a long list of improvements I wanted to make. Changes were happening, but they were happening at a snail's pace. Primarily, I wanted to change the Army National Guard's reputation for being an all-white male club. I was definitely in a position to help change that reputation.

In March of 2002, my divorce was finalized. It was such a relief to have that chapter of my life over and done with that the girls and I decided to celebrate. We took a trip to Disney World and the three of us lived it up for an entire week. Ending the brief marriage felt like a huge weight off my shoulders. After that relaxing vacation, I came back to the office ready to work and ready to plan a grand promotion ceremony.

And grand it was. In September 2002, Lieutenant General Schultz presided over the event in which the silver stars were pinned to my uniform. All of my siblings attended. Friends old and new came from all over to witness the big event. The ceremony and reception were an unforgettable way to celebrate my achievement.

Now my task list as a general officer grew longer. I was Special Assistant to the Director of the Army National Guard, Lieutenant General Schultz, who was a champion of diversity. His agenda was simple: work to ensure that the uniformed service members in the Army National Guard reflect the diversity of our nation. The Army National Guard, as a reflection of the rest of the nation, should be a beautiful patchwork quilt that is America, comprised of soldiers who are men, women, Native American, African-American, Hispanic, Asian, Caucasian and every other race, creed or ethnicity. That was General Schultz's vision and I was the person he tapped to implement that vision.

We began the initiative by issuing a proclamation that reflected his total commitment to the diversity effort and enlisted every Adjutant General in every state and the U.S. territories to agree to the wording and support the initiative. It took months of coordination on my part, hours on the phone, and personal visits to office after office, working to get everyone to buy into the idea. I racked up thousands of frequent flyer miles as I and my staff flew from one state to the next to discuss the long-term goals and to ensure everyone was on board.

Finally, after tons of rewrites and changes, we had a proclamation that clearly stated the diversity goals of the National Guard leadership. The Proclamation read:

> *The Chief, National Guard Bureau; Director, Army National Guard; Director Air National Guard; and Adjutants General*

are committed to Diversity Initiatives. The fundamental goal of Diversity Initiatives is to set the tone for our leadership to create an organizational culture where diversity is valued as a personnel readiness, combat multiplier contingent upon high performance.

Then the Proclamation listed several ways in which diversity would be implemented, including:

Diversity will enhance the recruiting and retention of highly qualified National Guard soldiers, airmen, their families, and their civilian employers.

Diversity of thought at all levels of the organization will position the National Guard to remain on the cutting edge of personnel management as America's Employer of Choice.

Once the proclamation was signed, we turned our efforts to organizing training to ensure the importance of diversity was taught and ingrained into the National Guard culture. Again, I hit the road, pushing training, encouraging leadership, speaking before large audiences to publicly state our goals. We wanted the National Guard of the 21st century to be different from the all-male, all-white Guard of the past, and I spent much of my time as a general officer working toward that goal.

RETIREMENT

My mother's health was an increasing source of worry for me. Home health care workers ensured she was well cared for, but there was no getting around the fact that our time with her was growing short. Much of my time was spent traveling the country speaking about equality, women's issues and the new Army National Guard initiatives. I was growing increasingly tired of being away from home much of the time. I knew that sooner or later, something had to give.

We were on a plane traveling somewhere when I finally decided to let Lieutenant General Schultz, the Director of the Army National Guard, know about my plan. I moved up the aisle of the plane and sat next to him.

"Sir, I've decided I need to spend more time with my mother. I've decided to retire by next September."

"Wait a minute, Julia. I was going to talk to you about nominating you for your second star."

It should have been exciting news, but it wasn't. Another star would mean a commitment of at least another year or two to the military. I wanted and needed to spend more time with my mom, and another two or more years seemed like an eternity.

"I'm sorry, sir. I appreciate your confidence in me, but I'm going to have to say no. We're a nation at war. You should give that star to one of these combat commanders."

"I don't suppose there's any way I can convince you to reconsider."

"No, sir. I've made up my mind. Please know that the star you pinned on my shoulder is beyond the dreams I had for this career and I will always be grateful to you for giving me the opportunity to be all that I can be."

Even though I had made the decision, retirement was something I had to plan for. I needed several months to go through all of the paperwork and steps leading to the end of my military career. I scheduled my retirement date for September 2004.

By this time, my mother's health was rapidly declining. Although Mom was getting fulltime home health care, she would stubbornly try to get things for herself and often would end up falling and hurting herself. She had diabetes, she would forget things, become confused and disoriented, and her general deterioration was a constant worry.

Ellen was aware of the changes and viewed every moment with her grandmother as more and more precious. Eventually, she was making the trip from San Francisco to Virginia so often it was becoming impossible to keep up with the schedule.

"I'm too far away, Mom," she said to me one day. "I know you and Dad loved San Francisco and I love my little apartment, but I'm tired of flying back and forth. I want to come back."

"Honey, you can come back anytime you want to," I said.

So she moved back. She encouraged me to end the evening-to-morning respite care for her grandmother, saying, "I'm here now, Momma. I can take care of her."

I took great pleasure in having those two women in my home. We enjoyed each other's company a lot. For the most part, our lives were harmonious.

Ellen and I had so many plans for my post-retirement life. She wanted to help me establish a business so that I could continue to do speaking engagements. I was often asked to speak to groups about the issues of diversity and women in the military. Ellen wanted to be a part of scheduling my time to ensure that, during months like Black History Month, Women's History Month, I could get the maximum use out of my schedule. In addition, she planned to set up a foundation in her father's name to do community work, and she wanted to write a book about me.

"Mom, your story is important. We *have* to write a book."

Ellen was an excellent writer. It seemed logical that she would be the one to tell my story.

"But just so you know, I've got to be able to do my own thing," she said. "I'm not just going to work for you."

She had writing goals of her own; she wanted to continue to teach and she wanted to travel. I had no problem letting her do what she could to reach any goal she wanted.

As I got closer to my retirement date, people approached me with job offers. Most of them were government contractors, hoping for input from a retired general officer, someone to serve on their staff, someone with the credentials to give them influence. They came in with pitches using my picture with a fancy title alongside their logo, plying me with compliments in hope that I would sign on. One particularly tempting job offer was a position in the personnel field with great money and a convenient location. Ellen was completely against my taking another job.

"Mom, don't sign any contracts. You were going to relax and do speaking engagements. I have to write your book. Don't take another job, please!"

She even began to cry, she was so desperate for me to listen to her. I had been working all of my life, from the time when I was a little girl running errands for Mrs. Greenwood. The reality that I suddenly wouldn't have a job to go to every day was sometimes a bit frightening. I laugh at it now, but at the time, I wondered what I would do with myself, if I would go crazy looking for things to do.

I made the decision to retire so that I could devote more time to my family, to spend time with my mother during her final years, to relax and enjoy time with my girls. It was a difficult decision. Somehow, I feel as if God had a hand in that decision, because only He could have known that I was about to be thrown the biggest curveball of my life.

In May, four months before I was to retire, Ellen came to me one morning while I was getting ready for work.

"Mom, what do you think this is?" She pointed to a lump on her thigh.

I sometimes wonder if I should have known immediately how serious that question was. It was so similar to the question her father had asked me, casually wondering about the lump on *his* thigh, unaware of the way the small thing would affect our lives. But I wasn't alarmed. For one thing, the lump didn't look anything like what was on Gus's thigh. It looked more like a small hernia, a strange looking fatty deposit.

But I question myself to this day. Was I so wrapped up in my retirement plans and worried about my mother that I couldn't see that lump for the threat that it was? Why didn't I make the connection between Ellen's lump and Gus's?

"I don't know, baby," I said. "How long has it been there?"

She shrugged, neither of us thinking about the significance.

"Well, we'd better make an appointment for you to see a doctor," I said.

Ellen shook her head. "It's just a fat pocket. I don't need to see a doctor."

Eventually I did convince her to see a doctor, but the results of that effort were insignificant. They didn't know what it was—a fatty deposit, a muscle strain or hernia, nothing to be alarmed about.

A few weeks later, Ellen pointed to the same lump again and said, "Mom, I felt a sharp pain that started at the lump and went all the way down my leg."

Pain? That alarmed me. It couldn't be a fatty deposit if she felt pain. It had to be something more serious. I used my command voice and wasn't about to hear any excuses.

"We're going to the doctor tomorrow. We're going to find out what that is."

I had a full schedule the next day, including going to the Pentagon to participate in the ceremony to promote a friend, and flying out of state to attend a funeral. Neither appointment could be canceled, but I was going to make whatever schedule adjustments necessary to ensure Ellen got to the doctor.

First thing in the morning, I dropped Ellen off at the emergency room at Alexandria Hospital and then rushed off to the Pentagon for the promotion ceremony. As soon as that was done, I rushed back to the hospital and found Ellen still sitting in the waiting room reading a magazine.

"Why are you still sitting here?"

"They ran some tests and asked me to wait," she said.

I spent some time telling the nurses that my daughter had been waiting a long time, but I still had to go home to gather my things for my out-of-state trip. I rushed home, changed clothes, picked up my luggage, then returned to the hospital to see what was going on.

Ellen was in radiology having x-rays, so I asked the doctor about her status.

"I've just finished conducting some tests, General Cleckley. Ellen's such a lovely girl. She's being very brave about this. We think it might be a sarcoma, so I'm sending her to Washington Hospital for more tests."

All I had to hear was that 'coma' ending and I knew she was talking about something much more serious than we had imagined.

"Are you saying that my daughter has cancer?" I whispered past the lump in my throat.

"Don't panic. We don't know that for sure. There are still tests we need to run. We'll send her to the cancer center at Washington Hospital and we'll know more after that."

"Did you tell my daughter what you thought it was?"

"Yes, she knows what we're dealing with."

When Ellen came back from the x-ray, she acted as if it was just another day.

"Hey, Mom," she said.

"Did the doctor tell you what was going on?"

"Yes. I have to go for more tests."

"Well, I'll cancel my trip and—"

"No, Mom. Go on your trip. I'll be okay. My appointment is two days from now, so it's no big deal."

Part of me wanted to argue with her, and the mother in me wanted to keep her from knowing how frightened I was. Despite her hours in the hospital, going through tests and waiting, she looked beautiful, healthy. Her long black hair was thick and curly; the kinds of curls women spend hundreds of dollars and hours in the salon to achieve. Hers were natural. Her fair skin was a smooth, nut brown with no blemishes and almost invisible pores. She was tall like me and her father, and slender, the kind of young woman who turned heads wherever she went. As I looked into her bright eyes that day, it was difficult to imagine there was anything wrong with her.

My trip was a two-day visit to San Francisco. As much as I didn't want to leave her, it was a funeral I felt I needed to attend.

Several years earlier, after I had been promoted to lieutenant colonel, I was invited to become a member of a group called Top Ladies of Distinction, an organization of professional and community-minded women who perform services for humanitarian causes. The president of the chapter I belonged to had died of cancer and, if it was in my power, I needed to be at her funeral.

The irony of that funeral wasn't lost on me. The entire time I was there, mourning a great woman who had died of cancer, all I could think about was the possibility that Ellen had the deadly disease, too. It was a killer that had already touched my life once. I prayed that the diagnosis was wrong, that even if it was cancer, it would be something we could beat. That day, standing in the chapel, being reminded of the reality of what cancer can do, my prayers began. I never stopped praying for many, many months.

When I returned home, Ellen had already been for her tests. The results would be available in a few days. At the appointed time, we returned to the hospital together and learned the news.

I had come to the appointment wearing my uniform, having left the office to pick Ellen up. Everyone in my office knew that I was taking my daughter to the doctor. My aide, Major Roger Etzel, knew just how serious this appointment was. I was only months away from retirement, a decision that seemed more and more like something fated, as if I had prior knowledge that I needed to immediately spend more time with my daughter.

"Don't worry, ma'am. We'll take care of things here," he said. "You go be with your daughter."

Standing there with my general's stars on my shoulders at the Washington Hospital Cancer Center, feeling powerless, I clutched Ellen's hand, using all of my will to stay calm, as the doctor confirmed the diagnosis of sarcoma. He said they wanted to send her to National Institutes of Health in Bethesda, Maryland for additional tests to determine the proper treatment. We left the hospital after asking a rash of questions and making appointments to see other specialists.

I felt dazed. Ellen and I walked close together as we made our way through the antiseptic halls of the hospital, people going about their business, the frequent *Good morning, ma'ams* all but ignored. Everyone was busily moving from place to place as if everything in the world were normal.

We stepped through the automatic doors, into the light of day, the first of hundreds of times I would walk in and out of those doors. It was June 2004 and our relationship with that hospital had only begun.

We made our way to the parking lot, and just as we were getting into the car to leave, the doctor called me on my cell phone. He asked us to come back to the office. I must admit, I felt a stab of hope—there must have been a mistake! The test results were mixed up with someone else. Ellen didn't have cancer. It was all just one big terrible mistake. Hope inflated me, buoyed me as we made our way back to the office. I didn't tell Ellen how much hope I felt, but I think she may have felt it, too.

"We've just received the results of the MRI," the doctor said. "We've found a small dot on Ellen's lung which leads us to believe the cancer may have already metastasized."

And just like that, the air was sucked out of the room. Hope leaked out of me like an untied balloon, sputtering and slow, but unstoppable.

"Can't you just cut my leg off? Just cut it off!" Ellen said. It was a horrible thing to contemplate, but suddenly it made the most sense to both of us. We looked at the doctor hopefully.

"If it's already spread, cutting your leg off wouldn't do any good. And besides, that's not something that we do. We'll need to treat the cancer to shrink the lump and get rid of the bit in your lung. Once we have things under control, we'll try to remove the lump."

In September, with the shadow of my daughter's illness hanging over our heads, I retired. Like all military ceremonies, the retirement ceremony is a traditional affair. A nation thanks the soldier for service and the soldier says goodbye to colleagues. I had attended many during my career and always found them to be respectful and emotional. The huge event took place at the Bureau and at ceremonial hall on Fort Myer, next to Arlington National Cemetery. My brothers Larry and Mickey and Mickey's wife Susan, my sister Bobbie, Ellen, Helene and my niece Lisa were all in the VIP section along with prominent officers from the

Pentagon and the National Guard Bureau. Old friends from Aliquippa and San Francisco also made the trip to be part of the festivities.

Lt. Col. Roger Etzel and his wife, along with Lt. Col. Al Durr and my friend Marybeth, had worked together and taken over the planning of the retirement ceremony. They had done a fantastic job. Their involvement released me from the need to worry about it, which was a very good thing because there were so many other things on my mind—the trips to the doctor, the nights in the hospital. Those final four months of my military career had been a blur of meetings scheduled around medical appointments for both Ellen and my mother, because my mother's health, which had prompted me to retire in the first place, was deteriorating as well.

One tradition of the ceremony is to recognize and present the spouse of the retiring soldier with flowers. Major Etzel had arranged that the flowers be presented to Ellen. The presentation is an acknowledgement of the role the spouse plays in support of the soldier throughout a military career. Ellen had played that role for me, acting as my sounding board, taking care of things at home when I was required to travel, offering her support the entire way. It was only right that she be recognized for the role she played in my successful career.

Row upon row of soldiers stood in formation on the parade field, flags waving as a military band played traditional marching songs. At the end of the program, the final Pass and Review was conducted. The platoons of soldiers marched across the parade field. Just as they reached me, standing with the other dignitaries, the officer at the front of the formation, wearing white gloves and a ceremonial sword, brought his sword up in front of his face in the parade salute and yelled the command, "Eyes right!"

Every head snapped in our direction. The soldiers marched by, erect, in perfect step, beautiful to behold. The marching band brought up the rear, maneuvering until they were directly in front of me. The drum major, with his tall, white, ostrich feather helmet, spun his long, gold-tipped baton, directing the band. As the final song drew to a close, the drum major stood at perfect attention and rendered me a slowly measured salute, the traditional last salute of my military career.

The ceremony was quite moving—one I will never forget. For many of my friends who came to celebrate with me, it was the first full military ceremony they had ever seen. They were probably surprised by the way the military pulls out all of the stops to recognize the service of a general.

The next day, at my retirement luncheon, Ellen addressed the crowd. She didn't use any notes, simply spoke from her heart, poised and calm as she stood there before so many people. Knowing she would lose it anyway, she had cut off her beautiful hair. She wore a wig that was similar to her own hair but could never replace the natural luxury of her long beautiful tresses. Still, she looked beautiful.

Of all the things I prayed for in those weeks and months, I was most grateful that I made the decision to retire when I did.

HOSPITALS AND DOCTORS

Failure was not an option for Ellen. I knew she would confront her cancer challenge with her usual determination to succeed. The frightening thing was that her intelligence, talent and beauty would have little to do with her survival.

When we received the news that the cancer had already metastasized, we went directly to the NIH where more tests were conducted. We waited four days for the results—four days that seemed an eternity. I went from home to work and back again, feeling more zombie-like than human. Worry is a physical thing. A knot in your stomach makes you want to fold in on yourself. If you could only reach inside and pluck it out, crush it with your fist, things would be better, but it's impossible. Such endless frustration. I couldn't help but think of Gus during those days. He was in my thoughts almost constantly as I worried about our child.

Lisa began making frequent trips from her home in Ohio to Virginia to help care for my mom and Ellen and to give me a chance to rest. Her visits were always welcomed. Lisa had her own trials and tribulations: she had two sons of her own, one getting ready for college and the other in his junior year of high school; her second marriage had failed and her mother continued to be resentful that she spent time with me and my family. But caring for her grandmother and spending time with us seemed to make her happy.

"I feel loved here," she said to me one day.

"You're always welcome and you *are* loved. You'll always have a roof over your head," I said.

I appreciated her help, but I mostly enjoyed her company. I now had a house full of women, women who loved each other's companionship. We shared laughter, love and patience with each other even though Mom and Ellen were sick. I could understand why Lisa visited so often.

The doctors had confirmed the cancer and the type—soft-tissue sarcoma, and now we waited to see what treatment they would use to fight it. After the interminable wait, we learned that the treatment needed to be as aggressive as she could handle. That June of 2004, she was checked into the hospital for a three-day series of chemotherapy and radiology treatments that sapped her energy and made her sick. It was the first three-day stay of many to follow.

Through those first days of tests and uncertainty, Ellen managed to keep her spirits up, to face the diagnosis bravely. She wrote a wonderful letter to family and friends to tell them what was going on, asking for their prayers and making light of the gravity of her condition.

> I was diagnosed with CANCER – specifically, soft-tissue SARCOMA in my right thigh. And to think…I used to complain about cellulite! Sarcomas, which represent less than one percent of all types of cancerous tumors, are considered quite stubborn. But so TOO am I!

Every other week for several months, the two of us checked into the hospital so that Ellen could undergo another three days of treatments. I stayed with her, spending the nights in a bed next to hers, holding her hand as the toxic chemicals were pumped through her veins.

When her hair began to come out in clumps, she said, "Mom, help me pull this hair out."

I was horrified. I was willing to do anything for my baby, but pulling her hair out seemed barbaric. Still she kept asking, "Mom, come here and help me."

I simply couldn't do it. She soon cropped it down very short, leaving a fuzzy blanket on her head. Her hair had always been so beautiful. Thick and long. Soft and curly. To see her without her signature locks was disheartening. And I regret, I so regret, that I didn't have the courage to help her with it.

Two weeks after my retirement ceremony, after she had delivered such a wonderful speech, the doctors decided the cancer had shrunk enough that they could attempt to remove it. The surgery was successful, and they were able to remove the tumor in her leg, but they continued the chemotherapy treatments, hoping that the chemical cocktail would rid her of the rest of the cancer.

"Mom, you've taken care of Grandma so long," she said one day. "You've cared for Helene all these years, and now you're taking care of me. You must be sick of all of this."

"No, you're my baby. This is my life. How could I be sick of it? Besides, I'm just glad I retired when I did so I can spend every day with you."

The treatments were hard on Ellen. What was supposed to help her seemed to be draining the life out of her. Each treatment made her weaker. It wasn't long before she was in a wheelchair, connected to an oxygen tank and barely able to move around on her own. Still, friends visited her often and she went out with me occasionally, sometimes to dinners or visiting. While Ellen's treatments were taking their toll, my mother's health continued to worsen.

Lisa visited often, driving more than five hours each way to help care for Ellen and to ensure that my mother got to her doctor appointments. Complications with my mother's diabetes medications and treatments had made her dangerously ill. We couldn't provide the constant care she required. I had never considered a nursing home for her, but her deteriorating situation forced me to find a place that would provide the round-the-clock care she needed. We managed to find a wonderful rehabilitation nursing home just minutes from my house. Two days after I retired, we moved my mother there.

Having two family members who are critically ill at the same time is almost impossible to manage. I needed help. Lisa did everything she could, but I had to call friends from time to time. Majors Durr and Etzel, as well as Major Etzel's wife Marybeth Marybeth, saved the day on more than one occasion. At one point, I was with Ellen in the hospital for an outpatient chemotherapy session when I received a call from the nursing home that my mother was critically ill. They wanted to admit her to the hospital. I had just been to see her that morning and had alerted the nurses that I thought she wasn't looking very healthy—her gray coloring and listless, borderline unresponsive behavior was alarming to me.

Ellen's treatment that day was almost complete, but after chemo she needed to be watched closely for adverse reactions. Who would do that while I went to see about my mother?

"Marybeth, my mother's sick," I said when I called her. "Can you stay with Ellen while I go to the emergency room?"

"Of course," she said. "I'll be right there."

I took Ellen home, gave Marybeth the instructions she needed, then raced to the emergency room to see about my mom. Her condition was indeed grave. I spent a couple of hours, calling my siblings, telling them that the doctors had decided they needed to amputate her leg because of complications from the diabetes. Marybeth continued to stay with Ellen until one o'clock in the morning, even though she needed go to work the next day.

Those were terrible days. I suffered from lack of sleep since the little time I did have for sleep was crowded with worry over my daughter and my mother. The hectic schedule meant I didn't even have time to get my car serviced, and several times it broke down. When that happened, Major Etzel would come to the rescue. At one point, he gave me the keys to one of his own cars. "Just take it, ma'am. Bring it back when things settle down."

I marvel now at how much Roger Etzel did for me. He had worked for me, yes, and he went on to assist me with so many things in my personal life, after my retirement. Etzel, his family and other folks in my military family, along with so many old friends had stepped up to help, but they couldn't do everything.

One day, while I sat with Ellen in the hospital, she complained that her hand was shaking.

"It's so strange," she said. "I can't control it."

Moments later, her eyes rolled back in her head and her body jerked uncontrollably. I knew it was a seizure because I had witnessed Helene's seizures.

"Help!" I yelled. "Someone help me."

Later, Ellen told me that she was completely aware of everything going on—my scream for help, the nurses rushing in, the prick of the needle as they administered the medication. She also told me, as if it were a gift she had been given, that having the seizure gave her an understanding of what her sister goes through when she has them.

Almost seven months after she was first diagnosed, in late October and early November of 2004, the seizures, far from being any sort of gift for her, were a devastating sign. That first seizure prompted further tests, which showed that the cancer had now metastasized to her brain.

The sickness, the treatments, the worry went on for months and months. How can a mother describe what it is to watch her daughter deteriorate before her eyes? So many people tried to offer comfort, so many came to visit and to help. Their kindness and thoughtfulness meant a lot to us.

Ellen's cousin and best friend Nicole visited from Philadelphia whenever she could. The girls would huddle together just as they did when they were younger, healthier and could plan their futures. They had been close since childhood and they talked on the phone often.

My old high school friend from Aliquippa, Blanche Roberts, and her husband Rob, lived in Newport News, Virginia. Ellen knew Blanche and Rob well and fondly called them Aunt Blanche and Uncle Rob. Blanche made the drive from Newport News to Alexandria to visit Ellen several times over the months of her illness. Visits from old friends like Blanche, their prayers and friendship helped me get through those difficult days.

Ellen's dog Gidget, a miniature schnauzer, at first brought lots of comfort, but as her illness grew worse and her treatments prevented her from cuddling Gidget, Ellen asked her Uncle Mickey and Aunt Susan to take Gidget to their home. When they visited, they always brought Gidget along. In small doses, Gidget brought joy to Ellen.

Still, the hospitals and doctors, the needles and the pain seemed ceaseless and I was left feeling powerless.

ELLEN

Ellen had always been intensely serious about her studies, about doing things the right way, about working as hard as she could once she made up her mind. While in high school, she applied for an exchange program that would take her to Japan for a summer semester. It was something she was determined to do and she spent hours on the application, ensuring everything was perfect, including the essay she was required to write about why she wanted to participate.

I was out of town at the time on a work trip and Lisa was staying with Ellen. Lisa called me in the middle of the night. "Aunt Judy, I'm worried about Ellen. She's still up. She's been working on this application for hours. She keeps reading it to me over and over again and I keep telling her its good, but she won't listen to me."

"That's just the way Ellen is," I said. "She'll go to bed when she knows she has it right."

I wasn't surprised when Ellen was accepted to the program and spent a life-altering semester living with a Japanese family in Tokyo. She came back from that experience much more mature than when she left, her bags filled with Japanese art and her mind filled with a new perspective on life. I still have those pieces of Japanese art in my house, and each one reminds me of Ellen.

Everything my daughter tried she not only succeeded at but excelled at. She faced every challenge with drive and determination, the same determination she drew on now as she fought her cancer.

By this time, Ellen had dark circles under her eyes and her once flawless skin was mottled and grey, a beautiful young woman bent under the weight of her illness. At home, she wasn't able to move around much, but she didn't want to be confined to her bed. We agreed that having her sequestered away from all the activities in our home would only make her feel worse. So I bundled her up and we went furniture shopping. She moved slowly through the stores, pulling her oxygen tank with her as she tried out different chairs, looking for the right piece, eventually finding a beautiful, overstuffed blue recliner she could sit and nap in throughout the day. That chair was so comfortable she even enjoyed spending the night in it, snuggled in her overstuffed throne.

Throughout the day, she lounged comfortably in her chair. At night, I found I had trouble relaxing, always worried that she would need me in the wee small hours of the morning. I brought home a baby monitor, leaving the transmitter part near her chair and placing the receiving speaker next to my bed. Oh, how she hated that monitor!

"Turn that thing off, Mom! You don't need to be listening all the time."

"But I just want to make sure you're okay."

"You need to get your own rest. Stop worrying about me all the time."

She was always telling me to rest, to relax, to not worry, but of course that was impossible. My own eyes had dark circles. Between my worries about my mother and those for my daughter, sleep was elusive. Exhaustion was a weight I felt down to my bones. Still, I never would have forgiven myself if she needed me during the night and I didn't hear her call for help. I kept that baby monitor on.

"We'd like to perform gamma knife surgery," the doctor said. "It's a non-invasive way to perform brain surgery using a precision beam, like a laser, to remove the cancer."

When the doctor explained the latest procedure to us, she went over a long list of possible side effects, all of them frightening. But I felt we had no choice except to follow the doctor's advice, so we agreed to try it.

Just a few weeks before Christmas of 2004, Ellen underwent the procedure. Lieutenant Colonel Etzel came along with us to the hospital to be by my side. Despite the fact that they were operating on her brain, the surgery didn't require an overnight stay and we took her home, still filled with hope that this Christmas wouldn't be our last one together. The doctor told me immediately following the operation that they weren't able to cut out the entire mass, but with continued daily radiation treatments, there was still hope they could stop the spread of the disease.

"Take her out. Do the things that she likes to do," the doctor said, when she had me alone.

"I don't want to hear that," I said. "You sound like you're giving her a death sentence."

"It's just that, we couldn't get it all and you should take this time—"

"I'm not listening to this," I said. "I want you to do everything you can. Do you understand me?"

"Of course. You know that we will. It's just that she should try to do things she enjoys while she can."

I never told Ellen about that conversation, choosing to prevent her from worrying about such things. At home afterwards, there was more bad news.

"Mom, I can't move my arm," she said to me the next day. It was one of the possible side effects of the surgery. They had warned us that she could lose the ability to speak, that she might not remember things, a whole list of horrifying possibilities we chose not to think about.

"The effects could be temporary," the doctor said when I called. "Just keep an eye on her and let me know if the condition worsens."

As frightening as the paralysis was, Ellen seemed in good spirits, tired and frail, but talkative and laughing, making jokes, teasing. Friends and family came by for holiday visits. She stayed engaged with the company, enjoying having people around, often looking wistful, as if knowing this could be her last holiday season and wanting to drink in every moment of it.

Lisa continued to be a big help, flying back and forth from Ohio, staying with us on weekends, even while her own job and family obligations were stressful.

The fear I carried around inside me had taken on a different presence. No longer was it simply fear of her leaving, of her dying. I now feared she would lose any quality to the life she had left. Seeing her so frail, the devastating sickness she felt from each treatment, the ever-present pain she tried to fight through, were all small tortures in themselves. Each treatment, each procedure seemed to worsen her condition, not improve it. I wondered how much more her fragile body could take.

Then, on Christmas Day, she was able to use her arm again.

"Look, Mom. I can move it again." She grinned like a small child who had accomplished a new feat. And I applauded her small victory in a struggle that seemed never-ending.

Two days after Christmas, Ellen wasn't feeling well so I took her to the Washington Hospital emergency room. Helene had come down from New York to spend the holiday with us and was patient with us while the staff went through the lengthy admission process.

I was grateful that Ellen had been well enough to celebrate Christmas Day at home, but she was too ill to be home for the rest of the holiday. Ellen sweetly complimented Helene for being so patient and brave while spending so much time in the hospital. I spent New Year's Eve and New Year's Day in the hospital. Most patients had been discharged so they could be home with their families. The building felt strangely empty and quiet while we were there. After the holiday, we said our goodbyes to Helene and she returned home to New York.

After that, Ellen and I had plenty of time to talk, laugh and pray. We spent *a lot* of time praying. The assistant pastor of our church, Reverend

Faye Gunn, often visited with Ellen, praying with us and offering her comforting support. Ellen and Faye were sorority sisters, so it was easy for Ellen to confide in her and receive spiritual guidance.

Perhaps it was Reverend Gunn's comfort that led Ellen to renew her campaign for me to become part of the Alpha Kappa Alpha sorority. Ellen had brought the subject up before, but now, with Reverend Gunn nearby, Ellen broached the subject again. Even after she was released from the hospital, she didn't give up trying to persuade me to become a member.

"Mamma, it's not too late. You can be an Alpha Kappa Alpha and then we'll be sorority sisters."

Joining a sorority while my daughter fought for her life seemed like the last thing I should worry about. To Ellen, however, it was important and the more I thought about it, the more it seemed like something I could do to make my daughter happy. And so in March of 2005, I was initiated into the Alpha Kappa Alpha Sorority, Incorporated.

Lisa told me later how difficult it had been for Ellen to muster up the strength to get out of bed, get dressed, get in and out of the car and into her wheelchair. She had almost given up, but she was determined to come to the celebration.

She had lost so much weight and there were dark circles under her eyes. The oxygen tubes across her face only enhanced her sickly pallor. It was torturous for me to smile as I stood with the other women, the ladies on either side of me clutching my hands in support, knowing how difficult the sight of her was for me to take. It was a happy occasion for all of them. For me, it was bittersweet.

Beyond doubt, the effort was worth it. Ellen was so proud that we could share being mother/daughter sisters and part of this wonderful organization. The friendship of Joyce Henderson and the other members was a tremendous help while we battled through the final stages of Ellen's illness.

The sorority events and causes continue to be a major part of my life. I look at my Alpha Kappa Alpha involvement as a gift from my daughter that continues to vibrate through my days.

In April of 2005, I was asked to be part of the retirement ceremony for Dorothy Barnes, my dear friend and the administrative assistant from the days when I was at Hampton University teaching ROTC. Mrs. Barnes had often watched Ellen during my years at Hampton and Ellen wanted to come with me on the two-hour drive. We were both excited that this would be her first chance to travel since she was diagnosed. She wasn't going to let the wheelchair and her oxygen tank get in the way. She was frail and there were days when she was completely devoid of energy, but the idea of a road trip was a boost to her spirits and she loved Mrs. Barnes. The decision was easy. We rented a car and hit the road for the two-day stay.

We took our time on the drive, stopping often to rest, and enjoyed relaxed chatter all along the way. Ellen watched the scenery going by, her first opportunity in many months to see unfamiliar things instead of the same old streets that led from our home to the hospital and back again. She slept often, but she was doing well.

My old friends, Blanche and Rob Roberts, lived near Mrs. Barnes and they invited us to stay with them during our visit. They bravely hid their sadness at their first glance at Ellen. As sick as she was, one couldn't help but be amazed at her spirit and her willingness to push on through her exhaustion.

It wasn't a trip where we could be involved in a lot of activities. In the end, Ellen wasn't feeling up to actually attending the retirement ceremony, but Mrs. Barnes came to visit the next day and stayed several hours with her.

After the trip, Ellen talked about how relaxing and fun it was and we immediately began to plan another trip. We talked about making the four-hour drive to Ohio to attend Lisa's son's high school graduation in June. Even when we knew time was short, we still couldn't help but make plans for the future.

By late April, we were in the hospital for one of Ellen's regular treatments. The doctors weren't happy with her blood work and decided she wasn't strong enough for chemotherapy. They wanted her to rest and get a little stronger. At one point during the day, Ellen demanded that the nurse leave the room. "Get him out of here, Mom."

She seemed excited for a moment, sitting up in bed. I hustled the nurse out of the room then sat at the foot of her bed, watching her. She sat quietly for about five minutes, isolated, as if nothing could touch her. Then she blinked several times and focused on me.

"Mom, I think I just saw God."

She said she knew it was me sitting on the end of her bed, but that I had a light around me. She sat there, as if in wonder, convinced that she had seen a heavenly vision. I didn't question her. The experience seemed to quiet her, make her more relaxed. If it could lighten her load, I had no objection to her belief that she had experienced a heavenly vision.

Nicole was scheduled to come visit us that weekend, and as we left the hospital Ellen turned to me. "Do you think I should tell Nicole that I saw God?"

"Honey, if you want to, you should."

"I don't know, Mom. Maybe He's calling me home."

I didn't want to think about that, but I wasn't going to discourage her from sharing her experience with her cousin. I was ready for anything, anything she wished, as long as it made her feel better.

Nicole arrived and the two of them laughed and talked all day Sunday. I had also asked Lisa to visit us. The fact that the doctors had withheld the treatment on our last visit made me nervous. I needed Lisa's support.

We all spent the day talking about the future and how we hoped the doctor would give us some positive news on Ellen's next appointment, which was scheduled for the next day. It was good to see the two young women together. Nicole seemed so healthy and vibrant sitting patiently with Ellen, so pale and drawn. Nicole was good medicine for Ellen that weekend. It would be the last happy visit the two would have together.

The next day, we arrived at the hospital for Ellen's regular appointment. Tests had shown that her blood count was low and the treatment could do more harm than good. She was obviously weaker, not showing any improvement. Worse, by this time, she was having two seizures a day.

"Mom, I feel a seizure coming on," she would warn. "Please don't get excited, just be calm, I'll be okay."

We waited in the reception area until we were called. Ellen looked frail and sickly in her wheelchair, so Lisa tried to keep us entertained with empty banter, but we were all on edge. Things hadn't improved since the treatment had been denied and we were worried. I had clasped my hands tightly in prayer and still hoped for the best, even as the doctor stepped into his office, bringing two other doctors with him.

Lisa began to cry almost immediately.

"I'm sorry to say that we can't give you anymore chemotherapy, Ellen. Your body is simply too weak. If we continue with the chemo, it could kill you. I would like you to consider hospice care and then, if you get stronger, we can consider more treatment later."

The words hung in the air like the death sentence they were. The surgery, the needles, the tests, pills, treatments and my prayers had all failed. By this time, Lisa was a complete mess, sobbing and hiccupping at the news. Two nurses came in and took her out of the room, thinking her reaction wasn't helping the situation.

My heart was pounding wildly in my chest. I held Ellen's hand, but she appeared to be calm, resolved, and far less upset than I was.

"I want to go home with my mother," Ellen said. "Can I have hospice care at home?"

I nodded. I wanted my baby's last days to be at home where she belonged.

"Yes, we can arrange for that. Then if things get better," the doctor said, "if your vitals improve, we can start the treatments again."

"Thank you for everything you've done," Ellen said. "I'd like to thank the nurses who have spent so much of their time taking care of me."

My heart was breaking. I wanted to let go, to wail and scream that it wasn't fair. I held it together through sheer force of will, clinging to my daughter's hand, fighting the desire to break down the way Lisa had. We were going to lose her. The reality was unspeakable. I stared at her, awestruck by her strength as she accepted the news.

The doctors left and one by one the nurses came in, some of them crying. They hugged Ellen, saying they would pray for her, that they hoped the best for her, words they had probably said in farewell to so many other patients. My Ellen smiled at them and thanked each of them. She didn't cry, only smiled, as if her goal were to provide comfort to her caregivers.

The medical staff talked about ways we could help keep Ellen comfortable, but we had already heard the worst. My baby girl was going to die and there was nothing I could do to stop that. Helplessness had become a constant companion. Over the months of treatments and increasingly bad news, my emotions had been stretched taut like the skin of a drum, every strike reverberating through my being. I struggled to hold myself together.

On the way home, Ellen had a seizure. I pulled over to the side of the road and held her until it passed. I wanted to go directly to the hospital, but she refused.

"No! No more hospitals. I want to go home."

She had another seizure when we got home and this time I wasn't taking no for an answer. I called 911 and the ambulance took her to the nearest emergency room. Ellen, stubborn now in her need to be done with doctors and hospitals, refused treatment.

"Mom, I don't want any drugs. Please, they're not listening to me."

Her pleas broke my heart. It was clear that she had had enough, but I refused to let the terrible news we had learned mean that we would give up completely. I asked the nurses to leave while I tried to reason with her.

"They want to give you something to calm you down, baby. You've just had terrible news. If they can calm you down, that will stop the seizures."

"I am calm. I don't want to be out of it, Mother. I want to be awake and aware. Don't let them drug me so that I don't know what's going on."

She was hungry for every moment, every second she had left. It would be easy to simply pump her full of drugs to ease her pain through her final days. I made a silent vow that I would only allow the use of drugs when it was absolutely necessary. At that moment, it was necessary.

"Don't worry, baby. They'll just give you something to relax you, nothing to knock you out. I understand what it is you want and I promise: no major drugs."

Eventually she relented and allowed them to give her an injection, which seemed to work, and we took her straight home.

The hospice workers soon had a hospital bed delivered and installed in the first floor of our townhouse in Springfield. The dining room became her space, a central location where she could stay in bed and still be aware of everything going on around her. Even as we made these arrangements, made plans for nurses to come in for hours each day, I still thought we had a few months, at least several weeks to say goodbye.

Over the next several days, hospice nurses came to the house, checking her vitals and helping with medications, but for the most part we tried to forget about drugs and treatments and to concentrate on making sure Ellen's every wish was taken care of.

She had been sick for so long and there were many times that we had spoken frankly about what she wanted, should the worst happen. I had never been able to have those conversations with Gus when he was alive. Although he had wanted to talk about funerals and plans for after his death, I couldn't bring myself to do it. I regretted that I hadn't been able to listen to him. With my baby, I knew I owed her my full attention, to hear her final wishes.

She had talked about having a party, something that would celebrate life rather than mourn her death. "I want to have one of those New Orleans-style funerals, where they play all of that rousing music and dance a parade through the streets."

She talked about throwing a party someplace very fancy, like the Ritz Carlton hotel down the road. "I deserve it. I want a big fancy party."

Like her father, Ellen had always loved the five-star treatment—thick carpets, expensive furnishings and impeccable personal service. I'm sure if she had lived, she would have wanted her wedding in a place with a large ballroom glittering with crystal chandeliers, filled with family and friends all dancing to a live band. As it was, she was now too weak for a big party, but she still wanted to say goodbye to everyone. So she instructed us to call friends, family, anyone who had helped care for her. She wanted us to open up the house so everyone could visit for one last time.

Lisa and Etzel worked the phones to pass on Ellen's wishes. For almost three days people came in a steady stream. Ellen laughed and talked to them, shared old stories, remembering how full her life had been. Her closest friends, Monica and Alexia came almost every day during this time. Ellen had been in both of their weddings and during one visit, Ellen had a chance to hold Monica's new baby in her arms.

Ellen's friend, Sharonda visited during this time. The two old friends laughed at the good memories they shared particularly when Ellen visited Sharonda in San Francisco.

Mickey and Susan brought Gidget as soon as I called them, providing Ellen the opportunity to be with her little dog for the last six days of her life. When Gidget came bounding through the door, yapping and excited to see Ellen, it nearly broke my heart. Ellen's face lit up like a star. The dog lay in the bed with her, often licking her hand as if knowing that Ellen needed the affection.

Colleagues of mine visited. Ellen would make them laugh, exchange small talk with them, kid them about having had to put up with me, then ask each of them to take care of me. She took every opportunity to tell the people closest to her that she loved them. She reached back to memories that brought her joy and shared them with the people who surrounded her.

Reverend Gunn talked to Ellen about her home-going ceremony—that's what she called it, a home-going, as if she were headed someplace she had already been, someplace welcoming and waiting for her. Ellen told her that she did not want a funeral, she wanted a happy event. She told Reverend Gunn, "I do not mind dying. But I'm going to miss my mom."

I had to hold back my tears.

Ellen continued to have a few seizures. They didn't seem to make her uncomfortable, but they alarmed her visitors. The seizures usually passed without her being conscious of them. We medicated her as instructed and maintained a constant vigil to ensure she was comfortable. We also wanted to squeeze out every single moment of time we could in her presence.

Three days after we received the news from the doctor, she could no longer speak. She would knock on the wall next to her bed to draw my attention.

"Can't you talk anymore, baby?" I asked her.

She shook her head slowly side to side. The bones in her face were almost visible through her transparent skin. I patted her hand to let her know she didn't need to try, not to waste her energy with that.

Still people came, sat with her, held vigil. Ellen was calm for the most part, resigned to what would happen.

My sister Cat was in prison at the time, but we wanted to give her an opportunity to speak with Ellen one last time. We had to arrange the call through the prison system. It was the first time Cat had talked to her in a long while. We held the phone to Ellen's ear and when Cat told her she loved her, Ellen mustered up enough strength to respond: "I love you, too."

Cat had quit drinking and was trying to clean up her life. I was glad she was making an effort to make her life better.

For the next couple of days, Ellen kept her eyes closed most of the time, but she could hear us and responded to questions with small gestures. When her eyes were open, she followed our movements, letting us know that she could still hear and understand. She would acknowledge that she recognized who was visiting, like her godmother Sonja, who came from San Francisco to see Ellen for the last time, and a high school friend, Naomi. Ellen had lived with Naomi and her family while she was an exchange student in Japan. Ellen always thought of Naomi as a sister after sharing that overseas experience in Naomi's home. Over the last days of Ellen's life, Naomi traveled from Atlanta to be by Ellen's side and to hold her hand.

I spent most of my time sitting next to Ellen's bed, holding her hand, gently rubbing ice across her lips to keep them moist, sometimes putting tiny chips of ice in her mouth. Susan and I were sitting with her when I was icing her lips and I became distracted with something.

"What happened to that piece of ice?" I asked Susan, panicked. I searched around, afraid that I might have dropped it, or worse, that Ellen might choke on it since it was too large for her to swallow. When my gaze met Ellen's, there was laughter in eyes. She opened her mouth to show me the chip of ice on the end of her tongue, her shoulders slightly shaking as she silently laughed.

"Ellen," I said, smiling, "I can't believe you're teasing me."

Ellen's spirit, in the end—the fact that she still *had* humor—still amazes me. My Gus had died with a smile on his face and laughter in his heart. His life ended just after we had expressed our love to each other and were bathed in the warmth of that love. It seemed that our daughter would leave me in the same way, with loving expressions and a happy heart.

Early the next day, the morning after Mother's Day, I was sitting next to her bed in the big blue recliner she had spent so many hours in. I must have dozed off, because the next thing I heard was Mickey calling my name. I heard him saying my name, but my first thought was of Ellen.

Oh, my baby's hand is so cold. Why is my baby's hand so cold?

I opened my eyes and looked at her. Her face was turned towards me, her eyes closed. I like to think that her last sight was of her mother sitting by her side, resting, the way she always demanded I should. My baby Ellen-Lizette passed from this earth on May 9, 2005.

The doctors had given the final diagnosis only seven days earlier. I had hoped for weeks more, perhaps even months, but was permitted only days. They had been days full of loving visits, special moments, lasting memories, but it wasn't enough. Could never have been enough.

SAYING GOODBYE

Ellen was very clear that she wanted to be cremated.

"And don't stick me in one of those urns and sit me on the mantel," she said. "I want to be spread in the river."

I stared at her, wondering if she'd gone a bit crazy. I knew she wanted to be cremated, but this was a new twist to that request. "You want to be sprinkled in the Potomac?"

She rolled her eyes. "No, Mom. Sprinkle me someplace nice. Wherever you want to."

When I saw my baby for the last time, she was laying on a draped table in the funeral home, dressed in white and surrounded by flowers. She looked peaceful. One could almost believe that a dreadful disease hadn't killed her.

"She looks beautiful," Mickey said as he gazed down at her. And she did. Released from her pain, relaxed and resting. Seeing her that way I felt a weight lifted off my shoulders.

"I'm okay now, Momma," I heard her saying to me.

I took some of her ashes to Gus's grave where I had them pull up his headstone and I buried the ashes near her father. I had Ellen's name engraved on the back of his headstone so that the two of them would be remembered together.

I took some of her ashes to San Francisco. Gus and I had met there and had spent several happy years there. Ellen had taught school there and loved the city as much as I did. Together with her godmother Sonja, we sprinkled some of her ashes in the bay just off the Presidio.

I've kept the rest of her ashes with me with the intention that when I go, some of her will be buried alongside my final resting place. Ellen made it clear that she didn't want to be kept in an urn on a mantle and I have followed her wishes.

For a while, I had a hard time simply being in my house. It was so empty, felt totally vacant without her. I spent all day every day with my mother at the nursing home. When I wasn't at the nursing home, I sat in Ellen's blue chair—the large overstuffed recliner made me feel close to her in some way. She had spent so many hours sitting and sleeping in that chair, in the center of the hustle bustle of the house, that I felt some remnants of her were somehow attached to it. After a little awhile, the comfort I received from the chair faded and I couldn't sit in it or look at it any longer. I couldn't simply throw it out, so I took it back to the store where we bought it.

As it turned out, the people at the store remembered me. They remembered Ellen in her wheelchair, attached to an oxygen tank, and how we had shopped for the piece of furniture she would rest in during her final days. In usual circumstances, I'm sure they wouldn't have allowed me to return the chair, but their memory of the transaction, and the realization that the sick young woman they saw with me that day had passed, moved them to agree to take the chair back.

Lisa still came to visit now and then, and Mickey and Susan would call on me often. But for the most part, I was alone, almost paralyzed with grief. I rarely left the house, usually only walking the mile to the nursing home where my mother was, to sit by her bedside, sometimes even spending the night there.

Even though her leg had been amputated, my mother continued to decline. But I knew Lizzie Mae Spencer-Jeter was a strong woman. And now I clung to her, the woman who had raised five children on her own, who was the only one to have the patience for the timid little girl who used to cling to her skirts. While she wouldn't totally regain her health, she would still be with us for three more years.

My sister Cat was finally released on parole and staying in a supervised living facility in Pittsburgh and attending regular Alcoholics Anonymous meetings. We made a written request to her parole officer who granted her permission to come to town to visit Mother. Cat stayed with me for four days. It was so good to see my baby sister looking healthy. She told me she was happy to be clean and sober, that life was much more enjoyable when she could remember everything she had done.

Several months later, on a Sunday, I was sitting with my mother in the nursing home. By this time, my mother wasn't speaking much. I would read to her but mostly just sit with her, letting her know I was there. On that Sunday, Cat called. We exchanged the latest news and I told her how Mom was doing. She sounded upbeat and happy, except for her health.

"My legs are so swollen," she said. She didn't understand why they were swollen, but it was obvious the condition was making her uncomfortable.

"You should go to the emergency room."

"No, I have a doctor's appointment tomorrow."

"Well, call me from the doctor's office when you get there. I want to know what that swelling is all about."

We talked for a few minutes more. Then I passed the phone to Mom. I could hear Cat say hello to her, asking how she was, not expecting a response. After a few minutes, I could hear Cat saying goodbye. "I love you, Mommy," she said.

My mother surprised us both by responding, "I love you, too, Cat."

"It's so good to hear her talk!" Cat said when I took the phone back.

We exchanged a few more words then signed off, Cat promising again to call me from the doctor's office. That was at around five o'clock in the evening. Around midnight that same night, I received another phone call.

"May I speak to Judy Jeter-Cleckley?"

A stranger calling in the middle of the night is never a good sign. I braced myself for bad news.

"This is the chaplain at the hospital. I'm sorry to tell you that your sister, Robbie Jeter, has passed away."

"What? I was just talking to her! This is crazy!"

"We're not sure of the cause at this point, but we believe it may have been an embolism."

The swollen legs, a blood clot. My sister Robbie "Cat" Jeter, who had such a hard time with drugs and alcohol and was finally free, died November 5, 2006. I traveled to Pittsburgh to take care of her home-going arrangements. Mickey, Susan and Lisa were there to support me.

My mother was a fighter. She stayed with us for almost two years longer. In her final days, she wasn't talking much but was aware of her surroundings. Mickey, Susan and Lisa were there with me during the last week of her life, sitting vigil with her around the clock. Lizzie May Spencer-Jeter died July 11, 2008.

I thought about her conversation with my recruiter and her surprising decision to allow me to become a WAC. It had been the singular most important moment in my life. Her decision to grant her permission allowed me to gain the education and experience required to care for my baby Helene; it provided me the avenue to leave the small town I had grown up in and make my own way in the world and put me on the path to Gustavus Cleckley and our darling Ellen-Lizette. One would think that after losing so many people who had meant so much to me, the loss of my mother would be one that I could best accept, but it wasn't. She was a lady to the end, and while I knew it was inevitable, I felt her loss gravely.

I asked Mickey to call the family with the news. By this time, the rift between me and Bobbie was such that we were barely speaking and when we did, it was always contentious. I sometimes thought she was angry about my relationship with Lisa. Other times I was simply baffled by the conflict, but at the time of my mother's death, I wanted to put all of that aside and give my mother a proper sendoff. Bobbie and Larry arrived at the funeral home to see Mom for the last time before she was cremated.

So much loss. So much grief. You can look around yourself at the people you love and know that they will all have to leave you, or you will leave them if that is the plan. You know these things in your head but can't face them in your heart. Is it the timing and the how of it that makes the passing of loved ones so hard? Or would it have been just as devastating if I'd lost Gus in an accident, or lost my mother later in life? These things are not for me to question. I can only feel my grief in the time allowed, then stand again and move forward.

What I do know is that it doesn't get easier. Losing my husband, losing my daughter, losing my sister, losing my mother. Each loss marks your soul in a new way and doesn't diminish, no matter how familiar loss may become.

Mickey, Susan, Lisa, Helene and I took Mom's ashes back to Aliquippa and held a memorial service for her. Father Darius Moss, Susan's brother, officiated at the service. He had been supportive during both Ellen-Lizette's and my mother's challenges and I will always love and respect him for his graciousness. Relatives and friends attended and I knew in my heart that Mom was finally at peace in the place she always thought of as home.

WHAT DOES A GENERAL LOOK LIKE?

Now that I'm retired and I don't wear my uniform anymore, it always amazes me how shocked people are when they learn that I'm a retired general officer. When you retire from the armed services, you're still entitled to all of the military protocol officers expect. For example, a general officer is granted distinguished visitor quarters when visiting Army installations. That's simply the way things are done.

I have a dashboard card—a red card with a white star in the center— which distinguishes my vehicle as belonging to a general officer. Most of the time, when the guards at the gate see the star, they make the assumption that I am the spouse of a general or even the driver for a general officer. It's not until they check my ID card that they realize *I am the general.* There's usually a look of surprise, then they gather their wits, snap to attention and salute. Time after time, the familiar scene repeats itself.

I use Bethesda Naval Hospital for my medical care. I would sit in the reception area with everyone else, waiting for my name to be called. When the nurse called for General Cleckley, I was always amused by the looks on people's faces as every eye watched me walk across the room.

Even when I was in uniform I didn't take advantage of all the perks that went along with my rank. I would show up at an appointment and be assigned an escort. They would go out of their way to be helpful, but these were not courtesies I expected or demanded.

During one visit to Bethesda, after having waited along with everyone else in the crowded reception area, a nurse stepped up and said, "Ma'am, you should use the executive service. You are aware of it, aren't you?"

I wasn't aware of it. Executive Service included priority treatment in appointments and not having to wait in reception areas. Initially, I would avoid all of the fuss, but when I saw how many times people were surprised by my position, how many times their relaxed state changed once they learned that I was, in fact, a retired general officer, I started asking myself, *Just what does a General look like? Why is everyone's first assumption always that I am a spouse and not an officer?*

I realize there's no way for anyone to know that I'm a retired general officer when I'm not in uniform. It would be impossible to know what my rank and experience has been, but it's quite another thing to be taken completely by surprise, to react with shock or awe as if someone who looked like me couldn't possibly *be* a general.

So I decided that I would always take advantage of the perks that go along with the title. I worked hard for my rank. I worked hard to get the training and experience I have. Not only that, but I'd like people to become more accustomed to seeing someone like me getting those perks. No one should be surprised to see me sitting in an executive waiting room, or being escorted down the hall, or seeing the red card with a large white star on my dashboard when I drive around post. I've *earned* those perks, so I'll take every last one of them.

LIFE NOW

Helene misses her sister, but just as she did when we lost Gus, she keeps her thoughts about Ellen to herself. There were no outward displays of grief, but she obviously understood the finality of the loss. Helene handles that loss in her own way.

Just after my mom died, I began my campaign to get Helene to join me in Virginia. Ellen and I had discussed this at great length before she became sick—we wanted Helene to move in with us. I knew it would take some convincing. My daughter loved New York City and couldn't imagine that she might be happy anywhere else. It took a bit of cajoling before she agreed to move, but she did finally come to live with me in Springfield. I enrolled her in an adult daycare program where she quickly made new friends. Change is hard for Helene to accept, but eventually she began to feel just as much at home in Springfield as she did in New York.

Around the same time I was trying to convince Helene to come home, I had a conversation with Lisa about her future. She had been traveling back and forth from Cleveland, first to help care for Ellen and then to visit her grandmother in the nursing home. Lisa was on the road constantly, driving several hours at a time or flying in for a visit. Her marriage had failed and neither her mother nor her older sister was speaking to her. We could not understand what had happened to those relationships and poor Lisa was heartbroken by their disregard.

"I don't want to stay in Ohio anymore," she said to me one day. "I'm happy when I come here. It's the only place I feel loved."

"Lisa, you can always move here. You'll always have a roof over your head with me and I'd be happy to have you."

That conversation planted the seed. Lisa continued to think about what she wanted to do with her future and came to the conclusion that as soon as her younger son graduated from high school she would relocate to Virginia to live with me. Just a few weeks before my mother died, Lisa moved in permanently. She took over the basement of our townhouse and called it her own.

After my mother passed, I decided I was done with stairs and wanted to sell my three-story townhouse. My knees were telling me it was time for single-level living. I sold the townhouse and had a new home built in Fredericksburg, Virginia. In August 2010, Helene, Lisa and I moved into our new home. We love our house. Lisa has an upstairs loft area that is fitted out like her own personal apartment. Helene has a lovely room that she enjoys spending time in. I like to think that we have a happy home. Lisa, Helene and I respect each other, laugh together, and share our thoughts, feelings, fears and accomplishments. We are three strong women making our way through life together.

Somehow, my retired life is even busier than my working life. I serve on several committees, some of them philanthropic, some professional, and all of them time-consuming.

Top Ladies of Distinction is a humanitarian and community group with the goals of helping young people achieve their aspirations through mentoring programs and activities like assisting senior citizens and recognizing accomplished women in the community. As a member of the Alexandria chapter, I conduct volunteer services and attend fund raisers, luncheons, and meetings. I'm one of the charter members of this chapter and enjoy spending time with community activities, top teens, and so many brilliant and distinguished women.

I served almost four years, from 2007 to 2010, on the Department of Veterans Affairs Minority Advisory Committee. Our mission was to report back to the Secretary of Veterans' Affairs about diversity and minority issues at VA hospitals and clinics and more importantly, on the wellbeing of veterans in the communities we visited. We traveled to VA facilities where there are large minority populations and spent several days listening to briefings and holding meetings with veterans and care-givers about issues unique to that particular VA facility. Typically, we hold town hall meetings to gain perspective from the clients of the services, and then we discuss issues, develop recommendations to solve concerns and complete a final report that is reviewed by the VA senior leadership.

We visited VA clinics, veteran benefit administration offices, hospitals, federal cemeteries and veterans' centers. The attention paid to our federal cemeteries is one of the things I'm sure most people don't realize. I was impressed with a veterans' center we visited in Baltimore where services are provided to vets who have been incarcerated, who are homeless and/or need mental health services and job training, all in an effort to help them live decent lives after the sacrifices, time and hard work they gave to their country.

While I was on the committee, Shoshana Johnson, a veteran of the Iraq war, became a member. Her story gained national attention when her convoy was ambushed and she and several other soldiers from her unit were taken prisoner. Shoshanna is the first African-American woman to be a prisoner of war. Since most of the committee members are Vietnam or Gulf War veterans, Shoshana's membership brought a valuable viewpoint from the current conflict.

Shoshana commented on the fact that she had had trouble navigating the paperwork and procedures necessary to get the veteran services she required. After working more than twenty-eight years in uniform, it would seem that I should have been more aware of the services available. But before my service on that committee, I had no idea how many services the VA provided. Our committee knows that education and information campaigns must be a major effort. Service members need to be schooled on the VA and VA services from the day they join the military.

Some of the issues we work on have been fascinating, like the recent increase of female veterans as patients in VA clinics that don't offer either the gynecologic/obstetric services women need or any sexual harassment and sexual assault counseling. As we review these issues and make recommendations, I believe we're making a difference in the kind of care veterans, especially female veterans, will receive for years to come.

In 2010, I was nominated to serve as a member of the Department of Defense Advisory Committee on Women in the Services or DACOWITS. We meet quarterly and conduct focus groups with service members from all branches at various military bases to collect data on programs and policies assigned to us. Our most recent project focused on how military assignments are made and on service-member wellness. During the assignments discussions, we naturally discussed the issue of women in traditional combat roles. I'm gratified that Secretary Panetta took steps in early 2013 to institute changes that will allow women to play a greater role than ever before.

I'm excited about serving on this committee and enjoy being an advocate for women in the services in whatever capacity I can serve. And I'm ready to do more.

Since 2011, I became a member of the Veterans Administration Homeless Veterans Committee. The Secretary's goal is to eradicate homelessness for veterans. It's a serious and pervasive problem and one I'm happy to help with in any way that I can.

In 2013, I was asked by General (Ret.) Eric K. Shinseki to serve on the Department of Veterans Affairs Advisory Committee on the rehabilitation of veterans. The committee meets quarterly to advise the VA Secretary on rehabilitation needs of disabled veterans and how veterans programs are administered.

My committee work keeps me busy, but it's the speaking engagements that would keep me constantly traveling if I allowed them to. When I was in uniform, I gave speeches all over the country and the U.S. territories, mostly about diversity, mentoring and EEO issues. Those were my areas of expertise and since there were so few high-ranking minorities in the Guard, I was frequently asked to speak on Martin Luther King, Jr. Day, during Black History month and Women's History month.

I always begin my speeches the same way: I thank the Lord for the life I have led.

> *To God be the glory. This is the day the Lord has made. Let us rejoice and be glad in it.*

The other message I always deliver is that opening doors for those who come behind you should be a goal for all of us.

> *The truth is, that being successful, which sometimes had its challenges and hard work, meant less to me than leaving the door open for the next woman or minority to follow. There are still many doors that need to be opened. I often tell those that I mentor, it's not always easy, but at some point you have to stop looking for the open door and start opening doors for yourself and for others. There are few things in life that can make you feel better than watching someone get an opportunity because you opened the door for them.*

And as Ellen suggested, I established Cleckley Enterprises, Ltd. to better organize my speaking engagements, my committee and board memberships, the personal and professional engagements I am called on to participate in.

The military will often request that a general officer sit down with a military historian to write a memoir. I turned down this opportunity knowing that my daughter would want to write my story. We often talked about the project, how we would go about it, what parts of my personal life would be included with the details of my military career, etc. Never once during these discussions did I think that Ellen would *not* be here to help me with it.

When I was first promoted to general, Ellen wrote an article entitled "General Mom," in *Parenting Magazine*. I found that title cute at the time; now I feel proud of it, glad that my daughter thought of me in that way. The article was a small example of her incredible talent.

From the day Ellen died until I started writing, I thought about the promise I made to her, that I would write the book and tell my story. It took four years before I felt comfortable enough to think that I could keep my promise.

For Ellen-Lizette and for Gustavus, this is my story. I hope they would both approve.

ACKNOWLEDGMENTS

It would take many pages to thank all of the people who have been there and supported me throughout this project. I'm blessed to have so many caring and loving friends who have touched my life in countless ways.

I must thank my Mom, Lizzie Mae Jeter, who always encouraged me to work hard, pray and keep the faith. I will always honor her and the life lessons she shared with me.

Heartfelt thanks to my late husband, Gus, and daughter, Ellen-Lizette, who both always had more faith in my abilities than I had in myself.

I thank my family, especially Helene Cleckley and Lisa Perkins Guilford, as well as lifetime friends, Sonja Johnson, Blanch Byrd Roberts and Phil Friedman, for their encouragement, love and continued support of me. Also thanks to the Reverend Dr. Faye Gunn for her spiritual guidance and friendship.

Thanks to my military family who have made significant contributions to my life and this project. A special thanks to Lt. Gen. (Retired) Roger Schultz for his leadership, vision, mentoring and encouragement.

Thank you to Col. (Ret.) Grethe Cammermeyer for reviewing the manuscript and providing profitable suggestions and recommendations.

Thanks to my many friends, neighbors and associates who reminded me often over the past couple of years that you wanted to read my story and have waited patiently to see it finally in print. Your interest kept me motivated.

I also want to thank Liz Trupin-Pulli, a great literary agent, for being so patient and helping me to navigate through this project.

My biggest thanks go to Mary Doyle, my co-author and new friend. Her patience with this first-time writer is to be commended. I wish my Ellen had lived to write my story, but since I can't have her, I'm so grateful and thankful for Mary.

ABOUT THE AUTHORS

Brigadier General (Ret.) Julia Jeter Cleckley served in the Women's Army Corps, the U.S. Army National Guard and 24 years active duty in the U.S. Army, for a total of 28 years in uniform in a storied and wide-ranging career. She currently serves on numerous advisory committees dealing with women's and veterans' affairs, is an active member of Alpha Kappa Alpha Sorority, Inc., and a charter member of the City of Alexandria Chapter of Top Ladies of Distinction. She is also a member of the National Parliamentarian Association. Julia is a pioneer, leader, coach, educator, mentor, key note speaker and survivor, who is remarkably successful at empowering and inspiring individuals to reach their potential. She lives in Virginia. Contact her at WWW.CLECKLEYENTERPRISES.COM.

M. L. Doyle has served in the U.S. Army at home and abroad for more than two decades as both a soldier and civilian. She co-authored the book, *I'm Still Standing: From Captive U.S. Soldier to Free Citizen – My Journey Home*, which chronicles the story of Shoshana Johnson, a member of the 507th Maintenance Company. She is also the author of fiction works in mystery and adult romance. She can be reached via her website at WWW.MLDOYLEAUTHOR.COM.

PHOTO ALBUM

My first official photo as a Private E-1.

My wonderful niece, Melissa (Lisa) Guilford. She lives with Helene and I and has been a great help to me.

My best friend, Sonja Johnson and me. We first met while I was serving as a WAC and have maintained that friendship over the years. She is also godmother to my daughters.

My official photo when I was Major Julia Cleckley.

Ellen and I at her Cotillion Ball.

One of the rare occasions when my whole family was together. My mom, Lizzie Jeter, is in the middle, surrounded by the rest of us. Robbie (Cat) Jeter, Barbara Williams, me, Larry Jeter and Robert (Mickey) Jeter.

Again, my mom, Lizzie Jeter is surrounded by us. Robert (Mickey) Jeter and his wife Susan, me and my brother Larry Jeter.

While I was a colonel, I had the opportunity to meet former secretary of state, Condoleezza Rice. I truly admire her tenacity and professionalism.

I was honored to serve as guest speaker during my high school reunion.

The is me with a Turkish guard at the embassy in Ankara, Turkey during the class trip I helped organize while in the Tuff's University Fellowship Program through the Army War College.

My official photo as a colonel.

My brother-in-law, Frank Cleckley attended Ellen's graduation from Cornell University with me. Frank was the first person I called when my husband died and he was very supportive.

My high school graduation photo.

My official photo as a Major.

The three of us, Helene, Lisa and I during Christmas 2011 in Florida.

Former NAACP Chairman, Julian Bond.

Ellen with family pet Gidget.

My brother Larry's son, Ty Law played cornerback for several NFL teams from 1995 to 2009. We are all very proud of him.

I served on a Veterans Administration committee with Specialist Shoshana Johnson, a former POW of the Iraq War.

I was a captain during this exercise at Fort Drum, NY.

My very good friends Vickie Blomquist and Otha Greer.

I am often invited to serve as guest speaker for a wide range of events. Here, I am the keynote speaker during a National Guard function.

Helene was excited to have a new baby sister. Here she kneels next to Ellen.

With my mother Lizzie.

Speaking at an event in San Francisco.

As a Brig. Gen. with Lt. Col. Durr.

I'm in the chair with my sister Barbara Williams.

I was a first lieutenant and the lead tactical officer at Empire State Military Academy (ESMA).

While a Brigidier General, I met with the former Secretary of Homeland Security, Janet Napolitano and Former Arizona Adjutant General, David Rataczak.

I presented Col. Roger Etzel with an award.

Phil Friedman is a great friend.

My handsome and loving late husband Gustavus Cleckley.

My lovely daughters Ellen and Helene during my promotion ceremony to Colonel.

I had the honor of meeting Massachusetts Governor Deval Patrick.

To celebrate Ellen's graduation from Cornell, we took a trip to Italy. Here, the two of us are toasting her success.

My beautiful daughter, Ellen with her friends Monica and Alexia.

Sisters Ellen and Helene at Mt. Vernon, Virginia.

I was a Lt. Col. when we took this photo with the late Senator Montgomery along with GI Bill recipients.

I am receiving the Legion of Merit Award from Lt. Gen. Schultz.